MacArthur

THE GREAT GENERALS SERIES

This distinguished new series will feature the lives of eminent military leaders who changed history in the United States and abroad. Top military historians will write concise but comprehensive biographies including the personal lives, battles, strategies, and legacies of these great generals, with the aim to provide background and insight into today's armies and wars. These books will be of interest to the military history buff, and, thanks to fast-paced narratives and references to current affairs, they will be accessible to the general reader.

Patton by Alan Axelrod

Grant by John Mosier

Eisenhower by John Wukovits

LeMay by Barrett Tillman

Omar Bradley by Alan Axelrod

Andrew Jackson by Robert Remini

ALSO BY RICHARD B. FRANK

Guadalcanal: The Definitive Account of the Landmark Battle

Downfall: The End of the Imperial Japanese Empire

MacArthur

Richard B. Frank

Foreword by General Wesley K. Clark

palgrave
macmillan

Jessamine County Public Library
600 South Main Street
Nicholasville, KY 40356
(859) 885-3523

MACARTHUR
Copyright © Richard B. Frank, 2007.
All rights reserved. No part of this book may be used or reproduced in any
manner whatsoever without written permission except in the case of brief
quotations embodied in critical articles or reviews.

First published in 2007 by
PALGRAVE MACMILLAN™
175 Fifth Avenue, New York, N.Y. 10010 and
Houndmills, Basingstoke, Hampshire, England RG21 6XS.
Companies and representatives throughout the world.

PALGRAVE MACMILLAN is the global academic imprint of the Palgrave
Macmillan division of St. Martin's Press, LLC and of Palgrave Macmillan Ltd.
Macmillan® is a registered trademark in the United States, United Kingdom
and other countries. Palgrave is a registered trademark in the European Union
and other countries.

ISBN–13: 978–1–4039–7658–1
ISBN–10: 1–4039–7658–9

Library of Congress Cataloging-in-Publication Data is available from the
Library of Congress.

A catalogue record of the book is available from the British Library.

Design by Letra Libre.

First edition: July 2007

10 9 8 7 6 5 4 3 2 1

Printed in the United States of America.

B
MACA

AUG 2 8 2007

3 2530 60622 6429

To my mother,
Lillian Frank,
a working nurse for fifty years

Contents

The photosection appears between pages 88 and 89

List of Maps

List of Tables

Acknowledgments

MY FIRST THANK-YOU HAS TO GO TO THE NATIONAL WORLD WAR II Museum, formerly the National D-Day Museum, in New Orleans. The museum planned an international World War II Conference for October 2005. I was asked to spe\\ak on the campaigns of Douglas MacArthur. Although I was well acquainted with MacArthur, this invitation prompted the gathering of information and a rigorous critical examination that proved the foundation of this work. Hurricane Katrina canceled the conference, but left me with a mass of material and new insights that proved readily adaptable to this biography.

Any biographer of Douglas MacArthur now walks in the footprints of D. Clayton James, whose monumental three-volume work is destined to endure for decades as the greatest study of that remarkable personality. Our differences on a number of factual and interpretative issues in no way diminishes my profound respect for his work.

My experience has taught me that any work benefits enormously from the input of other historians. I am fortunate in having a number of distinguished historians who were kind enough to take time from their busy schedules to look over all or parts of this work. My thanks go to Edward Drea, John Lundstrom, Richard Miexsel, Barrett Tillman, and James Sawruk. They provided invaluable encouragement, criticisms, suggestions, pointed out important source material, and saved me from many errors. Likewise, David Horner and William Stueck kept me out of trouble on some important issues where I was about to go astray. I am indebted to the staff at the MacArthur Memorial, Norfolk, Virginia, and particularly James Zobel, who reviewed a draft of this work, for their excellent and expert assistance. But my experience has also taught me that any work like this can also profit enormously from the input of nonprofessionals who are nonetheless well read in history and shrewd literary critics. Thus, I extend my deep thanks to my esteemed friends Gregory Embree, Dennis Fontana, Jerry Gough, and Robert Sullivan for reading the manuscript and guiding me on the shaping of this work. They also proved to be much better editors than I and salvaged many a phrase and sentence from mediocrity or incoherence. I also must note the useful insights into MacArthur provided by my former boss, Charles Craigin. Any remaining errors in this work are my responsibility alone.

I owe a salute to my agents, Robert Gottlieb and Alex Glass at Trident Media, and my editor at Palgrave, Alessandra Bastagli, for their patient nurturing of the book from inception to completion.

This work is dedicated to my mother, Lillian Frank, who completed training as a registered nurse in 1943. With time out to raise a family of four, she returned to that profession and in 2005 was recognized for fifty years of active nursing by the State of Missouri.

Finally, I lack the words to convey my full appreciation for all my wife Janet has done to sustain me through yet another book, as we juggle multiple jobs and the responsibilities of attending to my daughter Rachel and my son Mitchell in their academic pursuits and passions for ballet and tennis respectively.

Foreword

ON THE PLAIN AT WEST POINT IS A BRONZE STATUE OF DOUGLAS MacArthur, gazing into the distance. For cadets, he is the symbol of visionary leadership. But MacArthur is far more than a cherished symbol of the nation's Military Academy—he was a military commander whose legacy helped define a major region of the world and who also left a permanent mark on the military.

General of the Army Douglas MacArthur helped lead the rollback of Japanese conquest of the Pacific area in World War II, and masterfully shaped the emergence of a peaceful, post–World War II Japan, an engine of world economic growth and stability. His quick and decisive counterattack against North Korean aggression toward South Korea turned the tide of the war, sustaining the government of South Korea, and, ultimately, enabling a half century of containment of Communist China.

But despite these remarkable achievements, MacArthur emerged as one of the most controversial of our major military figures—both admired and distrusted. His achievements as well as the criticisms and controversies surrounding him are laid out clearly and persuasively by Richard Frank in this punchy biography.

As Frank notes, MacArthur was born with a head start on military achievement. His father was a general and Civil War Medal of Honor winner. He grew up immersed in military culture. He was also bright and charming in a robust, manly way. He demonstrated from his earliest experiences an incredible energy and ambition, and the vision not only to accomplish the mission, whatever it was, but also to place himself at the center of the action. He graduated from

West Point both first in his class academically and as the Cadet First Captain, a rare achievement. He carried with him a sense of destiny.

These qualities made him remarkably effective on the battlefield. He was one of America's most decorated military heroes in World War I. He was incredibly brave under fire, again and again. After the war, he became the US Military Academy's youngest superintendent. At West Point, he reformed the curriculum, helped create the Cadet Honor System, and inspired generation after generation of cadets to "compete on the fields of friendly strife" in other words, sports, in order to build qualities of character and leadership.

A few years later he was promoted to become the Army's Chief of Staff, its top leader. Here again he displayed sound judgment in implementing military reforms and adjusting to the tough budget realities confronting the Depression-era Army. MacArthur was the epitome of the military leader seized his opportunities and fulfilled his responsibilities.

But perhaps it was here that his military upbringing and sense of duty first collided with the realities of higher level political leadership. For in fact, these two worlds can be quite different: the military prizes officers who will step forward to assume responsibility for difficult and dangerous tasks, while political leadership demands an adroit sense of whether or not and how to take responsibility. The arrival of thousands of poverty-stricken veterans in the nation's capital in 1932 to collect their Veteran's Bonus brought about a collision of these two competing leadership styles, and led to sharp public rebuke for MacArthur.

As Army Chief of Staff, MacArthur accompanied a small group of troops sent to reinforce Washington police in clearing the unruly crowd of thousands of Bonus Marchers from Washington. When things got out of hand, he was responsible for the sickening sight of soldiers employing riot-control action, including the use of tear gas, against our own impoverished veterans and their families. MacArthur compounded his error by making inflammatory remarks to the press. Public detractors quickly emerged; his image was permanently clouded. But at a point where his military career should have ended, his greatest achievements were yet to come.

MacArthur left Washington, still too young to retire, to become advisor to President Quezon of the Philippines, with the title of Field Marshal. From here he went on to lead US and Philippine forces in the unsuccessful defense of the Philippines against Japan. Then, following his successful evacuation by PT boat, he commanded the island-hopping campaign that saw US forces recapture the Philippines, and move on toward Japan. It was MacArthur who accepted Japan's surrender aboard the US battleship Missouri in Tokyo Bay. It was MacArthur who guided the successful occupation of Japan and its transition from wartime dictatorship to peaceful democracy. He was now a five-star General of the Army and a recipient of the Medal of Honor.

In 1950, when the North Korean forces crossed the 38th parallel into South Korea, the task of defeating the attack fell to MacArthur. His forces conducted a brilliant, risky amphibious assault at Inchon, on Korea's eastern coast near the capital, Seoul, cut off the spearheads of North Korean forces already further south, rapidly destroyed the bulk of the North Korean Army, and advanced north to the Chinese border.

MacArthur had simply become a larger than life figure. He had often had his own way and publicly spoke his mind, in spite of the misgivings and even the direction of his superiors in Washington. Twice he had flirted with an all-out campaign for the Presidency as a Republican, even while on active duty and he had maintained his distance from successive Democratic Administrations. At the age of 70, he had outlasted all his military competitors save George C. Marshall, who became Secretary of State and subsequently Secretary of Defense.

Along the way, rivals, enemies and other controversies emerged. Rumors about him periodically surfaced—his creating his own uniform as Field Marshal, for example. He picked up a wounding nickname, Dugout Doug, for his failure to frequently visit his troops besieged on Bataan. Certainly he had confidence in his own judgment, on the battlefield and as a strategic commander, including surviving the terrible trials in the Pacific, but along with public acclaim he picked up a terrible reputation for vanity and egotism.

And in war, and especially theater command, leaders must understand the political environment and exercise intuition as well as hard military skills. When Chinese soldiers unexpectedly intervened in force in Korea in October, 1950, MacArthur faced an unprecedented reversal in war. He needed friends, close associates, and the deepest respect at home. Instead, he found himself out of step with Washington, and isolated in what looked to be a costly and losing war, and at a time when major concerns were focused on possible Soviet threats to Europe. His reputation, his character, his experiences, and especially his outspokenness in calling for victory at any price, worked against him. He was relieved for insubordination, and returned to the United States.

MacArthur's life and career are a moving testimony to his extraordinary talents and lifelong commitment to public service in the profession of arms—but also a signal reminder that there are political boundaries in American democracy which military leaders must not cross. Moreover, as MacArthur's experience demonstrates, the conduct of war is ever-changing, and not always straightforward. At the very highest levels it merges into statecraft, politics, and international strategy, and the greatest generals must take their direction from their government's leaders.

—*General Wesley K. Clark*

Introduction

GENERAL OF THE ARMY DOUGLAS MACARTHUR HELD HIS REMARKABLY well-preserved seventy-one-year-old frame erect as his limousine crawled along a nineteen-mile course through New York City on April 20, 1951. His unique and extravagantly gold braided dress hat served as a beacon, signaling to some the signature emblem of his public image and to others his gargantuan ego. Stone- and steel-sided caverns compressed the din of 7.5 million wildly cheering citizens who bombarded the cavalcade with over 2,800 tons of ticker tape, confetti, and paper. The parade set a city record for turnout and debris. It also etched a national mark for the most tumultuous ovation ever bestowed on an American just fired from his job.

This scene symbolized the truth that the one adversary Douglas MacArthur invariably routed was neutrality. Everyone agreed that he succeeded in his single-minded pursuit of greatness. But they differed sharply about whether he was great in matters that boded well or ill for the nation and the world.

It would be comforting to announce that more than a half-century later, only ashes of such fiery passions remain and that the task here is to articulate history's sober and evenhanded verdict on Douglas MacArthur with particular attention to his leadership traits. Unfortunately, the veracity of such a report would invite comparison to one of MacArthur's more suspect World War II communiqués. His thinning band of passionate admirers extols him as a military genius—biographer William Manchester's "American Caesar" at the center of media mogul Henry Luce's "American Century." His enemies revile him as a pompous, bumbling fraud—his heart filled with contempt for average

Americans and perhaps democracy—masking his ever more consequential failures in ever more egregious lies.

The reader need not fear that the verdict delivered or lessons extracted here will be bland pabulum of bite-sized judgments from each of these camps. There is a core vision to this work: Douglas MacArthur is best comprehended as a classic tragic hero. Like all tragic heroes, his great talents were more than matched by a ruinous flaw. That flaw was a conviction that he was an instrument of destiny and that by his will alone, he could turn his nation and history to fulfill his destiny. This belief plus an array of gifts drawn at birth and the molding by his remarkable parents propelled him to what are indisputably real triumphs—though often not those trumpeted by his admirers or dismissed by his detractors. Ironically, adaptability, not innate genius, hoisted him to his greatest accomplishments. Adaptability now reigns as the most indispensable trait for high military leadership in an era of technological leaps that guarantee the nature of war will radically change during the span of an ordinary career. No American figure better exemplifies this trait than the man who was commissioned before the Wright brothers' first flight but became a keen exponent of this entirely new dimension in warfare.

Douglas MacArthur's remarkably long life surged to three successively higher summits, any of which would have constituted the dazzling pinnacle of another man's career. The tug of war between his bountiful gifts and his flaws penned an enduring legacy swollen with positive and negative examples of vibrant or villainous leadership as well as a textbook on military and civilian relations. The reader should constantly examine episodes from MacArthur's life not only in the context of lessons offered by MacArthur himself, but also continuously reflect on how MacArthur's superiors did or did not reap the benefits and manage the detriments of so talented and challenging a subordinate. For generations to come, MacArthur's legacy will yield profitable—and entertaining—study to Americans in and out of uniform.

1

Beginnings

DOUGLAS MACARTHUR CLAIMED HIS FIRST MEMORY WAS "THE SOUND of bugles." This is the sort of unverifiable detail a man with an artistic approach to creating a legendary life could toss off with ease. So the first rule of writing about Douglas MacArthur is that he is a tempting resource for color, but for facts one should often look elsewhere.[1]

He was born on January 26, 1880, at the Little Rock Barracks, Arkansas. Douglas drew almost all aces at birth. Most biographies highlight his formidable intellect, his prodigious memory, his remarkable good looks, his dominating presence or charisma, perhaps nodding to his late-Victorian rhetorical skills. But arguably his most vital endowment was an astonishingly remarkable constitution. He maintained his physical and mental youthfulness for decades beyond his contemporaries and this extended his career for two encores beyond a normal span.

Without the slightest doubt, the most important human beings in his life were his parents. They molded Douglas and stored within him the ideas that served as his internal navigational gyroscopes. His father, Arthur MacArthur, distinguished himself as a Civil War Medal of Honor recipient and remained in the doldrums of the postwar army. In 1875, Arthur married Mary Pinkney Hardy ("Pinky"), a Confederate daughter of a Norfolk, Virginia family. They had three boys. The eldest brother, Arthur III, went to the Naval Academy and carved out for himself a distinguished career until appendicitis claimed him prematurely in 1923. The middle child, Malcolm, died in infancy. The baby was Douglas.

The MacArthurs spent the majority of Douglas's youth in the lonely posts faintly embroidering the West, where he witnessed the last twinges of three centuries of American frontier expansion. For the boy, it served as an idyll of barefoot explorations juxtaposed to an orderly daily regime of ceremony, drill, and brass buttons. Often the senior officer on the post, Arthur ruled the only universe Douglas knew and provided a profound example of what a soldier should be and do. He also instilled a very contrarian view during the time that America's destiny beckoned in the Far East, not Europe. During Douglas's life this view appeared bizarre to most Americans; it looks prescient now. If anything, Pinky's contribution loomed larger. She instilled the conviction that Douglas was an instrument of destiny. Pinky would hover near Douglas, often under the same roof, repeating this message for the first fifty-seven years of his life.[2]

Initially an indifferent student, Douglas bloomed in his teens. He entered the military academy at West Point in 1899; Pinky took up residence in a nearby hotel. This dogged maternal clasp was by no means eccentric for the time. Maternal harnesses yoked both Franklin Roosevelt and Adlai Stevenson far into adulthood. Rather than shielding him, Douglas's status as the son of a then senior officer made him the target of especially savage hazing. His bearing under this torment impressed his classmates, but much as Douglas loved the academy ever after, he loathed his mistreatment and when the opportunity arose, he would move to squash it. It is often claimed, but incorrect to say, that Douglas created an all-time record for academic excellence at West Point. Varying standards over the years preclude such a verdict, but he certainly towered above his contemporaries and graduated first academically in his class. Equally as important, his military bearing and character secured the coveted appointment as First Captain, the top post available to a cadet. This set of laurels formed the first milepost confirming that he was swaddled by fate for an exceptional life.[3]

His parents talked Douglas out of abandoning West Point to participate in the Spanish-American War. That war, however, vaulted his father from lieutenant colonel to lieutenant general and dispatched him to command the Philippines. Arthur behaved petulantly when William Howard Taft arrived to assume overall direction. The vindication of his judgment partly assuaged the sting of effective demotion. Taft promptly pronounced the Philippine Insurrection as waning; MacArthur insisted it was waxing; MacArthur was correct. Notwithstanding or perhaps because of his observation of the Filipinos he was fighting, Arthur developed a deep appreciation and respect for them that he passed to Douglas. But Arthur also bequeathed something else from the experience: Taft later would become secretary of war for Theodore Roosevelt and passed over Arthur for the appointment of chief of staff of the army. It left Arthur so bitter that he refused to be buried in his uniform. It instilled in Douglas a family grudge that crippled him with a hypersensitive vigilance to the possibility that he might be denied his rightful destiny by lesser men.[4]

As was customary in those days, as the top man in the class of 1903 Douglas took his commission in the Corps of Engineers. He fulfilled his first decade of assignments with distinction—except while distracted by his unsuccessful pursuit of a wife. In November 1903, during his initial tour in the Philippines, he encountered two armed insurgents, or possibly bandits. One fired a round that punctured MacArthur's hat—another event he read as a sign of destiny. MacArthur killed them both at close range with pistol shots. His most important assignment, he later claimed, was duty as an aide to his father during a tour of the Far East in 1905–6. When he attended the advanced course for engineer officers in 1908, he completed what turned out to be his last bit of formal schooling in his profession. He read prodigiously not only about military affairs, but many other subjects.[5]

The year 1913 found MacArthur as a Young Turk staff officer serving the dynamic chief of staff, Leonard Wood. For the next fifty years, Wood stood second only to his father in his imprint on MacArthur's thinking and behavior as an officer. Wood's odd career began as a contract surgeon, not as a field officer, much less a West Point graduate; thus MacArthur's admiration stemmed from shared ideas rather than shared roots. MacArthur harkened not only to Wood's call to make the army ready to fight a modern war, but also to his personality and methods. MacArthur particularly assimilated Wood's skillful manipulation of the press and open dabbling in politics.[6]

In 1914, the new president, Woodrow Wilson, faced a civil war in Mexico. Wilson detested the leader of one faction, General Victoriano Huerta, and sent American forces to Vera Cruz to deny him shipment of German arms. The situation careened toward a full-scale war, and Wood dispatched Captain

MacArthur to scout for prospective operations. In a swashbuckling adventure, MacArthur penetrated behind Mexican lines with several local railroad workers he bribed, and returned with three vitally needed locomotives. His report of the episode, however, further recounted three close-range gunfire exchanges with Mexican forces or bandits, during which at least four bullets pierced his clothes without seriously injuring him. As several officers, including Wood, agreed, if all of this was true, MacArthur deserved a Medal of Honor. MacArthur positively lusted for the award, both as proof of his worthiness as a son and as a coveted sign of his destiny. The nomination failed both because the only available witnesses were the bribed and thus compromised Mexicans, and on the pettifogging objection that MacArthur's deed lacked proper prior authorization. MacArthur filed the episode away in the large family trunk that stored festering grudges.[7]

✦━━✦

In April 1917, Wilson secured a declaration of war against Germany. The army realized, if the politicians did not, that American participation in World War I required a huge army. That meant conscription. Major MacArthur, now effectively the first public relations office in army history, performed stellar service in selling this idea. MacArthur exhibited keen vision when he advocated breaking up the tiny regular army into cadres for a much larger force of national guardsmen and conscripts. In order to highlight the role of the national guard and to avoid the political pitfall of favoritism of one state or region, Macarthur proposed creating a division of guard units "stretch[ed] like a rainbow across the United States." Hence was born the 42nd ("Rainbow") Division. Sixty-three-year-old Major General William A. Mann commanded the division, but MacArthur, with a spot-promotion to colonel, became the division's chief of staff. MacArthur switched his branch from engineers to infantry, a move that opened vastly expanded opportunities for advancement in wartime. With MacArthur's appointment to the Rainbow Division, at age thirty-seven he bid adieu to a bit player's role for the orbit of the powerful.[8]

The Rainbow Division was the second National Guard division (behind the New England-based 26th) and among the first four divisions to reach France in 1917. The commander of the American Expeditionary Force, General John J. Pershing, ignored sound advice from his allies that his divisional organization, with 28,000 men, was too unwieldy by over 10,000 men and woefully deficient of firepower. But the first challenge to Pershing's fetish for huge divisions was that his initial units all arrived well under authorized strength. Thus, ironically, the very first significant battle

MacArthur won in his military career was bureaucratic: thwarting Pershing's plan to break up the Rainbow Division to fill the ranks of the other three divisions. MacArthur prevailed because he went over Pershing's head to appeal directly to the secretary of war. The ploy worked but cost him in his relations with Pershing's staff.[9]

Pershing installed the 42nd Division into a front-line sector marked by little active fighting long before it completed training. MacArthur romped on two exhilarating adventures accompanying French troops on trench raids. His conspicuous bravery earned his first award of the Silver Star. The significance of this award and the ones that followed in France is much misunderstood. The hierarchy of valor awards now familiar to Americans only solidified after World War II began. In that hierarchy, the Silver Star Medal ranked third in the army behind the Medal of Honor and the Distinguished Service Cross. In World War I, however, the Silver Star was literally a small silver star device to attach to a campaign ribbon, not a separate medal. It really equated to a much lower level award, comparable to the British "Mentioned in Dispatches." MacArthur instigated the Silver Star Medal as chief of staff, and it was retroactively awarded to prior holders of the Silver Star. This is not to say that MacArthur's conduct did not merit the award of the Silver Star Medal as it later came to be understood, but the status and criteria for the award were much different in World War I.[10]

With the experience of the French trench raids behind him, MacArthur joined one mounted by the Rainbow's own Iowa-raised, 168th Infantry. At the appointed minute, MacArthur climbed out of a trench into No Man's Land between the lines and started forward. 'For a dozen terrible seconds," he recalled, "I felt they weren't following me. But then, without turning around, I knew how wrong I was to doubt even for an instant. In a moment they were all around me. I'll never forget that." MacArthur's dramatic leadership earned a Distinguished Service Cross for this action.[11]

An enormous administrative workload normally tethers a divisional chief of staff to a rear headquarters. In almost all other divisions in both world wars, few enlisted men could even name the divisional chief of staff. MacArthur managed to be not only a superb conventional chief of staff, but also a common presence in the front lines. Father Francis P. Duffy, later the Rainbow's illustrious chief chaplain, wrote in May 1917 that MacArthur "chafes at his own task of directing instead of fighting, and he has pushed himself into raids and forays in which, some older heads think, he has no business to be." Duffy went on to note that MacArthur's exploits were regarded by other officers in the division who were latter to become famous (notably William J. Donavan, a Medal of Honor winner who was the director of the Office of Strategic Services in World War II) as valuable in encouraging the men. But Duffy added that all of these officers, including MacArthur, "are wild Celts, whose opinion no sane man like myself would uphold."[12]

During his combat career in France, MacArthur refined a signature look that set him apart on the battlefield. After trying out a prototype at Vera Cruz, in France MacArthur perfected a distinctive image that remained with him ever after. He wore a shapeless hat far more often than a steel helmet (a helmet in his view was merely useful to keep away rain, not enemy projectiles) and a turtleneck sweater with a seven-foot-long purple scarf. Seldom burdened with a weapon, his swagger stick and calf-high boots spoke defiance of the realities of trench warfare. Even those who despised him—indeed, particularly those who despised him—recognized (or should have recognized) this distain for polish, stiff creases, and buttoned-down conformity as the mark of the quintessential casual American. It was the very antithesis of the European-style spit and polish, neck tie and starch of Pershing (and of Pershing's disciple, Patton).

His objective conduct seemed to reflect valor in spades. "All of Germany cannot fabricate the shell that will kill me," he allegedly declared. But this comment, if true, invites a philosophical question: Was he fearless or was he brave? If the definition of bravery is overcoming fear, then MacArthur's conduct lacked something critical. He truly believed he was an instrument of destiny and hence that he would be divinely protected until he fulfilled a huge predestined role. But even he recognized a border for his divine dome of personal grace. When a German prisoner disclosed a plan to shell a chateau MacArthur used as his headquarters with a huge howitzer, MacArthur discretely vacated the premises before it was pulverized. Twice he was gassed severely enough to be prostrated in the hospital for days. This type of incident will cure most men of the "it won't happen to me" world of denial, but it did not alter MacArthur's serenity under fire.

MacArthur's truly outstanding performance as chief of staff and in the front line won a recommendation for a general's star from his new division commander, Maj. Gen. Charles Menoher. The freshly appointed army chief of staff, Peyton March, was one of Arthur MacArthur's protégées. When Pershing failed to include Douglas on a list of men recommended for general officer appointment, March appended MacArthur's name—and deleted several of Pershing's staff officers. MacArthur received word of the promotion on June 26, 1918. He was only thirty-eight years old and had just begun his sixteenth year of active duty.[13]

On July 14, 1918, Bastille Day, the Rainbow Division withstood a ferocious attack. MacArthur was recommended for another Silver Star and the French Corps commander urged the award of the Legion d'Honeur. But this time MacArthur got a full ration of the sights and sounds of hideous squalid deaths, and said later that war was never the same for him again.[14]

On July 28, thinking the Germans were retreating, a French general flung the Rainbow infantrymen into an attack without their artillery. In fierce fighting against elements of four German divisions, Menoher relieved the commander of the division's 84th Brigade and replaced him with MacArthur. When the Germans did retreat, MacArthur saw the opportunity to pursue. By example and persuasion, he pitched the exhausted Rainbow men forward, lead by the Irishmen of the 165th Infantry. In seven days and seven miles, the division sustained 6,500 casualties. The battle's end brought MacArthur two more amply earned Silver Stars and the highest praise from Menoher. Moreover, MacArthur finally relinquished his job as chief of staff. The division's headquarters officers presented him with a gold cigarette lighter inscribed: "The bravest of the brave."[15]

For the first solo American offensive at St. Mihiel beginning September 12, 1918, Pershing massed a half-million Americans and 100,000 French soldiers to attack a German salient.[16] The mere 23,000 Germans in the salient were already pulling out when the American attack fell. MacArthur won a fifth Silver Star for personally leading the division into the attack. MacArthur was eager to take the strategic city of Metz and believed afterwards that Pershing's refusal to let him advance was a huge blunder. The reality was that MacArthur's men might have seized Metz, but surely would have been destroyed in the inevitable counterattack.[17]

After Pershing terminated the St. Michiel offensive on September 16, MacArthur's brigade took over sole responsibility for the Rainbow Division's sector of the front line, while the division's other brigade rested. MacArthur's men found their trenches subject to frequent shelling. During one such rain of German artillery rounds at the end of the month, MacArthur encountered George S. Patton, then commanding a tank brigade. Patton (who privately admitted fear, and therefore was unquestionably brave) wrote that as the creeping barrage marched toward them "I think each one wanted to leave, but each hated to say so, so we let it come over us. We stood and talked but neither was much interested in what the other said." When Patton flinched at a nearby shell burst, MacArthur assured him, "Don't worry, Colonel, you never hear the one that gets you." Patton, a connoisseur in such matters, anointed MacArthur "the bravest man I ever met."[18]

After St. Mihiel, Pershing's First Army shifted 500,000 men sixty miles into the Meuse-Argonne area. With a million men (eighty-five percent of whom were American), Pershing aimed to cut the railway line linking half the German front. Although he outnumbered the Germans here six to one, the German front comprised an intricate labyrinth of machine gun nests and mortar positions to place fire from high ground over dense belts of barbed wire, making it one of the strongest segments of the German line on the entire Western Front. The attack began on September 26 and careened into a vicious attrition contest. MacArthur's 42nd Division was rousted from a brief rest and flung into the maelstrom at what Pershing later labeled as the pivot point for the whole American advance: the Romagne Heights of Hill 288 and a low hill mass called the Cote de Chatillon. If one event can be identified as the most critical in MacArthur's subsequent rise, this was it.

The fresh but ruthless V Corps commander, Charles Summerall (former leader of the Rainbow artillery and then the 1st Division) told MacArthur on October 14: "Give me Chatillon or a list of five thousand casualties." MacArthur's come back was: "If this brigade does not capture Chatillon, you can publish a casualty list of the entire brigade, with the brigade commander's name at the top." MacArthur's rejoinder brought tears to Summerall's eyes.[19]

Ailing from a dose of gas, MacArthur still led the brigade forward in multiple futile charges. Summerall's relentless refusal to accept failure prompted him to relieve the commander of the other Rainbow brigade, the 83rd, and to deliver another tirade to MacArthur that he must succeed. These twin events powerfully implied that any further failure to advance might result in MacArthur's own relief and the permanent blighting of his career. Thus, October 16 proved the decisive day. In an episode that illuminates a fundamental feature of MacArthur's leadership, with his own career at stake, MacArthur displayed no qualms in accepting a daring plan authored by Lt. Col. Walter E. Bare, commander of the 167th Infantry Regiment, to slip one battalion through a weak point to unlock the German position and then stage a massive frontal assault. MacArthur then personally led the brigade to triumph. The 42nd Division lost four thousand men in these battles. Summerall recommended MacArthur for promotion to Major General and a Medal of Honor—and would be his champion for selection of chief of staff a dozen years later. Pershing concurred in the promotion and awarded MacArthur a Distinguished Service Cross. MacArthur was not promoted and received a Distinguished Service Cross, not the Medal of Honor.[20]

Following a desperately needed respite after de Chatillon, the Rainbow Division (under strength by some 120 officers and almost 7,500 enlisted men, a quarter of the division's total strength but a far higher percentage of its infantry) only reentered the pursuing front line of American forces on November 5. MacArthur became involved in a bizarre episode that easily could have turned tragic. In unthinking zeal to set foot in Sedan ahead of his French allies, Pershing goaded senior officers of the American First Army into launching several U.S. divisions off on a race for the city without regard to customary unit boundaries. Consequently, while on patrol the flamboyantly attired MacArthur was "captured" by soldiers of the 1st Infantry Division who had to be persuaded he was not a German. MacArthur added a seventh Silver Star to his history of exploits before the Armistice on November 11. MacArthur briefly led the 42nd Division (but not in combat) as Menoher went to a Corps command.[21]

Over the decades, MacArthur's critics subjected almost every facet of his life to scorching attack. The singular major exception is his record in France. He amply earned his six Silver Stars and two Distinguished Service Crosses. He very likely deserved the Medal of Honor for the Cote de Chatillon, but would not receive one. His driving personality undoubtedly played a key role in the fact that the Rainbow Division ranked as one of the top units in the American Expeditionary Force by all statistical measures. In casualties, it ranked third (behind only the 1st and 3rd Divisions) at 14,683 in only 162 days at the front. One particularly disinterested but keenly knowledgeable set of graders confirmed the accountants' lusterless accolades. Captured intelligence documents reflected that the Kaiser's officers consistently rated the Rainbow as one of the three or four American divisions they considered on par with the most elite British and French formations. A 1992 study determined that the 42nd Division stood second in combat effectiveness, behind only the 2nd Division, which was half Marine.[22]

The perverse reward for this excellence was assignment of the Rainbow Division as one of the nine divisions of the American component of the occupation army in a zone west of the Rhine around Coblenz. Meanwhile, many Yanks with far less arduous service headed for ships to take them home. After the great American journalist William Allen White visited the Rainbow Division during this duty, he declared of MacArthur: "I had never met so vivid, so captivating, so magnetic a man. . . . His staff adored him, his men worshipped him, and he seemed to be entirely without vanity." This interview with White surfaced two threads that loom as portents for MacArthur's subsequent triumphs and failures: MacArthur extolled the shrewdness of German women as voters, previewing his later support for the franchise for Japanese women; he also expressed interest in the radical movement in America, providing a dark hint of an obsession that would bear him to disaster as chief of staff.[23]

Finally, on April 18, 1919, MacArthur sailed with his brigade from Brest. A pelting rain provided the gloomy send-off from their adventure "Over There." When MacArthur and his men debarked in New York, he later recalled he expected a tumultuous cheering ovation. Instead, he encountered a child who asked who they were. When MacArthur replied that they were the famous 42nd, the child asked if they had been to France. This gangway incident presaged a vast reversal of the national mood. The market for ideals and crusades was bankrupt. The Republican nominee for the presidency, Warren G. Harding, marched under the banner of "a return to normalcy."[24]

Immediately upon MacArthur's return from overseas, the chief of staff, Peyton Marsh, selected him to become superintendent of West Point. This appointment proved absolutely critical in MacArthur's career. It guaranteed that MacArthur retained his one-star rank while dozens of other newly minted generals (including all but one of his contemporaries) reverted to lower grades.

At thirty-nine, MacArthur became the youngest superintendent since the revered Sylvanus Thayer, who made the academy a premier educational institution in America after the War of 1812. March instructed MacArthur to treat the faculty with diplomacy (some of them had instructed MacArthur as a cadet) but emphasized that the institution urgently required revitalization. During the war, March had converted West Point from a four-year military academy into little more than a year-long elite officer training program; to a large degree, March charged MacArthur with healing grievous wounds March himself inflicted.

While civilians might imagine that at the academy, as with all things military, the superintendent enjoyed vast powers to command fealty to his predilections, such was not the case. The democratic academic board formed the real locus of power. It comprised the superintendent, the commandant of cadets, and the heads of the departments of instruction. Each member exercised but one vote. The faculty deemed itself the guardian of the soul of the academy; that soul they identified as manifested by hallowed traditions. MacArthur's style emitted to the faculty early warning signs of his subversive intent. No grommet mustered his cap to attention. He was disposed to alarming familiarity with subordinates, like casually lighting their cigarettes for them (although he maintained a satisfactory distance from cadets).[25]

MacArthur's titanic clash with the academic board stemmed from a fundamental conflict of vision. MacArthur's war experience convinced him that West Point must prepare a different type of officer. Traditionally, West Point graduates entered a small regular army drawn from enlistees of very limited endowments who required strict discipline to become effective soldiers. MacArthur emerged from the war certain that he had seen the future: a mass army of National Guardsmen, volunteers, or draftees. Such men possessed far higher attainments and could only be commanded effectively by officers who enjoyed their respect, not officers who ruled by fear. MacArthur's experience in the occupation period also demonstrated that officers must be capable of dealing with problems beyond those of a strictly military character.

MacArthur's reform folio thus encompassed a comprehensive liberalization. He intended to broaden the curriculum to include social sciences and recent military history, provide cadets with more contact with American society, and bestow on them increasing levels of responsibility. Based on his own bitter experience as a victim of vicious hazing, he moved to stamp out such abuse which had careened dangerously out of control during World War I. While hazing did not wholly vanish—mainly because many alumni and not a few cadets viewed it as a valuable method of weeding out the unfit—MacArthur effected a fundamental change.

MacArthur did win some important victories at West Point. He formalized a longstanding but embryonic honor code which became a proud legacy for generations. He insisted that the notoriously inbred faculty visit other institutions of higher learning. Moreover, MacArthur brought many outside faculty members as well as political figures and military and other experts as guest lecturers to West Point. While these measures encountered resistance from the old guard, they were embraced by younger instructors. His other great timeless legacy was a comprehensive regime of intramural athletics. Over the gymnasium, MacArthur had inscribed his own words: "Upon the fields of friendly strife are sown the seeds that, upon other fields, on other days, will bear the fruits of victory."

MacArthur's zeal was unbounded when it came to football. He never missed a practice and writhed when Army could not defeat Navy during his tenure. But he began a program of recruiting skilled football players that would make Army dominant by the end of the decade. His opponents promptly killed some of MacArthur's reforms when he departed, but eventually the academy would adopt his vision and his reforms. The legacy of his comprehensive overhaul of academics, athletics and cadet life, ranked him as the most important superintendent of the Twentieth Century.[26]

The next years of MacArthur's rise form the only period apart from his childhood during which his personal life eclipsed his professional life. In September 1921, MacArthur met Louise Cromwell Brooks, a spoiled, alluring, rich divorcee ten years his junior who had two children. Her overpowering aura of sensuality poleaxed MacArthur. Louise proudly trailed a scroll of romantic victories over the likes of Pershing and Britain's dashing Admiral Sir David Beatty, but she was floored by the magnetic MacArthur. They married on Valentine's Day, 1922, sure that their union marked a divine fate reserved only for exceptional mortals. While his relationship with Louise was fueled by lust, MacArthur freely and genuinely bestowed his love on her children.

Louise interjected complications into MacArthur's career that provided a tangy source of gossip then and much historical smirking later. While Pershing had severed his romantic bonds with Louise, he was delighted when she took up with an aide he looked over with near fatherly regard, John Quekemeyer. Louise broke her informal engagement with Quekemeyer to accept MacArthur's proposal. This came within a few days of Pershing's writing to MacArthur that he was going to be transferred overseas, and so would have to terminate his appointment as superintendent of West Point far earlier than the normal four-year tour. The conclusion in army parlors was that these events formed a natural connection reflecting Pershing's spiteful attempt to sabotage MacArthur's marriage and career. The reality was that Pershing's letter predated the announcement of MacArthur's plan to marry Louise. The more likely explanation for MacArthur's removal from West Point was that Pershing's sympathies rested with the old guard.

MacArthur found that much had changed on his return to the Philippines in October 1922. Peace generally reigned. A Philippine National Assembly had exercised power since 1916. Its leader, Manuel Quezon, the rising star in the Philippine political firmament, worked assiduously for independence. Leonard Wood, MacArthur's old idol, commanded the Philippine Department.

MacArthur bore the official job title of commander of the Military District of Manila. In reality it was no job at all, but MacArthur used his idle hours to cultivate Philippine elites. Neither they nor the white colonial elite missed the fact that MacArthur treated upper-crust Filipinos as his social and intellectual equals. This endeared him to the Filipinos, but estranged many of the whites. Louise occupied herself with a social whirl, but almost entirely among the whites.[27]

Pinky became seriously ill and MacArthur retuned to Washington in February 1923. She recovered, but it was the last time Douglas saw his brother, who died that year of appendicitis. Soldiers of the elite Philippine Scouts staged a mutiny in July 1924 over the inequality of their pay, allowances, and benefits compared to white soldiers. MacArthur's known advocacy of equal treatment probably played a role in his replacement of the commander of the Philippine Division.[28]

Pershing retired as chief of staff in September 1924. Ten days later MacArthur's promotion to major general was announced. He left the Philippines in early 1925 to take command of the IV Corps area whose headquarters were in Atlanta. By the fall he took charge of the more significant III Corps area at Baltimore. Then came what he described as "one of the most distasteful orders I ever received." He became a member of the court martial of Brigadier General William "Billy" Mitchell. The trial presented no great legal issue: Mitchell's public denunciations of navy and army leaders undoubtedly constituted the offense charged. Mitchell and his supporters, however, exploited the event to propagate for air power, in general, and an independent air force, in particular. MacArthur maintained a sphinx-like silence during the trial; he and Louise passed the hours exchanging loving glances. He and others later claimed—or seemed to claim, for the matter is still unresolved—that he voted for acquittal. This is unlikely. But MacArthur probably did labor to block Mitchell's dismissal from service.[29]

The MacArthurs' marriage crumbled in Baltimore. The official reason for their divorce in 1929 was the patently ludicrous charge of "failure to support." Both later characterized the failure as due to "incompatibility," which was all too true. If the Jazz Age still flickers in history from the glow of a set of hedonistic spirits burning their candles at both ends, Louise Cromwell provided one of the particularly incandescent tapers. There was no niche in the staid army for a spoiled, willful, fabulously wealthy woman-child of advancing years. Obviously recognizing the trajectory of their relationship, she tried to persuade MacArthur to leave the service and become a (very, very rich) businessman, but he refused: his life and destiny was the army. MacArthur closed a door on his first marriage and virtually never mentioned it again. Perhaps the deepest wound from this adventure was the separation from his stepchildren, for whom he had developed genuine affection.[30]

An uneasy union of several hundred sports organizations huddled under the umbrella of the American Olympic Committee. When the committee president died suddenly, MacArthur's well-known commitment to athletics at West Point secured an offer to replace him for the 1928 games. The new Chief of Staff, General Charles P. Summerall (the man who demanded MacArthur take de Chatillon), likewise advocated athletics and authorized MacArthur to take the job to provide the army with much-needed favorable publicity in an era when there were many who wished to avoid any reminder that peace might not be permanent. MacArthur threw himself into the role with the bright eyed zeal of a boy who finds a train beneath the Christmas tree. He tamed the egos of the rival cardinals of sports denominations while he exhorted American athletes toward triumph. In one flamboyant vignette, he had his driver steer his limousine down a road alongside the waterway as to his exhortations an underdog American rowing team pulled in the gold. His team won the games, an accomplishment that simultaneously provided balm to his soul after the wounds of his broken marriage and polished his reputation just as he approached his chance for the ultimate prize in an army officer's career.[31]

2

Chief of Staff

DEVASTATING FLOODS IN 1927 PERSUADED PRESIDENT HERBERT Hoover ("the Great Engineer") that he needed a dynamic new chief of engineers to spearhead a massive program of flood control. Hoover offered MacArthur the post. MacArthur wisely but politely turned the offer down, recognizing it as a potential cul-de-sac that would foreclose his rise to the coveted job of chief of staff, the jewel that escaped his father.

As Summerall's term expired in 1930, MacArthur occupied a commanding but not impregnable position. Four years constituted the customary "tour" for a chief of staff. None of the six major generals senior to MacArthur had at least this remaining length of service. Of the eleven major generals with at least four years service remaining, MacArthur ranked as the youngest; the best known, publicly; and the most conspicuously decorated. His recent triumph with the Olympics further burnished his name. General Pershing reputedly championed Fox Connor, but preoccupation with battlefield monuments in Europe left Pershing ill-positioned to press his favorite's case. Finally, MacArthur enjoyed the active support of Summerall and the dashing secretary of war, oil tycoon Patrick Hurley. Hoover's high opinion of MacArthur clinched the case. MacArthur took the oath of office on November 21, 1930. He moved into the quarters at Ft. Myers in Virginia just outside Washington; his mother accompanied him.[1]

Finally obtaining the top professional job that eluded his father infused MacArthur with pride, but in reality he donned a veritable crown of thrones. Failures overshadowed his successes during his tumultuous tenure. The opponent MacArthur faced was the Great Depression. In military terminology, events cast him as a beleaguered commander fighting a bitter rear guard action, not as a dashing cavalier galloping forward in a triumphal advance.

Providing a vision for the army constituted perhaps the most consequential of MacArthur's plethora of tasks as chief of staff. MacArthur's vision was wholly conventional. He aimed to secure a balanced, broad-front advance of all arms and services. Representative Ross A. Collins, the leader of the House sub-committee on military appropriations, entered the lists as one of MacArthur's chief antagonists. Collins offered a radically divergent vision of a future dominated by mechanization and air power. MacArthur refused to award priority to either.

Nonetheless, it would be unjust to present this clash as a cartoon with MacArthur as a troglodyte. Economic stringency drove army appropriations down dramatically. With so few dollars available, any initiative with costly new equipment mandated a significant reduction in manpower and/or training. After World War I, Congress calculated that the minimum size of the army should be 18,000 officers and 285,000 enlisted men. MacArthur took over an army numbering about 12,000 officers and 125,000 men. MacArthur believed that the attenuated size of the army, and particularly the officer corps, left him with no margin for a trade-off. As he put it succinctly in one letter to Congress: "Trained officers constitute the most vitally essential element in modern war, and the only one that under no circumstances can be improvised or extemporized."

MacArthur fought desperately not for hardware, but to maintain, and in fact hugely improve the army's officer educational system. Indeed, one could make the case that MacArthur's towering achievements and only area of radical innovation prior to World War II involved education. His choice was vindicated when the money spigots finally opened and the army generally proved capable of reforming doctrine and fielding modern equipment rapidly as well as conducting a gigantic mobilization (at peak strength in 1945, the army was nearly *sixty times* larger than the force MacArthur led as chief of staff). But all of this rested on a core of professional officers with advanced training who could not be "improvised or extemporized" in an emergency.[2]

MacArthur's initiated two reforms of note. One was a reorganization of the general staff itself, which greatly improved coordination and efficiency. More important proved his plan to consolidate the army's nine corps areas into four armies. These armies in turn became the basis for mobilization, training, and tactical employment. Army historians extolled this "as a monumental step towards readying the Army's tactical organization for its gigantic tasks in the global conflict soon to come," and saw it as the germinal stages of the organization George Marshall would employ for the great World War II expansion.[3]

MacArthur played a key but wholly inadvertent role as a booster of air power. In 1931, MacArthur wangled an accord with the navy on the roles of each service's aviation. MacArthur secured for the army the mission of coastal defense with aircraft. This mission thus provided army flyers with the license for an aircraft capable of long-range "coastal defense." In 1933, they triggered a design competition that resulted in the B–17 "Flying Fortress," the plane that finally permitted army flyers to realize their dreams of strategic bombing.[4]

With regard to mechanization, MacArthur managed to both ameliorate and exacerbate an intractable problem he inherited. As historian George Hoffman observed, severe budgetary restriction that ruled out large scale mechanization "did not preclude the Army's leadership from modernizing the mind." The National Defense Act of 1920 created a fundamental impediment to American armored warfare development by abolishing the independent Tank Corps where advanced concepts were germinating. The act instead relegated control of tanks to the infantry branch largely dominated by officers who envisioned mechanization in terms of direct support of the rifleman. In 1931, MacArthur disbanded a recently formed experimental mechanized brigade. This one step backward permitted two important steps forward. He perceived correctly that rather than expending his limited funds to maintain antique vehicles unsuited to the coming high-tempo warfare, the monies were better employed on prototype versions of new, fast, robust tanks that led to the vehicles used in World War II. More significantly, he ordered all branches to develop mechanization. This proved crucial, for it was the cavalry branch that would originate most of the advanced doctrine employed in World War II. But MacArthur's balkanization of mechanization by separate branches retarded development of combined arms techniques, and neither he nor his successors foresaw the very deep mobile penetration operations on the German and Soviet model.[5]

Amid all his other travails, MacArthur found time to honor the request of a religious journal publisher for a response to a poll of American clergymen that demonstrated pervasive pacifist ideology. MacArthur mounted a muscular excoriation of those he labeled as seeking privilege without attendant responsibility. This provoked one anonymous pacifist to discover an exemption in his creed that allowed him to send MacArthur a death threat.[6]

MacArthur was as close to a friend of Hoover as the distant and frigid president permitted. They saw each other as consummate professionals in their respective fields, soldiering and engineering. For MacArthur, the fact that Hoover was not a professional politician ennobled him. MacArthur's few articulations of his philosophy outside of soldiering bore marked resemblance to the "rugged individualism" portrayed in Hoover's *American Individualism*. This was an idealistic system that rejected European examples of both birth caste and socialism. He believed that the government's legitimate goal was to permit each individual to attain his highest rise in accordance with "his intelligence, character, ability and ambition." The government should also act as a referee to prevent domination by any political or economic faction that would thwart individual opportunity. In return, the individual owed the community a sense of social responsibility, such as caring for the less fortunate—but without corrupting their self-reliance and initiative. This brand of philosophy rejected Adam Smith's laissez-faire, but approached government intervention in social and economic affairs as a cure to be used very sparingly, with great caution and skepticism. In copying Hoover's philosophy, MacArthur provided another example of his penchant for adapting the ideas of others rather than innovating his own. More practically, these principles rendered MacArthur totally incompatible with fascism, a military coup, or mindless worship of big business.[7]

Once he became chief of staff, MacArthur discovered the then obscure Major Dwight D. Eisenhower. The younger officer displayed a mastery of detail, a willingness to accept responsibility and possessed an engaging personality that meshed easily with civilians. But most of all MacArthur noted Eisenhower's fluid pen. After exploiting the ambitious major with repeated special assignments in addition to his regular duties, in February 1933 MacArthur placed Eisenhower in his office, just a slatted door away, as an aide. Eisenhower discharged this role for almost seven years.[8]

The complexity of their relationship and Eisenhower's attitudes about MacArthur fascinate. Eisenhower's various contemporary and retrospective comments disclose a sweet and sour salad of admiration and disgust. MacArthur's intellect awed Eisenhower ("My God, but he was smart," remarked Eisenhower.) Eisenhower's ego sprouted up to the sun of MacArthur's disarming charm, a potent component of which was flattery. (MacArthur once commented that a paper of Eisenhower's was "much better than I could have done myself." No normal mortal would fail to find such words from the brilliant chief of staff intoxicating.) For MacArthur, Eisenhower provided a polished voice coupled with the rare ability to anticipate and to project perfectly the view point of the chief.[9]

On the other side of the ledger, Eisenhower found MacArthur's towering ego and pomposity deeply repugnant. MacArthur's cavalier willingness to violate army norms and engage in political partisanship alarmed Eisenhower. Another soul-deep fissure between them was that Eisenhower outwardly remained a seemingly unpretentious professional officer whereas MacArthur disported himself regally like some consummate dramatic actor, always on stage, no matter the size of the audience. MacArthur, under full sail, stoked up purple prose with exaggerated body movements and invocations of the Almighty when speaking in public. In private, MacArthur's' references to himself in the third person amused the son of a Kansas farmer.

There were also several conspicuous contrasts between Eisenhower's experience under MacArthur and later under General Marshall. Unlike Marshall, MacArthur mounted no effort to teach his protégé; he simply gave Eisenhower the opportunity to observe. On the other hand, MacArthur actually bantered jokingly with Eisenhower and met socially with Eisenhower and his wife, things Marshall avoided. MacArthur would write in one of Eisenhower's efficiency reports: "This is the best officer in the Army. When the next war comes, he should go right to the top." But MacArthur never envisioned Eisenhower, even at the "top," as his peer. His years with MacArthur taught Eisenhower far more than how to be a field marshal of paperwork. From MacArthur Eisenhower developed a whole approach to command. It began with detailed mastery of subject matter (though Eisenhower learned to carry this lightly at times) followed by a persistent and rigorously logical presentation of facts in an authoritative but not bombastic voice. Dealing with MacArthur's *Hindenburg*-size ego left Eisenhower superbly prepared to confront Churchill and British General Bernard Montgomery. In other words, Eisenhower as a student learned important lessons from both his teacher's virtues and flaws.[10]

━━◄═══►━━

In the United States as in the rest of the world, the economic calamity of the Great Depression fostered political unrest. MacArthur stood adamantly against entangling the army directly into relief work, such as various congressional proposals for an enlisted reserve corps to perform public works. MacArthur also forged a close friendship with his number-two man, Major General George Van Horn Moseley. A virulent nativist, anti-Semite, and scourge of communists, Moseley showered MacArthur with warnings about the rise of radicalism and saw such forces behind every public disturbance.[11]

In 1924, Congress had rewarded some 3.5 million World War I veterans with "adjusted compensation certificates." The average certificate would have a value of about $1,000 when it was redeemable as Congress promised in 1945. In the depth of the depression, this represented a very substantial sum, and unemployed veterans agitated for immediate redemption of "the bonus." After Congress provided a half-payment over Hoover's veto, in 1932, Congressman Wright Patman advanced a bill to pay the balance of "the bonus." Thousands of veterans, some with their families, headed to Washington to lobby for the measure. Later MacArthur and Hoover administration officials contended that few of these men were actual veterans, but studies demonstrated that as many as 94 percent were. Hoover, Secretary of War Hurley, and MacArthur saw the gathering bonus marchers as the fruit of a conspiracy. There had been a series of disturbances and marches on Washington that Hoover and his subordinates were convinced communists had orchestrated.[12]

An ex-sergeant in the American Expeditionary Forces (AEF), Walter W. Williams, lead the "Bonus Expeditionary Forces" (BEF), which numbered perhaps as many as 22,000 by June. A charismatic man with a skillful tongue, Waters enforced discipline and order. He publicly rejected the idea that his legions represented radicalism. The man carrying the burden of dealing with the BEF was the police commissioner, Pelham D. Glassford. In the history of this episode, he glimmers as the hero. A brigadier general in the World War I, Glassford correctly perceived that the marchers' need was support, not suppression. He used his influence as well as about $1,000 of his own funds to provide them with food and care, and employed his considerable charm and verbal skills to encourage them to return home.[13]

The Senate defeated Patman's bill in mid-June and Congress provided money for those marchers who wished to go home. This measure, along with an ensuing sense of despair, reduced the BEF to approximately 10,000 by mid-July. From Hoover down to the commissioners of the District of Columbia, patience expired by late July. Glassford was told to clear the bonus army marchers from buildings they occupied on Pennsylvania Avenue by July 21 and to have them out of town by August 4. Glassford successfully pleaded again for delay, but on July 27 Hoover issued a firm order that the BEF must go.[14]

When Glassford began to clear the marchers from Pennsylvania Avenue, on July 28, violence erupted. Even after a brick seriously injured Glassford, he carried on. What happened next marks just the first of a series of disputed events. Glassford wrote later that at the time he reported that his police retained control of the situation, but that he intended to defer further evictions until the next day. The district commissioners maintained that Glassford actually requested federal troops. The commissioners forwarded a troop request to Hoover. About 2:15 P.M. the situation lurched out of control as a disturbance led police to shoot two marchers fatally. [15]

This incident prompted Hoover to seek aid from the army. At 2:55 P.M., Hurley, stating that the civil government could not maintain law and order, ordered MacArthur to send troops to the scene, "[s]urround the affected area and clear it without delay." Hurley further directed that prisoners would be turned over to civil authorities and that women and children "be accorded every consideration and kindness. Use all humanity consistent with due execution of this order."

By 4:00 P.M., a squadron (battalion) of cavalry, a battalion of infantry, a tank platoon, and motor transport company waited on the ellipse south of the White House. Against the sound advice of Major Eisenhower, MacArthur accompanied the troops, who directly answered to Brigadier General Perry L. Miles. MacArthur explained his presence to Hurley on the grounds that he should be there to make "necessary decisions" beyond the purview of Miles. To Eisenhower, MacArthur justified his presence on the more visceral grounds that "incipient revolution [was] in the air."[16]

By 5:00 P.M., the troops cleared the Pennsylvania Avenue arena of conflict with minimum injury, although some shacks were set afire. By nightfall, nearly all the marchers retreated across the Anacostia River via the Eleventh Street Bridge. Troops employed much tear gas in his last stage. One infant died from the fumes.

Had events halted at this juncture, only mild controversy at most would have ensued. But they did not, and the reason they did not forms the eye of the subsequent storm. Hurley dispatched two messages to MacArthur containing Hoover's order not to pursue the marchers across the Eleventh Street Bridge. Eisenhower later insisted that in neither instance did MacArthur "hear" the orders. Miles likewise vouched that no such instruction reached MacArthur. The source for the story that MacArthur deliberately violated the president's order, the version that became gospel for MacArthur's critics, was Van Horn Moseley.

But the assistant secretary of war for air, F. Trubee Davidson, contradicted Moseley. The most likely reality is that Moseley did in fact fail to forward the *first* message. But later Col. Clarence Wright tried to deliver the *second* message. Eisenhower recalled, "I went up to the General and said, 'There's a man here who has some orders about this.' He said, 'I don't want to hear them and I don't want to see them. Get him away.' He wouldn't listen to these instructions, and so far as I know he never heard them." Thus, by Eisenhower's account MacArthur technically did not defy a direct presidential order. But even this most favorable version of events indicates that MacArthur sensed that Wright's instructions would have defeated or retarded him in his self-determined objective of routing the marchers. Hence, he refused to listen to Wright, which for practical purposes equated to defiance of civilian authority.[17]

MacArthur later claimed that he told Glassford that he should instruct the veterans to clear the area, that the army would proceed slowly and that nothing would happen until after the troops were fed. This delay did occur. Miles took his men over the bridge about 11:15 P.M., pausing briefly again to permit the marchers to clear the area. Whether due to angry defiance by the marchers, or possibility as a result of the pyrotechnical effect of tear gas grenades, the encampment erupted in flames. Thousands of choking, frightened, veterans and their families, many of them destitute, fled at the midnight hour. By that time, MacArthur, again ignoring Eisenhower's advice, launched some pyrotechnics himself in remarks to the press. He questioned the bona fides of the marchers as veterans; proclaimed that they had mistaken the consideration with which they had been treated as weakness; insisted that revolution was imminent; and opined that had the government not acted, far worse consequences would have ensued.

The whole episode was a deadly blow to the army's image, and still worse for MacArthur's. Much of the press, and what would soon be a small army of detractors, interpreted MacArthur's efforts to provide a ringing endorsement of Hoover's call for decisive action as a mask for his own initiative in creating the horrible scenes of that night. The core truth here is that MacArthur (as well as Hurley and Hoover) genuinely but quite mistakenly believed the bonus marchers were communist puppets. They thus saw the episode in vastly more sinister terms than the facts justified. By the magnanimous standards set by Glassford, the flight of the bonus marchers and their families appeared unforgivably brutal. What little to be said for MacArthur in this episode is that, apart from the one accidental death of an infant, the police, not the army, inflicted all the fatalities.[18]

The other leitmotif of the Bonus Army March for MacArthur's reputation ever after harbored by liberals, including Franklin Roosevelt, is that it exposed MacArthur's barely veiled aspirations to become the man on horseback. Roosevelt famously remarked to an aide that Huey Long was one of the two most dangerous men in America. When the aide asked the identity of the other individual, Roosevelt replied "Douglas MacArthur." (In the frequent retellings of this episode, Roosevelt's further comment that MacArthur's threat was merely latent is routinely omitted.) If it is correct to call MacArthur hysterical on the topic of communist influence in the United States—and it is—it is likewise hysterical for his critics to charge that he harbored ambitions of becoming a dictator when no evidence of this exists in any known writing or utterance.[19]

<hr>

If there was any doubt, the rout of the Bonus Army guaranteed the election of Franklin Roosevelt. As MacArthur rode his stallion at the head of the inaugural parade, he could no more foretell than anyone else what the new president would be like. Columnist Walter Lippmann famously assessed Roosevelt as "a pleasant man who, without any important qualifications for the office, would very much like to be President." MacArthur and Roosevelt's relationship went back prior to World War I. Of it, MacArthur claimed "Whatever difference arose between us, it never sullied in slightest degrees the warmth of my personal friendship for him." Oddly enough, Roosevelt did have a reservoir of actual respect for MacArthur. They related as two great aristocratic actors sharing a grand stage—but each always looking to outdo the other, with Roosevelt usually triumphant.

Two matters stood between them. Professionally, MacArthur represented the armed service Roosevelt disfavored, for the president deeply loved the navy and occasionally spared some fond thoughts for the Army Air Corps. Ideologically, they habituated entirely different planets. Nonetheless, the ability of both men to work around these divisions became manifest almost immediately. Roosevelt's fertile imagination envisioned taking the idle hands of legions of unemployed men and turning them to healthful, productive outdoor tasks in conservation. Congress authorized the Civilian Conservation Corps (C.C.C.) at the end of March 1933. Roosevelt wanted a quarter-million men deployed by July 1. MacArthur tasked the general staff with implementation plans even before the act passed, and secretly alerted the corps commanders to start preparations. Initially, Roosevelt limited the army's role to inducting, conditioning and deploying the men to work locations supervised by other agencies. When the other federal agencies conspicuously floundered before the challenge, on May 10 the army got the whole job.

In a brilliant effort the general staff generated a master plan in less than two days that vaporized a two-month-old cloud of confusion. MacArthur delegated actual implementation to the corps commanders. This enormously accelerated the enterprise and minimized bureaucratic sclerosis. Between May 17 and July 1, the army mobilized 275,000 C.C.C. recruits. This not only exceeded the president's goal, but outdid the record of mobilization in the first six months of World War I. FDR was delighted. MacArthur cited the episode as exemplifying the value of general staff planning and a large and capable officer corps.[20]

This triumph may have saved MacArthur's job, for around this time his budget struggles reached a searing confrontation. In March 1933, Congress authorized the army a mere $277 million for fiscal year 1934. Then the administration proposed to reduce this by a further $80 million. In desperation, MacArthur and the new Secretary of War George H. Dern met with Roosevelt. The encounter was heated and Dern wilted before the full blast of Roosevelt's scorn. At this point, MacArthur stepped forward, and according to his recollection:

... I spoke recklessly and said something to the general effect that when we lost the next war, and an American boy, lying in the mud with an enemy bayonet through his belly and an enemy foot on his dying throat, spat out his last curse, I wanted the name not to be MacArthur, but Roosevelt. The president grew livid. 'You must not talk that way to the President!' he roared. He was, of course, right, and I knew it almost before the words had left my mouth. I said that I was sorry and apologized. But I felt my Army career was at an end. I told him he had my resignation as Chief of Staff. As I reached the door his voice came with that cool detachment which so reflected his extraordinary self-control, 'Don't be foolish, Douglas; you and the budget must get together on this.'

Dern had shortly reached my side and I could hear his gleeful tones, 'You have saved the Army.' But I just vomited on the steps of the White House.[21]

MacArthur repeatedly warned that the army rested at half the strength contemplated by the National Defense Act of 1920 and that its equipment overwhelmingly was comprised of World-War-origin relics. But the appropriation for fiscal year 1935 was a mere $280 million. In what was probably a bitter pill to swallow, MacArthur found himself beholden to the Public Works Administration for millions of dollars of expenditures for army construction.[22]

MacArthur's travails expanded to a new front in 1934. Of the many rival contenders for the title of MacArthur-hater-in-chief among the liberal press, Drew Pearson was at least a finalist. Typical of Pearson's methods, he uncritically accepted Louise Cromwell Brooks' bitter ranting about her former husband MacArthur. Pearson published accusations that MacArthur was vain (true), incompetent (false), and disloyal to Roosevelt (true politically but not professionally). He did not print, but disseminated Louise's further vicious jibes that MacArthur was sexually dysfunctional. (The letters they exchanged left no doubt that this was far from the case.)

The published charges prodded MacArthur into the horrendous mistake of suing Pearson for defamation. Pearson at first thought his defense would be simple: put Louise on the stand to repeat her stories of "the truth" about MacArthur. But Louise, now tormented by alcoholism and imprisoned in a very unhappy third marriage, balked, probably because she retained enough sense to see how quickly her stories would crumble if challenged. Pearson appeared to be confronting ruin when Congressman Ross Collins, MacArthur's nemesis on Capital Hill, handed Pearson a deadly weapon.

While still in Manila in April 1930, MacArthur had fallen for Isabel Rosario Cooper. She had a Scottish father and Filipina mother, modest singing and dancing skills, and made her way in life as a chorus girl. Then fifty; MacArthur styled his sixteen-year-old paramour his "baby girl." When MacArthur left Manila to take up his post as chief of staff, he brought Isabel along and installed her in convenient locations in Washington that became the destinations he preferred when the demands of his job and Pinky permitted. When they were apart, he showered her with letters, leaving no doubt about their relationship. Though MacArthur professed to Isabel that their relationship was love, most of their hours together were passed horizontally.

Isabel, young, neglected and soon bored, sought some course work to while away her lonesome hours waiting for MacArthur's increasingly infrequent visits. Predictably, she met and fell in love with another student her age. Meanwhile, MacArthur broke off the crumbling relationship and paid Isabel's passage back to the Philippines. But Drew Pearson located Isabel before she left. She not only had the epistolary evidence of the affair, but also offered to recite much of MacArthur's boastful and damaging bedroom talk demeaning other public figures. The legal case was settled; MacArthur dropped the suit for one dollar and acquired Isabel's affidavits from Pearson's attorney. Isabel received $15,000 in exchange for a pledge never to ask for money again. She failed in an attempt to restart her career in Hollywood and in 1960 committed suicide.[23]

✛━━✛

By tradition, not any formal stricture, the term of a chief of staff was widely viewed as four years. Thus, November 1934 loomed as MacArthur's nominal date of relief. In the social whirl that lubricated official relations in Washington, MacArthur was an outsider with the coming of the New Deal. One journalist witness portrayed him "as a lonely figure. No one spoke his language. No one wanted to speak it." Senator Gerald Nye, who spearheaded a congressional investigation that purported to prove that arms manufacturers had conspired to dupe America into entering World War I, depicted MacArthur as a warmonger and stooge for arms merchants. Roosevelt entertained no doubt of MacArthur's rigorous ideological opposition to the New Deal, which the president could rightly consider in view of the army's unprecedented role in the administration's relief effort. Nor could the president miss the fact that MacArthur maintained relations with his old West Point cadet friend Robert Wood, of Sears, Roebuck and Company, who also led a prominent anti-New Deal business organization. Then there was the Bonus March, proof positive to Roosevelt's most committed followers that MacArthur was little short of a fascist viper. All of this made it appear highly unlikely that Roosevelt would fail to find a successor promptly.[24]

MacArthur supporters were few, but significant. First, he continued to retain support in the army. Second, key democratic legislators (conspicuously including men who had crossed swords with MacArthur in hearings) nonetheless urged MacArthur's reappointment. Another factor may have been that one leading candidate to replace MacArthur, Stuart Heintzelman, a personal friend of Roosevelt's since their days at Groton, became progressively debilitated and would die in 1935. Other candidates were no warmer to the New Deal than MacArthur. In a typical Roosevelt maneuver to placate the rival views, he announced that MacArthur would continue as chief of staff until a successor was appointed, but made it clear that he was not reappointing MacArthur to a full term. Thus, it is quite mistaken to regard this as a sterling vote of confidence in MacArthur; certainly it was not, as sometimes alleged by MacArthur's advocates, a "reappointment" as chief of staff.[25]

It was in this rump season of MacArthur's tour as chief of staff that he regained a fraction of the ground lost since his accession. The darkening international atmosphere proved his most potent ally: Japanese aggression in Manchuria and Hitler's rise in Germany reversed the anti-military tide. For fiscal year 1936, the army's budget jumped up to $355.5 million. MacArthur lost a struggle to increase the officer corps, but did maneuver an increase in enlisted strength to 165,000. He further shepherded through a cherished revision of the officer promotion system intended to speed promotions, particularly for promising officers.[26]

One final note must be added about MacArthur's tenure. George Marshall's skilled biographer, Forrest Pogue, examined and dismissed the malicious charge that MacArthur deliberately sabotaged Marshall's career. MacArthur was hesitant about jumping Marshall over many senior officers, for reasons quite apart from any animosity. Indeed, MacArthur proposed Marshall's promotion to brigadier general in 1935 and elevation to Chief of Infantry, a major general's slot. This did not happen, probably because of Roosevelt's manipulation of the date of MacArthur's succession, and Marshall only gained his first star after MacArthur's tour as chief of staff ended. [27]

3

From the Center to the Fringe

THE PHILIPPINE ARCHIPELAGO IS A ROUGH SEVEN BY SEVEN: ABOUT 7,100 islands about 7,000 miles from the United States. The eleven largest islands claim 94 percent of the total area of 115,000 square miles. The two largest islands are Luzon (40,420 square miles) and Mindanao (36,527 square miles). These populous isles anchor the poles of a 1,150-mile-long north-south axis stretching from Formosa (Taiwan) to Borneo. The Philippines lay only 500 miles off the Asian continent. They straddle a natural crossroads between Japan, China, Indo China, and the Netherlands East Indies.[1]

The United States acquired the Philippines after defeating Spain in the Spanish-American War in 1898, but established effective control only following a brutal war against Filipino insurgents. (Whether one regards this as commendable or lamentable, absent American control, the Filipinos would have tasted first German and then Japanese conquest.) In 1934, the Tydings-Mc-Duffie Act authorized a plan for Philippine independence in 1946. The next year free elections selected Manuel Quezon as president of a commonwealth.[2]

For sober Americans and Filipinos, the Japanese domination of Manchuria in 1931 and temporary seizure of Shanghai in 1932 raised the specter that Philippine independence might be brief. Even before the Filipinos faced the world on their own, the United States struggled with the long-running quandary of its obligations. In that era, the highest authority for American military planning was the Joint Army-Navy Board. It assigned potential enemies color codes. Japan was "Orange"; hence the plan for a hypothetical war with Japan was "War Plan Orange." This blueprint allocated the army the mission of holding Manila Bay for approximately six months, until a navy relief expedition arrived. For decades, however, senior officers recognized that neither the army forces in the Philippines nor the Pacific Fleet was strong enough to discharge its responsibilities under the plan. Indeed, despairing army officers seriously mooted the idea of withdrawing all forces. The navy insisted on continuing a military presence, hoping that someday the United States would commit the forces to make defense viable. As Japan's aggressiveness increased, the State Department incoherently advocated a strong foreign policy but not the force to back it up.[3]

━━

While he presented himself as the "Paladin of Philippine Freedom," Manuel Quezon actually favored a dominion status over complete independence. Moreover, he maneuvered in these stormy times to keep his people under an umbrella of a United States security guarantee. Nature dealt him one bargaining chip in the attractiveness of air and naval base rights in such a strategic location; he decided to create a second chip in the form of Philippine armed forces that could do double-duty in defending the islands, and, as a powerful inducement to a continued American protectorate, by guarding U.S. bases. He denounced critics who detected such aims and who decried "militarization" and the diversion of resources from social welfare programs, but he was careful not to publicly rule out the continued presence of an American naval base. Moreover, MacArthur's private remarks leave no doubt that he saw the same dual purposes.

Thus, when Quezon decided to hire a military adviser from the United States he aimed not just to procure a capable officer to supervise the creation of the new republic's armed forces but also to further his pursuit of continued American defense ties. MacArthur, who shared Quezon's thinking, emerged as a most felicitous choice for this role, as his selection bestowed valuable benefits on all the interested parties. For MacArthur, it meant he would not have to step down from the pinnacle of chief of staff and wait for retirement in a subordinate role. For Quezon, MacArthur's professional attainments, undoubted commitment to the Philippines, and understanding of Quezon's hidden

Parshall 2007

agenda ideally satisfied his requirements. For Roosevelt, the move furthered broad U.S. interests, but also secured the president's own narrower political interests by removing a potential political rival from the scene. The wily president continued MacArthur as chief of staff officially until October 1935. Roosevelt's motivation for this move probably was that it assured that George S. Simonds, MacArthur's favorite, lacked the requisite four years of remaining active service. Roosevelt picked Malin Craig as MacArthur's successor.[4]

MacArthur's contract with the Philippines guaranteed him an annual salary equivalent to $18,000 per year plus $15,000 in yearly allowances. This was on top of MacArthur's full pay as a U.S. major general, since he would remain on active duty. He thus became the best-paid soldier in the world. The title of field marshal appealed to MacArthur as another marker as his status as the preeminent world warrior. Internationally, it was the highest possible rank; but democratic America conspicuously eschewed such honorifics. A journalist planted the seeds of a persistent myth that with the pay and title went a new uniform adorned to MacArthur's gaudy taste. The reality was that the journalist mistook a new U.S. Army uniform for the dress of a "Philippine Field Marshal." But freshly minted regulations authorized current and former chiefs of staff to create distinctive uniform items. MacArthur exercised the unique privilege to devise a special hat wreathed extravagantly with gold braid. This headpiece became a signature component of his public image for the rest of his life.[5]

MacArthur's formal title was military adviser to the commonwealth government. MacArthur assembled a small staff, the key officer being Eisenhower. With the help of input from the Army War College, MacArthur and his staff drafted a plan to provide the Commonwealth with national security by 1946—and to manufacture a bargaining chip for Quezon. The essential features of the plan were: a small regular army (10,000 men); a conscription system; a ten-year training program of two 20,000-man classes a year (five and one-half months of training) to create a reserve force (the goal was 400,000 men); a small air force (100 fast bombers); and a fleet of 36 small torpedo boats. Tactically, the army comprised divisions of about 7,500 men with armament suitable to the terrain and the Philippine purse. The scheme marked another example of MacArthur's adaptability, for the basic idea originated with Leonard Wood's concept of a Swiss-style citizen army, ideally strong enough to deter aggression without incurring undue national burden.[6]

Critics fretted that unlike mountainous Switzerland, the Philippine archipelago was inherently much more vulnerable to an enemy—like Japan—with naval and air power. Some of the doubters may have harbored a low, and possibly racist, opinion of Filipino soldiers. The record demonstrated clearly, however, that properly trained and equipped, the Filipinos were excellent warriors, a fact MacArthur never doubted. It cannot be definitively concluded that MacArthur's overall scheme was sound and would have been effective. What can be said is that the plan never got a fair test, for it was not supported, and particularly, funded, as envisioned. Forces beyond MacArthur's control contributed the most to defeating his scheme. Even so, MacArthur must take responsibility for glaring flaws within his span of influence and an ominous failure to recognize the difference between his expansive ideals and reality.

The most basic underlying problem proved to be cohesion. After forty years of American rule, about 27 percent of the population spoke English and 3 percent Spanish. Tagalog was the language of the influential residents of central Luzon. It became the national language in 1937. But elsewhere, over sixty-five dialects divided Filipinos. MacArthur and his staff failed to make adequate allowance for this linguistic barrier, which erected a huge obstacle to creating a national army, since recruits from other islands could understand neither English nor Tagalog, the tongues of most Filipino officers.

Moreover, the lack of an adequate cadre of trained officers threatened the whole program. MacArthur probably anticipated that the Philippine Scouts, an elite body of well-trained Filipino enlisted men under U.S. officers serving as a component of the U.S. Army, would be transferred to the commonwealth's fledgling army and thus meet the need for a cadre of qualified instructors. But this did not occur. Not only did the five- and-a-half-month training cycle prove inadequate to imprint permanently its lessons on raw recruits, but also at one point army training was diluted to allow for basic educational and vocational subjects in deference to critics of "militarism." Despite warnings from Eisenhower about serious deficiencies, MacArthur did not exercise close supervision or take corrective action. It may well be that MacArthur pressed for large recruit classes from the start, an unwise move in terms of creating effective soldiers, because he believed that standing up a large force swiftly would aid Quezon's pursuit of continued U.S. security ties.[7]

The new military adviser soon discovered that adequate funding would not materialize. At the outset, Eisenhower estimated that it would take $25 million per year to give the fledgling republic an adequate defense force. But the Philippines could only provide about $8 million annually, and the U.S. did not fill the gap. Even with its extraordinarily limited budget, the U.S. Army provided almost $220 per man per year for each national guardsman. Not only did the army fail to give the Philippine Army equal treatment, it rejected MacArthur's plea for just $50 per Filipino. Hence, it proved impossible to house, equip, and conduct more than rudimentary training for each class of reservists. U.S. parsimony in providing low-cost weapons and munitions further exacerbated MacArthur's woes.[8] The story of the other components of the commonwealth's armed forces was, if anything, worse. The Philippine air force received just minuscule numbers of cast-off American aircraft. Despite spirited exertions, efforts to build a fleet of motor torpedo boats were almost entirely vain.[9]

Worse still, rifts between Quezon and MacArthur appeared. Like the leaders of many other small nations in that era, Quezon faced agonizing choices in how best to safeguard his people. The triumphs of the axis powers, the feeble resistance of the democracies, America's palpably inadequate investment in guarding the islands, and apparent U.S. disinterest in a continuing security arrangement all combined to propel Quezon to consider appeasement over resistance. He flirted with obtaining Japanese assurances of safety in exchange for Philippine neutrality. Even after the international situation took an unmistakably ominous cast with the German triumph in Europe in 1940, Quezon dithered.[10]

━━◆━━◆━━

In this interval, MacArthur's personal life underwent a profound transformation. The first and most devastating event was the death of his eighty-four-year-old mother in December 1935, just five weeks after they reached the Philippines. It was a crushing blow. Eisenhower noted that her death "affected the General's spirit for many months." Moreover, it followed upon the divorce from Louise and the disastrous entanglement with Isabel Cooper Rosario, to make MacArthur's cup of woes with the opposite sex run over.

Yet in a twist that seemed the intervention of guardian providence, stepping into MacArthur's life at this same time was the woman who became the fount of domestic bliss that stabilized his later life. On the ship out to the Far East, MacArthur met Jean Marie Faircloth of Murfreesboro, Tennessee. She was thirty-seven, never married, attractive, enchanting in personality and conversation, and with a regal bearing. On top of all this she possessed independent wealth (more than $2 million) and was as immediately smitten with MacArthur as he with her. When MacArthur took leave in April 1937 to return his mother's remains for burial with his father's, at Arlington National Cemetery, he married Jean in a civil ceremony in New York. She bore him a son, Arthur IV, in February 1938. MacArthur's genuine and unrestrained outpouring of love for his new wife and son appears as though some internal dam ruptured to release emotions long constrained by his Victorian upbringing.[11]

But an ominous change emerged during MacArthur's years as military adviser. In World War I, MacArthur exemplified the go-forward, direct-observation, personal command style. By the 1930s, as chief of staff, he became accustomed to managing a large institution and gathering facts second-hand. This style of leadership left his effectiveness hostage to the care and perception of subordinate officers, a number of whom lacked his intellectual gifts and energy.[12]

Like many a powerful man, MacArthur's vanity and ego long disposed him to present his own accomplishments in a bright light. But prior to this time, there was no marked *pattern* of egregiously misleading or flatly dishonest pronouncements. Beginning at least as early as his April 1936 report of the progress of the creation of the Philippine Army, MacArthur began to generate a steady stream of falsehoods. He may have been attempting to build support for something he sincerely believed was for the ultimate benefit of the Philippine people; he further believed, perhaps, that he had to place a false face on the project to support Quezon's pursuit of a U.S. alliance. But Eisenhower clearly informed him of the already manifest shortfalls in the scheme. MacArthur chose to begin announcing that things were as he wished them to be rather than as they were. Once he started down this path, he did not, and perhaps could not, stop.[13]

Why this later change occurred is critical to understanding what his admirers viewed as the underside of his subsequent triumphs and what his critics seized upon as his fundamental characteristic. Its exact origins are obscure, but likely linked to several obvious factors. Probably foremost was that his unique position freed him from the firm constraints of ultimate civilian supremacy that bound him in the U.S. Army, even as chief of staff. Indeed, from this point on he acted as though he regarded civilian authorities as, at best, colleagues (Quezon, Roosevelt, Secretary of War Henry Stimson, and Emperor Hirohito), and sometimes as inferiors (President Harry S. Truman). Moreover, because of his meteoric rise, and then his continued career long after his contemporaries retired or even died, he really had no remaining true peer, much less a superior, in the army whose opinion he respected. During World War II and thereafter, he officially was subordinate to the chief of staff. But when MacArthur had been chief of staff, these men had held the lowly ranks of colonel (George Marshall), major (Eisenhower and Omar Bradley) and even captain (J. Lawton Collins). This background placed these men in an extremely awkward position. MacArthur's physical distance from sources of restraining authority clearly played a role. He conspicuously resisted any suggestion and even orders that he return to the U.S. from 1935 to 1951, with the minor exceptions of his own trip to bury his mother in 1937 and the Pearl Harbor meeting in 1944. With the passing of his mother, the prospect that he might provoke her criticism ended and this also may have lifted his inhibitions about redefining the truth.

Another related source of this change was his façade of austere haughtiness that warded off intimacy. Outside his immediate family, he permitted only a handful of individuals to penetrate the façade. Like FDR, he played many roles and even his intimates were baffled as to who the "real" MacArthur was. One officer commented, "Who were his close friends? His key staff members, whoever they were at any given moment." This insight may shed light on a significant facet of his command conduct. He was famous, or infamous perhaps, for maintaining a staff that George Marshall compared to a court. Usually, his retention of some mediocre (or worse) staff officers has been attributed to his requirement for adulation over competence or a fear that to dismiss an inadequate officer might signal that he had erred in his selection of staff. While these and other reasons may be true to one degree or another, unlike other leaders, MacArthur secured an unhealthy and disproportionate number of his friends in his staff.[14]

That staff underwent key changes in 1939 and 1940. Eisenhower finally obtained a return to duty in the United States. He later denied that he parted with MacArthur in a state of enmity and acknowledged how his administrative experience with MacArthur prepared him for the great challenges awaiting him. Replacing Eisenhower as MacArthur's chief of staff was Lt. Col. Richard Sutherland, a Yale-educated infantry officer. Sutherland coupled complete loyalty with genuine talent as a staff officer. These attributes redeemed him in MacArthur's eyes, but Sutherland's extraordinarily abrasive, sarcastic management style left him with no friends. Worse yet, Sutherland exacerbated rather than ameliorated MacArthur's often divisive relationships with other military and naval leaders. A quartermaster corps officer, Lt. Col. Richard Marshall proved an adroit planner who enhanced his value by providing balm for the wounds Sutherland routinely inflicted. Major William F. Marquat ("an oasis of wit in a wilderness of stuffed shirts," quipped one observer) joined as anti-aircraft officer. He played a key role in the war and in Japan. While deprecating the talents of MacArthur's staff has provided sport for decades to historians, no one doubts that Captain Hugh Casey, an engineer officer who rose to become MacArthur's chief engineer, was extraordinarily capable and would have been an asset to any command. Then there was German-born Lt. Col. Charles A. Willoughby, who became MacArthur's erratic intelligence officer. Willoughby matched intelligence with a mercurial personality. (Nothing further need be noted now about Willoughby, but readers should begin to gird themselves for the trials ahead.) These officers and several others who joined MacArthur at this time would form an inner circle that surrounded MacArthur for the whole war, and some remained close well beyond.[15]

In an obscure Washington power play, MacArthur was forced to leave active army duty in 1937. Two years later, his increasingly strained relationship with Quezon foretold an end to his role in the Philippines. Thus by 1939, the tide of events seemed to be inexorably bearing MacArthur off the main current of history. He should have become one of countless once-powerful individuals whose lives are known only to a handful of history professors. One of these professors might have suggested MacArthur's life as a subject of a master's or doctoral dissertation to a student (these days a less promising student). But Japan and Germany changed everything. MacArthur joined a disparate but intriguing company of men whose seemingly dead careers the war resurrected: Winston Churchill, Henry Stimson, Admiral Ernest King, British Admiral Bertram Ramsey, and Australian General Thomas Blamey.[16]

From July 1937, Japan waged full-scale war against China. Although staunchly isolationist, the American people donated their sympathy to the Chinese people. President Roosevelt shared this outlook and took steps to support China and deter Japan, but solely with diplomatic and economic measures. These failed to dissuade Japan, and Tokyo further alienated Americans by allying itself with Germany and Italy.

The German triumph in Western Europe in 1940 shocked America from its slumber and prompted the first serious efforts to arm since World War I, but Roosevelt failed to mobilize the Philippine Army in 1940 on the grounds that such a move would be provocative. This was a major mistake. An extra year of properly funded preparation time could have greatly complicated Japan's problems. Washington only crossed the real Rubicon with Japan in July 1941, when Japanese forces occupied southern French Indo-China. Roosevelt reacted with what he intended as a creative and potent set of economic sanctions, which included threat of an oil embargo. Roosevelt conceived the program, as H. P. Willmott phrased it, as "an extremely sensitive instrument of torture, to be applied or slackened depending on Japanese behavior." But Roosevelt's characteristic vagueness boomeranged and eager subordinates interpreted his words as meaning an immediate and total oil embargo. Overnight, Roosevelt's stance became inflexible and marked a line in the sand from which neither side could retreat without humiliation.[17]

The diplomatic shift accompanied an abrupt and radical change of strategic policy. As recently as May 1941, official policy reaffirmed the long-standing view that successful protection of the Philippines was impossible. Now just two months later, Washington executed a total about-face and prepared to defend the commonwealth with a trio of decisions on July 26. First, all American and Filipino forces were placed under one unified command, the U.S. Army Forces in the Far East (USAFFE). Second, MacArthur was recalled to active duty (first as a major general, but shortly as a lieutenant general), and entrusted with the unified command. Third, now in the eleventh hour (and fifty-ninth minute) Washington decided to fund fully the mobilization of the Philippine Army.

Washington did not stop there. Over the next several months, MacArthur's American component received major reinforcements and supplies. At one point, the deployment of one U.S. infantry division was contemplated. This action was deferred and instead, MacArthur received an infusion of anti-aircraft, aviation, logistical, and small tank units. These reinforcements bolstered his U.S. Army component (which included the Philippine Scouts) from 22,532 to 31,095 men.

MacArthur's air arm grew even more. By early December, the Philippines hosted at least 181 aircraft. Moreover, it possessed thirty-five B–17s and sixty-seven P–40Es, the most modern aircraft in the army inventory, while Hawaii had only twelve and thirty-nine respectively. But the air warning and anti-aircraft services lagged behind the aircraft build-up. Only two radars were in operation in early December.[18]

The rationale for this set of decisions remains unclear. The most logical interpretation is that Washington finally grasped that deterring Japan mandated not only a fleet at Pearl Harbor, but also powerful forces in the Philippines. This rational deduction merged unfortunately with a leap of faith. The object of Washington's worship was the Boeing B–17 "Flying Fortress." The entire top tier of army decision makers as well as the president became convinced that with enough B–17s in the Philippines, Japan would be deterred in the short run. This would buy time for complete American mobilization, which would assure long-term deterrence. Roosevelt would later imply that MacArthur's erroneous assurances about the defensibility of the Philippines led to these decisions, but the record is clear that leaders in Washington made foolish miscalculations without prodding from MacArthur. Secretary of War Stimson admitted that the reasons for the about-face in Washington were at least twofold: (1) MacArthur's optimistic reports and (2) faith in the B–17.[19]

This is not to deny that MacArthur's statements to other American officials in 1941 demonstrate his grossly unrealistic assessments of the capability of his forces to shield the Philippines. Right through to the early days of the war, MacArthur floated upon a sublime cloud of confidence about his command and grossly underestimated the Japanese. Ironically, particularly given his attitudes toward the Soviets, MacArthur was nearly alone among senior Western military officers in predicting that the Germans would not conquer Russia in 1941. This fact suggests that MacArthur's military judgment could be excellent when his own interests were not at stake.

But MacArthur's prognostication about the Russian campaign may contain a clue as to why he deprecated the Japanese. The Soviets trounced the Japanese in two major border battles in Manchuria in 1938 and 1939. Finnish reservists, in turn, checked and severely handled the Soviets in the winter of 1939–40. These events provided a sort of logical progression that reflected poorly on the Japanese.[20]

The reality in 1941, which MacArthur should have recognized, was that he lacked the resources to defend the Philippines successfully. The islands featured a longer coastline than the United States and were almost surrounded by Japanese bases. Nor did the Americans make any meaningful effort to coordinate with the Dutch and British.[21]

But the realistic appraisal of the prospects for the Philippines in 1941 was refracted through MacArthur's brain and emerged as the conviction that Japan would not attack until April 1942, after he would have corrected all the manifest deficiencies apparent upon mobilization. Money now flowed freely, but it was far too late. By the time the war broke out, not one of the ten reserve divisions was at full strength; most hovered at 50 to 75 percent of their authorized manning. Clothing and all forms of equipment were scarce or deteriorated—some men went barefoot. Most of the 120,000 mobilized Filipinos retained little of their prior training; Major General Jonathan Wainwright singled out gross deficiencies in marksmanship, scouting, and patrolling. Only one or two regiments of the three assigned to each division had received any refresher training prior to outbreak of the war. The virtues of the Filipinos were few but important: a burning desire to learn, and a ready obedience that made disciplinary problems virtually nonexistent.[22]

Even had all the Philippine Army reserve divisions boasted fully trained soldiers, their authorized equipment left them grossly outmatched against the Japanese. A full-strength rifle regiment of 92 officers and 1,620 men had 1,437 Enfield rifles with stocks too long for handling by the average Filipino. Worse, the regiment possessed merely thirty-six automatic rifles and only twenty-four 30-caliber machine guns. A Japanese regiment possessed over three times the automatic firepower and this ratio applied right down to the level of the rifle company. No Philippine division possessed an antitank battalion. Only two of the ten divisions received the full complement of twenty-four howitzers authorized for its artillery regiment.[23]

The experience of the 31st Philippine Army Division illustrates the breadth of failure. The division's 31st Infantry Regiment was mobilized on September 1. The 33nd Infantry Regiment began its call up on November 25. The 32nd Infantry Regiment joined the division only on December 6, 1941. The division's artillery regiment possessed only eight World War I-vintage 75-mm guns. There was only one Browning automatic rifle per company, not the authorized four. In one regiment, soldiers in one battalion fired fifty rounds in practice; a second battalion, twenty-five; and the third, none. Many Filipino soldiers entered combat never having fired a round in practice.[24]

Though much of the shortfall of the Philippine Army can be charged elsewhere, MacArthur himself contributed one hugely disastrous strategic misjudgment—although contrary to conventional wisdom it was not his novel idea. Senior American army officers in the Philippines, generally, had subscribed to a war plan that called, upon outbreak of hostilities, for an immediate withdrawal of all forces to the Bataan Peninsula and the island of Corregidor to hold Manila Bay. But MacArthur in the 1920s and the officers who commanded in the late 1930s espoused a more aggressive variant vested in beach defense against a landing. Only if that effort failed would there be a phased withdrawal into Bataan and Corregidor. Major General George Grunert, the last commander of the Philippine Department, rewrote the formal plan to reflect this much more belligerent stance. MacArthur adopted Grunert's plan as his own.[25]

This major switch in Philippine defense plans also reflected MacArthur's underlying premise that he would have until April 1942 to prepare, when he would have 200,000 trained men. MacArthur divided his forces into the North Luzon Force, the South Luzon force, and the Visayas-Mindanao regions. But the new scheme contained a crucial error: supplies were dispersed away from Bataan and Corregidor to locations where they could sustain a beach defense strategy.[26]

In an interview just before war commenced, MacArthur declaimed to journalist Theodore White that destiny brought him to Manila. On the morning of December 8, 1941, destiny arrived.[27]

4

Catastrophe

WORLD WAR II IN THE PACIFIC COMMENCED IN CATASTROPHE FOR Douglas MacArthur, though unlike Admiral Husband Kimmel and General Walter Short in Hawaii, MacArthur would not be disgraced, much less held accountable (or scapegoated) for the terrific losses his air command suffered in the initial Japanese attacks.

Unofficial news of the Japanese attack on Pearl Harbor reached MacArthur (across the International Date Line) about 3:30 A.M., December 8, 1941, about two hours before the official War Department notice. From 5:00 A.M., MacArthur's chief airman, Major General Lewis H. Brereton, repeatedly beseeched MacArthur's headquarters for authority to strike Formosa with his B–17s. Brereton initially proposed attacking Japanese *shipping*, not airfields. He did not know that Formosa hosted 500 Japanese planes, but that a fog blanket grounded a planned massive dawn Imperial Navy strike on the Philippines. Not until 10:14 A.M. did MacArthur personally call Brereton to authorize the strike.

Meanwhile, a small raid of Imperial Army planes from fog-free bases on Formosa struck northern Luzon and triggered an alarm. The B–17s at Clark

Field lumbered aloft for protection at 8:45 A.M. When the delayed Imperial Navy armada of 192 planes arrived at 12:35 P.M., they caught the B–17s back on the ground refueling. The attackers eliminated twelve of nineteen B–17s and thirty-four of the ninety-one P–40s—MacArthur's best bombers and fighters. The raiders destroyed between twenty-eight and thirty-three additional aircraft. (Another sixteen B–17s already had been sent south to Mindanao and survived.) The Japanese demolished the sole operational radar set, thus blinding the Americans to future Japanese raids. The Japanese lost just seven fighters. Morale took a tremendous blow. The official U.S. Army historian concluded that "the Japanese had removed in one stroke the greatest single obstacle to their advance southward."[1]

Washington immediately subjected the Pearl Harbor disaster to investigation, and continued the process culminating in massive postwar congressional hearings. It was impossible practically to dispatch investigators to the Philippines during the war, or to recall the principle officers, and the episode received no comparable postwar scrutiny. Thus, the facts surrounding the Philippine debacle were never fully established and leveling final judgment remains difficult. MacArthur bears responsibility for failure to authorize immediately Brereton's Formosa raid that might have avoided destruction of a dozen B–17s on the ground. Since Brereton initially targeted shipping rather than airfields, the idea that the strike might have inflicted one of the few significant setbacks Japanese arms experienced in the opening five months of the war appears a myth. But this barely begins a catalogue of blame.

The roots of the disaster grew from July 1941 decisions made in Washington. Leaders, starting with President Roosevelt, elected to try to unfurl air power in the Philippines for political deterrence of the Japanese, not for military effectiveness. They emphasized offensive air units over defensive ones. They then compounded this error by rushing offensive airpower to the Philippines without providing adequate airfield defense (or even adequate space for dispersal—a twenty-four ton B–17 was not an easily moved art deco lawn ornament).

A vital and underappreciated element in American miscalculation was technological surprise. U.S. airmen advised MacArthur that it was impossible for Japanese fighter planes to escort bombers to central Luzon from Formosa. Therefore, an attack by unescorted Japanese bombers was unlikely. The only serious peril would be if the Japanese managed the feat of providing carrier-based fighter escorts for their Formosa-based bombers. What no American airman knew (or would have believed) is that the Mitsubishi A6M Type "Zero" fighter plane was the world's first fighter plane with the strategic reach to fly such an astounding, 500-mile mission from Formosa. Indeed, unlike a carrier raid on Pearl Harbor, which the U.S. Navy itself foreshadowed in several pre-war exercises, the ability of the Zero to reach Clark Field from Formosa was completely unprecedented. Thus, assurances of relative immunity from Formosa-based bombers, coupled to warnings to be on guard for Japanese carriers that might approach from virtually any point on the compass, go a long way to explain MacArthur's fateful hesitation.

At the second tier of failure, Army Air Forces officers failed to extract the best use of what defensive resources they possessed. At the proximate end of the chain of causation, air force commanders egregiously bungled the interception of the Japanese attack. Finally, fortune favored the Japanese: The Americans braced for a dawn attack just as the Japanese intended, but bad weather forced postponement of the onslaught, and human error on the American side did the rest.[2]

The allegation that this disaster, as bad as it was, amounted to a "second Pearl Harbor" is preposterous. Senior American leaders in 1941 invested wholly misplaced confidence in the vaunted B–17s. War experience demonstrated that the Flying Fortresses proved virtually useless in attacking moving ships and displayed little effectiveness, especially in small formations, even against stationary targets afloat or ashore. Thus, it is ridiculous to suppose that one group of thirty-five B–17s would have altered materially the course of the Japanese surge. The official U.S. Army history went so far as to conclude that "the possibility of a successful raid [on Formosa] by the B–17s seems extremely remote." Indeed, in the entire opening phase of the Pacific War, about eighty B–17s reached MacArthur's area. They sank exactly two ships and all but ten were lost from various causes. It was the loss of the defensive fighters and the key radar unit that really struck a lethal blow at MacArthur's airpower.[3]

+⊨══⊨+

MacArthur's forces on November 30, 1941 numbered 31,095 members of the U.S. Army. Exclusive of the excellent Philippine Scout units, the vast bulk of the American servicemen in the Philippines in December 1941 manned coast defense, aviation and service support units. Very few Americans were trained or served as front-line fighters. The sole American infantry regiment (the 31st) in the Philippine Division numbered only 2,100. The 4th Marines, a "regiment" just arrived from China mustered just 750 men. The 11,957 Philippines Scouts (about half of whom were recruited only in 1941) possessed an outstanding standard of training and discipline, but they added only about another 7,240 front-line fighters.

The Philippine Army on paper comprised ten reserve divisions. There was also one nominally "regular" division in the Philippine Army, but in reality its ranks were filled with many reservists. A second "regular" Philippine Army division was cobbled together from police units. Altogether, Philippine Army forces numbered about 120,000 men, scattered throughout the Philippines. Thus, of his over 150,000 men, MacArthur's true strength of trained and equipped front-line fighters amounted to merely 10,100. His other first-class assets comprised four American or Philippine Scout artillery battalions and a tank group of two light tank battalions which performed extremely well when fuel supplies and terrain permitted.[4]

Lieutenant General Homma Masaharu commanded the Japanese Fourteenth Army. It numbered about 43,110 men, with 34,856 in combat elements; the others filled shipping and aviation elements. Homma's major combat units comprised the 16th and 48th Divisions, the 65th Brigade and the 4th and 7th Tank Regiments. He enjoyed huge artillery superiority.[5]

Initial Japanese landings by battalion- and regimental-size elements occurred at Aparri and Vigan in Northern Luzon on December 10 and at Legaspi in Southern Luzon on December 12. Between those dates and December 22, Japanese airmen established their complete mastery of the skies over the Philippines. Brereton took his surviving B–17s to Australia. The icy politeness of MacArthur's relations with Brereton contrasts with his fiery exchanges with the commander of the Asiatic Fleet, Admiral Thomas Hart, who headed south on Christmas Day. From the start, Hart viewed the Philippines as a lost cause. He wasted no time in sending his limited surface forces south—where most perished heroically around Java. An enraged MacArthur remained convinced that the navy could have done much more. MacArthur was wrong about Hart's cruisers and destroyers, which could have done little but sacrifice themselves, but MacArthur had a case with regard to Hart's considerable force of twenty-nine submarines. The scandalous failure of the American undersea craft to inflict any significant damage stemmed from faulty equipment (torpedoes mainly), tactics, and what proved to be a chronic problem of finding aggressive skippers. MacArthur did admire the squadron of six motor torpedo boats under the colorful Lt. John D. Bulkeley and about 4,300 sailors and marines who stayed on to fight.[6]

The main Japanese landings arrived at Lingayen Gulf on December 22—ironically the date MacArthur was promoted to four-star rank as a general—and on December 24 around Lamon Bay, seventy miles southeast of Manila.

Homma's approximately 25,000 men at Lingayen Gulf brushed aside three Philippine army divisions. Around Lamon, the Sixteenth Division, with another 7,000 combat troops, moved rapidly toward Manila. In their initial contacts, disintegration and desertions plagued the novice Philippine Army divisions. There were plenty of Filipinos with courage, but few of them with training or adequate weaponry. "They were a mob," complained one American officer. Further, they fed MacArthur's headquarters grossly exaggerated reports that the Japanese invasion force mustered 80,000 men, and these fallacious figures spawned subsequent false claims that MacArthur's forces were greatly outnumbered.[7] MacArthur carefully kept his best units in reserve, except for the Philippine Scout 26th Cavalry Regiment and tank units, which fought well, although the scouts sustained serious losses.

The collapse of the Lingayen defenses on December 22–23 finally shocked MacArthur out of his illusion that the Japanese would not strike before April 1942, by which time the Philippine Army's deficiencies in training and weapons would be corrected. On December 23 MacArthur abandoned beach defense as futile and ordered the phased withdrawal to Bataan. Any urge to commend him for decisiveness in discarding this plan must be suppressed, because he had clung irrationally to the scheme despite the obvious fact that the Philippine Army was far from ready.

The new plan fused two equally vital components. One was a carefully orchestrated withdrawal of the defenders from Northern and Southern Luzon. MacArthur devised the overall plan and selected the leaders. He then experienced for the first time the agony of high command, as he waited, with little useful to do, to see if his plan worked. Amazingly, it appeared as if American officers, foremost Major General Jonathan Wainwright in Northern Luzon, managed successfully to maneuver what amounted to a Philippine militia through a multistage withdrawal against a far better-trained and better-equipped foe. An American officer who participated in the event, however, said it could better be described as a disengagement, with the credit for any delay awarded to engineer demolition work and two battalions of self—propelled 75mm guns on half-tracks. Wainwright reached Bataan with about 15,000 of his original 28,000 men. The Southern Luzon force did even better, arriving with 14,000 of its initial 15,000. Homma's limited forces and his misjudgment of MacArthur's intentions provided much needed succor. The Japanese commander expected a battle for Manila and ignored evidence of a withdrawal into Bataan. This misjudgment perhaps explains the otherwise inexcusable failure of Japanese airmen to inflict severe losses on the virtually bumper-to-bumper traffic and packed humanity crawling defenselessly along the two roads leading to Bataan.[8]

But the second vital element of MacArthur's new plan involved stocking Bataan with adequate supplies. This was a disastrous failure. Supplies originally earmarked for Bataan under standing plans had been dispersed to support the new beach defense strategy. It proved impossible to retrieve all of these supplies or to exploit other sources. The first reason for this catastrophic mismanagement was MacArthur's vacillation until December 23 to revert to the original plan, an irretrievable delay. The second reason was a gross shortage of quartermaster troops (only about 1,300 of MacArthur's forces), transportation, mismanagement, and, in some cases, Philippine objections or obstructions designed to spare the civilian population. Three Philippine divisions were guarding the central and southern Philippines, so they imposed no logistical burden on Luzon, but contrary to plans, no fewer than 26,000 civilian refugees fled to Bataan, in addition to about 70,000 military and naval personnel, seriously compromising the already inadequate food and medical supply situation. From January 5, MacArthur ordered half-rations and thereafter the supply situation spiraled downward until food, not the Japanese, became the central concern of everyone on Bataan and Corregidor.[9]

During this period two of MacArthur's key decisions reflected his rejection of a total-war philosophy. Primarily due to his abhorrence of aerial bombardment of cities—a theme recurring repeatedly in this war and Korea—MacArthur declared Manila an "open city" and thus tried to shield it from Japanese bombers. Second, during the frenzied efforts to move supplies into Bataan, MacArthur deferred to the demands of President Quezon that nothing should be done that would seriously compromise the welfare of the Philippine civilian population. Consequently, MacArthur's quartermasters were barred from seizing readily available stores of civilian foodstuffs. No commander of Hirohito, Hitler, or Stalin would have exhibited such tenderness.

⊹≻══≺⊹

The Bataan peninsula stretches about twenty-nine miles from north to south, but MacArthur pitched the initial "main line of resistance" astride Mt. Natib, about eleven miles down the peninsula. Wainwright's I Corps held the left and Major General George Parker's II Corps the right. The Japanese judged that only about 25,000 to 45,000 dispirited defenders occupied the peninsula (the real number was about 70,000) and figured that Lt. Gen. Nara Akira's 65th Brigade of 6,500 men (composed mostly of men with only one month of basic training) and one regiment could end the campaign.

American officers left a two-mile-wide gap in the center of the line because they deemed the densely jungled Mt. Natib impassible. The Japanese thought otherwise. The Japanese attacked on January 9, with their main effort along the obvious east coast main road. Checked there, the Japanese launched a complementary attack on the west coast. The defenders held until the Japanese managed to get a battalion astride the primary road in the west and exhausted Nipponese soldiers lost for days on Mt. Natib finally materialized on the American flanks on January 16. MacArthur's forces withdrew to a final defensive line about six miles to the south. Some Philippine army units again experienced much confusion and even disintegration, but the spent Japanese could not exploit it. The local commanders managed the battle, with MacArthur's prime contribution a timely authorization for the withdrawal.

The next Japanese strokes ended disastrously. Two battalions of the 20th Infantry Regiment were virtually annihilated when they mounted amphibious end runs on the western coast of Bataan in what became known as the Battle of the Points. Meanwhile, Japanese efforts to again punch through the center of the new line culminated in the Battle of the Pockets, in which the third battalion of the 20th Infantry was mauled.[10]

Cracking the first defensive line cost Homma's Fourteenth Army ruinous—and needless—casualties. Once the Japanese pushed the American and Philippine forces into the Bataan cul-de-sac, the Japanese needed only wait for hunger and disease to do the hard work of compelling capitulation. But as Homma well knew, patience gained no honors in the Imperial Army. Despite the fact that Tokyo stripped him of the 48th Division (his best unit) and the 5th Air Division for the onslaught against the Dutch, Homma recognized that he was expected to force a decision quickly with his remaining forces. Thus, he threw his available units into the January attack. By the end of the offensive, Homma estimated that his effective strength equaled only the equivalent of three battalions. Homma was forced to order a withdrawal to a more defensible line. This was the only occasion in all of Japan's initial campaigns in which the Imperial Army deliberately gave up ground already seized.[11]

Consistent with his behavior in World War I, MacArthur set a powerful personal example of courage under fire at his headquarters on the island of Corregidor, frequently standing erect in a casual pose as Japanese shells and bombs crashed down. A correspondent called his wife Jean "one of MacArthur's finest soldiers," as she regularly toured the battered topside conversing with soldiers. But this same period spawned perhaps the most wounding slur of his life. For reasons that MacArthur never revealed, he managed only one trip to Bataan in two and half months. His absence gave rise to the nickname "Dugout Doug." The most likely, though speculative, explanation for this is that MacArthur's physical courage (or fatalism) transcended his moral courage. He could not look his doomed men in the eye.[12]

+≡≡+

While MacArthur retreated to Bataan, Roosevelt and Churchill met in Washington in what was known as the Arcadia Conference. This meeting reaffirmed the overall "Germany First" strategy. Although this precluded the slightest chance of relieving the Philippines, for weeks after Pearl Harbor senior American officials deluded themselves that MacArthur could be rescued. Much worse, public statements, press releases, and even messages from Marshall could be and were read as promises that "help is on the way." President Roosevelt on December 28 quite falsely asserted that the navy was pursuing an "intensive and well planned campaign . . . which will result in positive assistance to the defense of the Philippine Islands." Marshall's dispatch on January 4 was particularly egregious. Although acknowledging worldwide commitments and the fact that powerful naval forces could not be massed in the Western Pacific, Marshall's message nonetheless clearly implied that powerful air units were en route to Australia from where they would blast open a relief route to the Philippines. MacArthur reasonably construed other messages itemizing men and planes earmarked for the Pacific as the vanguard of a relief force when they were, in fact, defensive garrisons positioned to hold open the sea routes to Australia and New Zealand. [13]

In this miasma of hopes and illusions, one man emerged who insisted on clear thinking. Newly promoted Brig. Gen. Dwight D. Eisenhower answered Marshall's preemptory summons to come to Washington and take charge of Pacific war plans. Eisenhower's long association with MacArthur and knowledge of the Philippines fitted him uniquely to provide advice. After a review of the situation, in what was perhaps the most critical interview of his life, Eisenhower told Marshall that the Philippines were lost. America must concentrate on defending the defensible. He emphasized, however, that the people of Asia "may excuse failure but they will not excuse abandonment." Eisenhower counseled that the United States must attempt visibly to bolster MacArthur while preparing Australia as a base for future operations. It took weeks for many to face up to what Ike grasped immediately. It was February before Secretary of War Stimson would write in his diary, "There are times when men must die."[14]

MacArthur displayed sensitivity to the political components of high command when he deferred to President Quezon's demand that the stocking of Bataan not be accomplished at the cost of Philippine civilian needs. But how MacArthur handled Quezon's next major interpolation is not to his credit. Disillusioned by what he justifiably regarded as the abandonment of the Philippines, in February 1942 Quezon cabled Roosevelt proposing that since further resistance was useless, the United States should grant immediate independence so that the Philippines could be neutralized. Secretary of War Stimson found that MacArthur's accompanying estimate and comments went "more than half way" in supporting Quezon. FDR fired back a rejection of Quezon's proposal, coupled with an order to MacArthur to "keep our flag flying in the Philippines so long as there remains any possibility of resistance."[15]

MacArthur complied with a further directive from Washington to evacuate Quezon, but failed to respond to probes by Marshall concerning his own evacuation. The prospect of a former chief of staff becoming a Japanese prisoner, particularly after his reputation had been hugely elevated, was intolerable. On February 22, Roosevelt ordered MacArthur to go to Australia. In the evening of March 11, 1942, MacArthur, his immediate family, and key staff officers boarded Lt. Bulkeley's four surviving motor torpedo boats to begin the epic adventure of his escape from the Philippines.[16]

Rain clouds hid the small flotilla from Japanese shore batteries and the naval blockade as they scampered out to the open sea. But the torpedo boats bucked ceaselessly, throwing spray that competed with rain squalls to keep all the seasick passengers soaked. MacArthur compared their plight to a "trip in a cement mixer." A mishap at the way point of Tagauayan at the south end of the Sulu Sea cost one of the boats, but the other three pressed on. The surviving boats reached Mindanao on March 13. To MacArthur the fact that they had broken the blockade provided damaging evidence against the navy. When he eyed the ailing B–17s and their inexperienced crews sent to pick him up and carry him to Australia, he was enraged. While he waited for better planes, MacArthur used the interval to implement a very ill-considered division of command in the Philippines. He limited Wainwright's authority to only Bataan and Corregidor. He designated separate commanders for the Visayas and for Mindanao. The primary reason for this scheme was MacArthur's unease over Wainwright's well-known alcoholism.[17]

It was the evening of March 16 when suitable B–17s arrived to move MacArthur to Australia. After the pilot consumed eight cups of coffee to revive himself, they took off just after midnight for Darwin. Over Australia, a Japanese air raid forced the party to fly on to Batchelor Field, about forty miles further south. MacArthur reluctantly agreed to take a C–47 to Alice Springs, but thereafter insisted on proceeding only by train. When he reached Adelaide on March 18, he met reporters for the most famous interview of his life. He explained that President Roosevelt had ordered him to Australia, "for the purpose as I understand it, of organizing the American offensive against Japan, a primary object of which is the relief of the Philippines. I came through and I shall return." MacArthur's personalization of the "I shall return" commitment reverberated through U.S. strategy for the next two and a half years.[18]

When MacArthur finished his press conference, he met with one of his staff officers who briefed him on the situation. To his amazement, MacArthur learned that there was no massive relief force gathered.

<hr />

The Philippines marked MacArthur's first wartime venture in high-level command. Typical as to all judgments of MacArthur, it produced sharply antagonistic assessments. During the actual campaign, it was widely extolled in allied nations as masterful defense against overwhelming odds. Postwar, Charles Willoughby would claim that the protracted defense in the Philippines exerted a powerful effect inhibiting Japanese efforts into late 1942 during the struggle for Guadalcanal and Papuan phase of the New Guinea campaign. U.S. Army historians disproved the lingering belief that MacArthur was outnumbered. They also found no evidence of a protracted effect, or indeed of much effect at all, on Japanese operations, for the Japanese effectively bypassed MacArthur's army to go on to seize other targets, including the prize of the resource areas in the Dutch East Indies. A second official U.S. Army volume on the retaking of the Philippines would condemn MacArthur's generalship by implication, by commending the Japanese commander for not withdrawing his forces into Bataan, but instead holding out in the mountains of Luzon. The Australian official historian tartly dismissed MacArthur's conduct of the campaign with the assertion that the much higher-quality Japanese forces in Malaya actually required only the same number of actual combat days to take Singapore as the lesser-quality Japanese forces did to capture Bataan and Corregidor.

Any judgment of MacArthur's performance in the Philippines must be made in context. It has become very difficult to recall the bleak record of anti-

Axis forces from the mid-1930s to early 1942. Ethiopia, Spain, and Poland fell, followed by the stunning collapse in just six weeks of Western European nations that had held out for four years in World War I. The opening days of the Pacific War added more black pages at Pearl Harbor, Hong Kong, Guam, Wake Island (after a shinning moment of triumph over the initial Japanese invasion), and the Dutch East Indies. The defense of Bataan glowed as an almost solitary beacon of hope for the future. Bataan held out for almost two months longer than Singapore and a month longer than the Dutch. As H. P. Willmott shrewdly noted, "The Americans believed they had done well on Bataan, and this was as important as actually doing well."[19] This was an undeniable benefit to the allied cause. Practically speaking, the protracted defense of the Philippines did not discomfit Tokyo in any major way. The original timetable anticipated it would take only about fifty days to secure the Philippines, but it eventually took six months. It says something, however, that in August 1942 Imperial Headquarters placed the victorious commander, General Homma, on the retired list, ending his career.

This is by no means to claim that the Philippines witnessed MacArthur at his best, for his achievements were more than balanced by grievous mistakes. The decision to defend the beaches did not get a fair test because the Japanese struck four or five months before the date MacArthur expected. Consequently, the training and equipping of his Philippine Army units was far less than he anticipated. MacArthur carries the responsibility for the grossly negligent failure to properly stock Bataan and Corregidor with supplies. He further bears ultimate responsibly for the losses his air force sustained on December 8, but the errors of Washington and his own airmen, plus bad luck, substantially mitigate this.

The actual conduct of the defense of Bataan and Corregidor inevitably must be compared to the abysmal defeat of a numerically much superior garrison of 130,000 in Malaya. Although some of the Australian, English, and Indian troops defending Singapore were plagued by training deficiencies, they eventually numbered five divisions and an armored brigade, and unquestionably possessed vastly more trained and equipped front-line fighters than MacArthur ever fielded. Only about 10,100 of MacArthur's men, roughly one in eight of his total force on Luzon, were really trained and equipped for modern front-line fighting. To believe as some did and continue to do that MacArthur's performance was mediocre if not abysmal, one would further have to conclude that a sound soldier like Marshall missed the failure. On the contrary, although Marshall accepted the notion that Macarthur was "outnumbered," he must have recognized that the impressive raw numbers of

MacArthur's command concealed a paucity of trained infantrymen, and, judged MacArthur's performance accordingly. So should we. [20]

But if the core of MacArthur's performance warrants some respect, that core arrived in hideously repulsive wrappings. Of 142 communiqués issued by MacArthur's command between December 8, 1941 and March 11, 1942, no fewer than 109 named only one individual: MacArthur. Even this astonishing vainglory was surpassed by a pervasive infection of falsehoods, the worst of which was perhaps a claim that Homma had committed suicide. MacArthur became a superhero in the eyes of vast swaths of the American public due to these dispatches, but this ignominious behavior alienated both senior leaders in Washington and his own troops. [21]

The bow around the wrapping was known to only a select few, and concealed for decades. On February 13, President Quezon signed an executive order authorizing payment from Philippine funds of $500,000 to MacArthur, and a total of $135,000 to three of his staff officers. The sum may have equaled the salary due through 1945 plus a performance bonus contemplated under MacArthur's contract with the Philippines. That contract's provisions also draped a cloak of technical legality over the payment, if approved by his superiors, which it was. (The acquiescence of Roosevelt and Stimson in the transaction smacks of guilt over their strategic judgment to abandon the Philippines.) The payment to the three staff officers (including Sutherland) may have correlated to sums due from the Philippine government, but gave off the powerful odor of "hush money." MacArthur's critics could justly claim that the episode's appearance alone is indefensible, whatever its technical legality. It further clouded the question of MacArthur's motives in supporting Quezon's neutralization proposal and his initial opposition to evacuating Quezon. It stands as an eternal example of how no American officer should behave. [22]

5

An Expensive Education

PRIMARILY IN ORDER TO DEFEAT EXPECTED AXIS PROPAGANDA savaging MacArthur for "abandoning" his men, General Marshall spearheaded the successful effort to bestow the Medal of Honor. The award represented either a travesty (for there existed no valid grounds for the decoration in the new war), or rough justice (for MacArthur had earned the honor in World War I, if not also at Vera Cruz).[1]

MacArthur's melodramatic journey from Corregidor to Australia by torpedo boat, aircraft, and train consumed eleven days. Upon his arrival, American Ambassador Patrick J. Hurley (the Secretary of War in the Hoover Administration) informed MacArthur that his name now soared into the sort of orbit of public adulation previously enjoyed by only Admiral George Dewey, General John J. Pershing and Charles Lindbergh. The main batteries of anti-Roosevelt press, the publications of William Randolph Hearst, Col. Robert McCormick and Henry R. Luce trumpeted MacArthur.[2]

MacArthur's name suddenly graced babies, flowers, dances, parks, streets, and buildings beyond counting. Indian tribal tributes (much appreciated given MacArthur's boyhood), university degrees, memberships in prestigious and not-so-prestigious organizations cascaded down upon America's superhero of the hour. Republican and even some Democratic politicians acted like spigots spraying out effusive tributes. Some counseled that MacArthur should be brought home to direct the armed forces. Others went further and began to see MacArthur in Roosevelt's job.[3]

Ambitious politicians recognized the opportunity to gather some stardust with a visit to MacArthur's front. Congressman Lyndon B. Johnson of Texas traded his business suit for the uniform of a naval reserve officer and hooked himself to a Washington-launched field trip. Johnson and a Pentagon colonel volunteered to fly on a bombing mission to the stoutly defended Japanese airbase at Lae on New Guinea. Japanese fighters shot down the colonel's plane; the whole crew was lost. Johnson's plane developed engine problems and aborted the mission before any encounter with Japanese planes. MacArthur decorated Johnson and another much more useful visiting congressman in uniform, Melvin Maas, with the Silver Star Medal. Most accounts of this episode grossly mangle the facts and their significance. First, the faint of heart did not venture near Lae at that time. Second, by far the most reliable evidence shows Johnson's plane did not engage in combat. Third, MacArthur decorated Johnson before the Silver Star Medal achieved its later high place in the hierarchy of valor awards. To MacArthur, the award he bestowed on Johnson (and Maas) meant as much as the World War I Citation Star.[4]

MacArthur's fame powerfully enhanced his fortunes. On March 30, Washington promulgated the new command arrangement for the Pacific. Sound logic dictated a single supreme commander for the theater, a role that appeared to MacArthur and the army as his due. But the navy, led by Admiral Ernest J. King, the Commander in Chief, U.S. Navy, deemed MacArthur unfit by age and demonstrated abilities (or lack thereof). Moreover, the sailors possessed the powerful argument that only an admiral could command effectively a vast oceanic theater demanding sea fights and amphibious operations. The upshot was a compromise. The great majority of the Pacific became the domain of Admiral Chester W. Nimitz. His overall command was titled Pacific Ocean Areas (POA), subdivided into a trio of subordinate areas: the North, Central, and South Pacific. MacArthur became commander of the Southwest Pacific Area (SWPA). This comprised Australia, the Philippines, New Guinea, the Solomon Islands, the Bismarck Archipelago, and the Netherlands East Indies, save Sumatra.[5]

On April 18, MacArthur appointed an Australian, General Thomas A. Blamey, as his ground forces commander. Lt. Gen. George H. Brett became his air force commander and Vice Admiral Herbert F. Leary (soon replaced by

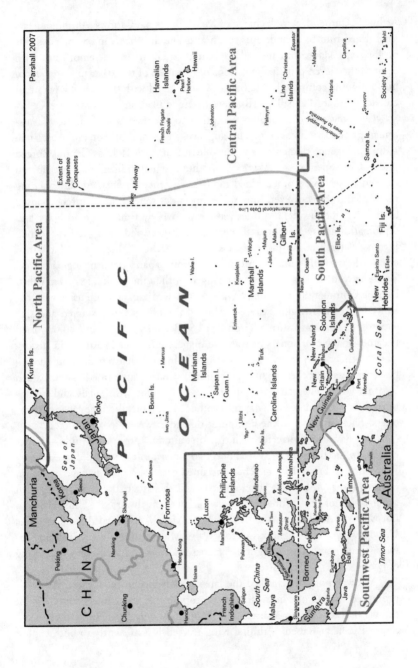

Arthur S. Carpender) took charge of MacArthur's naval forces. Although Marshall urged him to include Australian and Dutch officers in senior positions on his staff, MacArthur instead appointed an all-American senior staff, with eight of the eleven principal positions to members of the "Bataan Gang" from his Philippine command. The Bataan Gang shared with their chief a paranoid conviction that Marshall and Roosevelt were implacable enemies.[6]

One key and conspicuous exception to MacArthur's shunning of Australian participation concerned intelligence. American, British, and Australian radio intelligence elements were consolidated in April 1942 as Central Bureau under Col. Spencer B. Akin, MacArthur's signal officer. Central Bureau worked closely with other Allied radio intelligence services. At this opening phase of the war, however, Imperial Army codes were almost entirely a closed book. Decrypts in 1942–43 derived almost wholly from Imperial Navy and diplomatic messages. A critical breakthrough occurred in April 1943, when Japan's Water Transportation Codes were breached. Thereafter, MacArthur obtained extremely valuable information about Japan's seaborne logistics.[7]

The whole course of the war changed in the nine weeks after MacArthur became Commander in Chief, SWPA. A renewed Japanese offensive with the equivalent of nearly three divisions forced the now severely starved and sick garrison of Bataan to surrender on April 9. Between 70,000 and 80,000 men became Japanese prisoners of war, the biggest surrender in American history (though the vast majority of these were Filipinos). What remained unknown, however, was that these men then endured what became titled as the Bataan Death March. The Japanese pummeled Corregidor with shells and bombs until it too surrendered on May 6. Another 11,000 men became Japanese prisoners. The remainder of the Philippine defenders were also surrendered.[8]

The day after Corregidor fell, the first aircraft carrier clash in history occurred. In the Battle of the Coral Sea, two American carrier task forces, led by Rear Admiral Frank Jack Fletcher, sustained greater tactical damage by loss of carrier *Lexington,* but the Japanese sustained their first strategic reverse when the invasion of Port Moresby on New Guinea was thwarted. (Thus, Fletcher, not MacArthur, deserves the title of "The Man Who Saved Australia.") The U.S. Navy won a tremendous victory off of Midway in the Central Pacific between June 3 and 7, sinking four Japanese carriers and a cruiser while losing only one carrier and a destroyer.[9]

Midway not only checked the Japanese advance in the Central Pacific, it prompted MacArthur immediately to propose that the United States exploit the victory at sea with a direct assault on the main Japanese bastion in the South Pacific at Rabaul. Admiral King reacted just as swiftly to both exploit the victory and keep navy control of the Pacific War. He prevailed with a July 1942 plan to launch a three-phase campaign. The ultimate objective remained Rabaul, but there would be two preliminary steps up the Solomon Islands, starting at Guadalcanal. King insisted that the Navy must command this offensive; theater boundaries were adjusted to place Guadalcanal in the South Pacific subdivision of Nimitz's overall command.[10]

In all of his nearly forty years as a professional soldier, MacArthur had never experienced anything remotely on the scale of his failures in the first six months of the Pacific War. His ego precluded him from finding serious fault with his own actions. Consequently, he viciously attempted to shift blame to others, and wrote a series of hysterical and paranoid messages back to his superiors. He bombarded Washington with predictions of disaster if the "Germany First" decision was not reversed to accord priority to him. More startlingly, in setting up the Guadalcanal campaign, Nimitz proposed using air and naval assets assigned to MacArthur. King also communicated directly with MacArthur's naval commander rather than routing messages through MacArthur. These actions formed the specifications for MacArthur's radioed charges to Marshall that they proved the navy's ambitions extended to "general control of all operations in the Pacific." Moreover, MacArthur fulminated that this was part of a conspiracy—which he had discovered "accidentally" while he was chief of staff—for the navy to gain complete dominance over national defense and reduce the army to a training and supply organization.[11]

The failure of Roosevelt, Stimson, and Marshall to rebuke and censure MacArthur immediately for these hysterical charges and provocations contributed powerfully to a decade of defiance, culminating in MacArthur's firing. Very belatedly at the end of 1942, Stimson finally acted. He summoned Eddie Rickenbacker, America's top ace in World War I. Rickenbacker nearly matched MacArthur in public fame and had impressed Stimson with his candid reports on the situation of the army air force units in England. Entrusted with a verbal message from Stimson and under a pledge not to divulge its contents to anyone but MacArthur, ever, Rickenbacker boarded a B–17 for Australia. En route, the plane ditched and Rickenbacker spent twenty-four days in a raft before his miraculous rescue. When he finally reached MacArthur in November, he delivered Stimson's message demanding that MacArthur cease his campaign to generate personal publicity for himself, desist from his complaints that his theater received only limited resources, and halt his personal criticism of General Marshall. In addition to these prohibitions, Stimson ordered MacArthur to work harmoniously with the navy. Sadly, when this rebuke proved at best transitory, MacArthur's superiors failed to enforce his subordination. Their dereliction stands as an important lesson in the management of willful subordinates.[12]

＋━━━＋

A common misconception about the Pacific War is that following Midway, the Japanese reverted to the defensive. In fact, the Imperial Army remained very much on the offensive. Having rejected as infeasible an Imperial Navy proposal to invade Australia, the Imperial Army embarked on a more practical strategy of advancing southeast through the islands of New Guinea, New Caledonia, Fiji, and Samoa so as to cut the lines of communication to Australia and New Zealand. This would preclude their use as springboards for an Allied counterattack.[13]

New Guinea sprawls some 1,300 miles, like some primitive bird with its head to the northwest and tail to the southeast. Its mountainous jungle forms a glacis protecting Australia from the north. In 1942, the Pacific War focused on Papua, the southeastern tail. The Imperial Army chose the South Seas Detachment under Major General Horii Tomitaro, a well-balanced force of about 10,000 men with five battalions of infantry, accompanied by artillery, engineer, pioneer, and signal elements, to take Port Moresby with a 200-mile overland march from Buna on the northern coast of Papua.

MacArthur, however, initially faced major handicaps in meeting the Japanese threat. His air units could muster but eighty to one hundred operational aircraft with exhausted crews. The two U.S. Army divisions, the 32nd and 41st, were not ready for combat. Available Australian units defended Port Moresby and Milne Bay, respectively on the southern side and eastern tip of Papua. Central Bureau could not read Imperial Army codes and relied very heavily on the work of navy radio intelligence, but naval radio intelligence after May 1942 worked almost entirely from traffic analysis rather than decryption, forcing them to hedge their predictions. Paucity of means, uncertainty in the intelligence picture, and the cloak of bad weather grounding Allied planes prevented MacArthur from forestalling the July 22 Japanese seizure of Buna on the northern coast of Papua.

Throughout the war, Col. Charles Willoughby, MacArthur's intelligence officer, sifted information through a filter of his own judgments of appropriate strategy and tactics. Willoughby believed the "correct" Japanese move was to use Buna as an advanced airbase, not as a jump-off point for a land attack across the Owen Stanley mountain range to Port Moresby. He discounted a rare decrypt in May that warned of Horii's objective. Then Willoughby

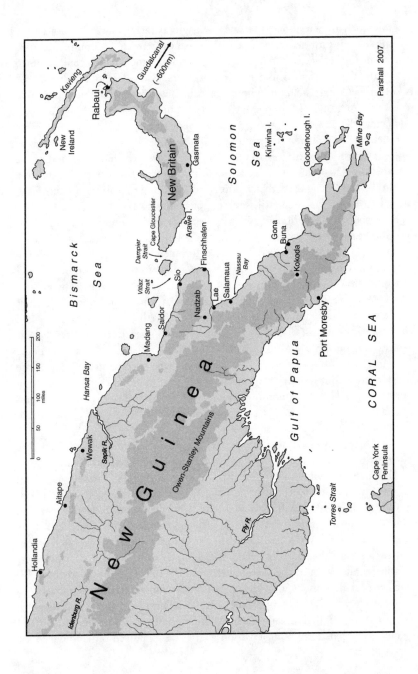

Parshall 2007

grotesquely underestimated Japanese strength as mere companies, not battalions. This in turn persuaded MacArthur that the retreat of outnumbered Australians in the face of the Japanese advance along the Kokoda trail stemmed from a failure to fight and deficient leadership. MacArthur told Melvin Maas, a visiting Congressman in uniform, that the Australians would not fight.[14]

By August 1942, both MacArthur and his Australian land forces commander Blamey knew that they must deliver a victory on New Guinea or face relief. In September, MacArthur contrived to have Australian Prime Minister John Curtin order Blamey to New Guinea to take personal command of the situation. This made no sense, as Blamey bore much wider responsibilities, but Blamey recognized that failure would certainly result in his dismissal, while MacArthur could still shift responsibility to the Australian. Inexcusably, neither MacArthur nor Blamey went forward to see the actual horrendous situation the troops faced on the Kokoda trail. The trail was really a narrow path scaling peaks that "rose turbulently to the clouds," skirting 4,000-foot sheer drops, crossing angry spray-enshrouded torrents (Horii would drown in one such stream), and compressed and shadowed by walls of jungle. The only means of supply were man packing or air drops. Ironically, due to a change of emphasis to Guadalcanal, the Imperial Army halted Horii's advance just as Blamey headed to New Guinea, but even after the tide turned Blamey succumbed to MacArthur's ill-founded criticism and pressure. Blamey unjustly relieved several Australian commanders to placate MacArthur and save his own career, actions that have blighted his reputation ever since. There was nothing wrong with the Australians, as they demonstrated in crushing a rash Japanese landing around Milne Bay at the eastern tip of Papua in July and August.[15]

Once Australian reinforcements halted and then drove the Japanese thrust back along the Kokoda trail, MacArthur launched his own offensive. Although advised to send the better-trained U.S. 41st Infantry Division, MacArthur instead deployed the U.S. 32nd Infantry Division under Major General Edwin F. Harding to attack Buna, while Australian troops aimed at nearby Gona. Both the American and Australian troops confronted brilliantly conceived and constructed defenses as formidable and sophisticated as entrenchments in World War I. As at Bataan, MacArthur failed to go forward for a firsthand review of the situation. Instead, he relied upon the advice of his chief of staff, Sutherland, who believed quite wrongly that it was infeasible to get artillery forward to support the attacks, and information from Willoughby, who grossly underestimated Japanese strength. To give just one example of how ill-prepared the 32nd Division was, a dye employed on clothing to aid concealment rendered the garments nonporous and thus nearly unbearably hot. Without supporting weapons or even elementary tools like flamethrowers and demolitions, and soon riddled with disease, the American and Australian forces sustained severe casualties. MacArthur blamed the leadership and the troops. He was humiliated by reports that American soldiers had abandoned weapons and fled from the enemy—there was an isolated instance of this amid much valor. MacArthur relieved Harding and sent Lieutenant General Robert Eichelberger forward in November with orders to "take Buna or don't come back alive." This is the absolute nadir of his generalship.[16]

Buna finally fell on January 2, 1943. Although Eichelberger coupled competence with ample courage (his aide was shot while standing next to him), what really changed was major bolstering of the combat power of the 32nd Division with an infusion of supplies plus artillery and tanks. The Japanese fought with their astonishing standard of heroism. In one place, defenders donned gas masks to struggle on amid the stench of their unburied slain comrades. In other places, starved Japanese resorted to cannibalism. When Eichelberger gained the opportunity to inspect at leisure the conquered Japanese defenses, he was stunned at their "complexity, depth and ruggedness." The last Japanese positions in the area fell on January 22.[17]

MacArthur issued a communiqué claiming that "[o]ur losses in the Buna campaign were low." He further asserted that the two major reasons for these "low" losses were that "there was no necessity to hurry the attack because the time element was of little importance; and second, for this reason no attempt was made to rush the positions by mass and unprepared assaults." Among a plethora of false statements profusely littering MacArthur's wartime communiqués, this one was a prizewinner. MacArthur had bombarded his local commanders with demands to finish the campaign quickly so he could achieve victory before Admiral William F. Halsey, Jr. secured Guadalcanal. Japanese losses, almost all fatalities, totaled about 12,000 of between 16,000 and 17,000 troops committed. American ground losses numbered 2,848 total, with 930 dead. The Australians carried a far heavier load and sustained 5,698 battle casualties, including 3,896 dead. Allied total ground losses were thus about 8,546, with 4,826 dead. By contrast, American ground fatalities at Guadalcanal reached 1,769 soldiers and marines. Since only about 33,000 allied troops were committed in Papua, compared to about 60,000 on Guadalcanal, the overall rate of loss was nearly six times greater under MacArthur. Besides at least seventeen Americans who died of scrub typhus, illness produced 24,234 medical admissions for infectious diseases among allied troops in Papua, although some of these were readmissions. In view of this fact, the official U.S. Army history called the victory in Papua as proportionately "one of the costliest of the Pacific War."[18]

In January 1943, Douglas MacArthur ended the worst thirteen months of his life. Most men of his age would have been crushed by the experience. MacArthur was not. But how far he could rebound from this low point remained to be seen.

6

Parameters

CHARLES WILLOUGHBY DECLARED THAT MACARTHUR FOUGHT A "war of distances." The vast span of MacArthur's domain—only a fraction of the Pacific itself—still dazzles. Twenty-five states the size of Texas would drop comfortably within the borders of the Southwest Pacific, and Texas is bigger than France. As William Manchester noted, MacArthur in Brisbane scheming to defend New Guinea was like a general in New Orleans orchestrating the defense of the United States-Canadian border.[1]

Water constituted the overwhelming majority of this expanse. For landlubbers, depth is the defining characteristic of the Pacific Ocean. For sailors, however, its dominant trait is a plethora of charted or uncharted rocks and reefs patiently awaiting a moment's ignorance or carelessness to rip out a ship's bottom. The cliché that the ocean constituted highways for movement houses a portion of truth, but if one lost command of the sea, the water served equally as imprisoning fortress ramparts.

Yet for anyone contemplating military operations, the most singular feature of the theater was neither distance nor water but nothingness. Virtually any other locale on the globe will provide such essentials as: collections of human habitation from mud-hutted villages to steel and concrete cities; paths or roads for men, beasts or vehicles; wharfs for dingy fishing craft to vast ports for fleets of cargo vessels; local foodstuffs readily exploitable by fighting forces; plentiful and healthy drinking water; and controlled or suppressed diseases. But in the Southwest Pacific, scarcely any of these existed; man's imprint only faintly altered the most primitive face of nature.

Virtually every item MacArthur's forces consumed in their campaigns had to be shipped to the theater. Staff officers in Washington calculated in 1942 that with due regard for time and distances factors, the same amount of shipping that would move two men to the Southwest Pacific would serve to shuttle five to Europe, and it actually required less shipping to sustain those five men. ("Germany First" not only made sense from a strategic perspective, but it delivered a bonus in logistics.) Thus, it is not just the distances, formidable and wholly out of scale with European battles, it is the sheer void of the theater that presented MacArthur with challenges that men like Eisenhower, Patton, Rommel, and Soviet Marshal Georgi Zhukov never faced.

This void made MacArthur especially dependent upon two services usually slighted. Behind everything MacArthur accomplished were the achievements of his engineers, led by the stellar General Hugh J. Casey. Casey estimated that about 20 percent of MacArthur's troops should be engineers, a figure never reached (it did hit 13.4 percent). MacArthur, like other theater commanders, compounded this error by habitually according shipping priority to combat troops over service troops, usually in the hope that later shipping allocations would make up the difference.[2]

The second service that played a huge and unsung role for MacArthur was the medical corps. Only the Middle East and African theater had a higher sickness rate. On an annualized basis, eight of every ten men in the Southwest Pacific on average spent some time in a hospital each year, a rate 75 percent above that in Europe (Nimitz's Pacific Ocean Area command, by contrast, was on par with Europe and lower than the continental United States). Likewise, on an annualized basis, one in every thousand men assigned to MacArthur died of disease, the highest rate in the whole army and nearly double the rate in Europe.[3] One of the few criticisms of MacArthur's otherwise incredibly resourceful and energetic engineers is the low priority they awarded medical facilities. Consequently, medical corps personnel of all ranks found themselves often constructing their own facilities. In fact, medical personnel alone built the U.S. Army's largest overseas facility, the 3,500-bed 54th General Hospital—with professors of surgery manning cement mixers and driving bulldozers.[4]

In the subtle but critical element of morale, MacArthur's challenges grossly exceeded those of his peers in Europe and were rivaled only by commanders in China. No American serving MacArthur could intuitively sense that his location directly connected to the defense of his home. A serviceman assigned to the Southwest Pacific plunged into an extremely primitive and alien environment. There was no human habitation at hand with familiar streets, houses, stores, theaters, bars or restaurants. No Caucasian women, except a rare glimpse of a nurse or Red Cross worker. Rain and pestilence remained constant companions. The War Department attempted to initiate a rotation policy for men in hardship areas, like the Southwest Pacific, of 1 percent per month. But MacArthur was forced to cancel this because he received no shipping to perform the rotation. How he handled this blow to morale is instructive. Commanders all over the Southwest Pacific received sealed parcels from theater headquarters with instructions not to open until a specific date. When they did, they found inside a letter to "Soldiers of the Southwest Pacific" explaining the decision. Every one of the hundreds of letters posted on company bulletin boards was personally signed by MacArthur.[5]

<hr />

Morale connected directly to a festering and never-solved problem. As the official U.S. Army history admitted:

> For reasons that went deep into contemporary medical beliefs and assumptions, neuropsychiatric casualties—the nation's leading cause of nonbattle disability separations—might almost be called the definitive American medical problem of World War II. MacArthur's command had the worst record of any theater in handling NPs. During 1944, problems defined as psychiatric accounted for almost 33 percent of all evacuations to the United States; intra theater evacuation also were heavy. The reasons were depressingly familiar—jungle warfare, the tropical environment, the conviction of many GIs that they would never see home until the war ended. The number of evacuees swelled because commanders used medical channels to eliminate their undesirables. In additional, doctors who lacked neuropsychiatric training misdiagnosed NP disorders and, like the commanders, dispatched puzzling or incomprehensible cases to the rear.[6]

MacArthur began his SWPA theater command with just two American divisions in 1942. During 1943, his U.S. elements expanded by only three divisions as well as the equivalent of one more in three separate regiments. MacArthur's expanding campaigns in 1944 warranted more forces and he received them, but many of the eleven additional divisions came to him as the South Pacific command ceased offensive operations and Australian and New Zealand units replaced them. Three more divisions came under his command in 1945. Thus, MacArthur would eventually have under his command prior to the planned invasion of Japan fifteen U.S. Army divisions and the equivalent of one more in separate regiments. Eisenhower's ground command in Europe was over five times larger. *

A look behind these numbers is revealing and provides a concrete example of why MacArthur believed he had real enemies in Washington. During World War II, the U.S. Army raised ninety-one divisions from three sources: sixteen regular units (18 percent) existing at the time of Pearl Harbor, nineteen (20 percent) mobilized national guard units and fifty-six (62 percent) wartime "Army of the United States" or "draftee divisions." Of these sources, senior army officers regarded the first as the best, the draftee divisions as the next best and the national guard units as the least desirable, although there were outstanding exceptions (and personnel policy and combat attrition usually made all three types indistinguishable after a while in combat). Over 50 percent of MacArthur's divisions (eight) originated as national guard units. Reflecting deep-rooted prejudice, army leaders rated a fourth informal type of division as virtually useless: three black divisions. Of these, one was disbanded before combat, one fought in Italy, and the 93rd Infantry Division went to MacArthur. The 93rd was never used in combat as a whole. Thus, overall 60 percent of MacArthur's U.S. divisions came from sources the army deemed least desirable. (By contrast, Eisenhower commanded sixty-one American divisions in north-

---

* For the record, in 1942 MacArthur gained the 32nd and 41st Divisions. In 1943, the three divisions sent to SWPA were the 1st Cavalry, 24th Infantry Division and (temporarily) the 1st Marine Division) as well as the equivalent of one more in three separate regiments (158th Infantry, 112th Cavalry and 503rd Parachute Infantry). MacArthur gained the following divisions in 1944: 6th Infantry Division (January), 31st Infantry Division (March), 40th Infantry Division (April), 33rd Infantry Division (May), 11th Airborne Division (May-June), 38th Infantry Division (July), 43rd Infantry Division (August), 96th Infantry Division (September), 37th Infantry Division (November), 93rd Infantry Division (November), 25th Infantry Division (December) Joining MacArthur in 1945, were Americal Infantry Division in January, and the 77th Infantry and 98th Infantry Divisions in July.

west Europe; of these just eight, or thirteen percent, were of national guard origin and none was black.)[7] Ably filling the gap in 1942 and 1943 was the Australian Army. Eventually, seven Australian divisions would serve under MacArthur. New Zealand contributed a two-brigade division that served in the Solomons. What lingers as a source of great anger is that in his wartime communiqués MacArthur masked the huge contribution of Australia and New Zealand to his campaigns by usually referring to their units as "allied troops," while he customarily was explicit about according credit to American units.[8]

MacArthur's forces afloat formed the Seventh Fleet. Although there were Netherlands and even Free French vessels, the U.S. Navy provided the bulk of the assets, supplemented by stalwart ships of the Australian and New Zealand Navies. The very word "fleet" implies powerful forces, including capital ships and aircraft carriers. The U.S. Navy, however, withheld from MacArthur any ship more powerful than a heavy cruiser until mid-1944, and even then, he only obtained the loan of elderly battleships and small escort carriers. Naval officers rigorously kept the prized new battleships and large fast carriers from MacArthur's command.

Adding insult to injury, the signature ship of amphibious operations in World War II was the attack transport, usually a vessel capable of transporting an infantry battalion and then landing it on the beach with its own landing craft. Again, the navy denied MacArthur virtually any of these vessels until 1944, and then largely on loan. As late as early 1944, a census of the Seventh Fleet turned up only two heavy and three light cruisers and a collection of U.S. and Australian destroyers—plus a motor torpedo boat command. The VII Amphibious Force comprised flotillas of landing ships and craft and a very few transports. Perforce, most of MacArthur's landings through mid-1944 were of the "shore-to-shore" variety, with troops loading directly onto landing ships and craft that then hauled them to the target beaches.[9]

On formation in September 1942, the Fifth Air Force numbered three fighter and four bomber groups on paper; operational strength was much less. Its main combat elements at full strength in January 1944 numbered six fighter groups, five light and medium bomber groups, and four heavy bomber groups. Rounding out the Fifth Air Force were two reconnaissance groups, five transport groups, and three night fighter squadrons.

When Halsey's South Pacific command ceased offensive operations in early 1944, the Thirteenth Air Force was transferred to General George C. Kenny, whose formal title in August 1944 became commander Far East Air Forces, effectively the Fifth and Thirteenth Air Forces, which retained independent identities.[10] The Thirteenth Air Force swelled Kenney's command by two fighter groups, one medium bomber group, and two heavy bomber groups, plus two night fighter, one separate heavy bomber, two reconnaissance, and one transport group.[*][11]

It was only in this area that MacArthur would enjoy consistent numerical and (after 1942) qualitative superiority. But even so, at peak he had only 13 percent of the fighter squadrons and 10 percent of the heavy bomber squadrons Eisenhower commanded on D-Day. The skill and heroism of MacArthur's aviators was outstanding, but three other factors powerfully enhanced their dominance over their adversaries. First, during the early months radio intelligence experts rifled Japanese aerial communications networks to work out accurate order of battle and more important, operational activity. Thus, Kenney's flyers gained more warning of incoming raids than even radar could supply. Second, the Japanese would have been far better off trading several hundred aircraft dispatched to New Guinea for a dozen bulldozers. The American capacity to build and maintain airstrips completely outclassed the Japanese. Third, likewise, American mechanical dexterity and its wide dissemination within the population proved a great asset.

The most significant and least heralded part of MacArthur's strategic direction concerned logistics, a subject intimately entwined with the political dimensions of his command. Put bluntly, if MacArthur had relied solely upon a supply pipeline from the United States there could not have been any extended offensive operations in the Southwest Pacific. "Reverse Lend Lease" from Australia provided the essential foundation for all of MacArthur's combat operations. Agriculture, supplemented by some raw material production, dominated the economies of Australia and New Zealand. Neither possessed an industrial sector that could begin to sustain both the populations and MacArthur's forces.

---

* MacArthur's Fifth Air Force units were: the 8th, 35th, 49th, 58th, 348th, and 475th Fighter Groups; the 3rd, 38th, 312th, 345th, and 417th Medium or Light Bomb Groups; the 22nd, 43rd, 90th, and 380th Heavy Bomber Groups. (In addition, the battered 19th Bomb Group from the Philippines served MacArthur until withdrawn in late 1942.) Rounding out the Fifth Air Force were two reconnaissance groups (6th and 71st), five transport groups (2nd, 314th, 374th, 375th, 433rd) and three night fighter squadrons. The Thirteenth Air Force contained two fighter groups (18th and 347th), one medium bomber group (42nd) and two heavy bomber groups (5th and 307th), plus two night fighter, one separate heavy bomber, two reconnaissance and one transport group (403rd).

Thus, the situation dictated an exchange whereby the commonwealth nations provided MacArthur with housing, sustenance, clothing, and myriad miscellaneous supplies, while MacArthur's extremely scarce shipping allocations delivered war material like planes, vehicles, and heavy equipment.

MacArthur's much overlooked role in this was to make determinations as to requirements and final allocations as to both military and civilian Lend Lease supplies. Working smoothly with the Australians, MacArthur achieved a level of pooling of resources and the conservation of shipping such as was achieved in no other theater, according to the official U.S. Army history. Moreover, as one American administrator pointed out, "Australia was the one country that actually returned more in Lend Lease goods than we gave them."[12]

MacArthur's achievement in this realm stemmed directly from his exceptional relationship with Australian Prime Minister John Curtin. MacArthur's political Hooverism and Curtin's avowed socialism appeared to foretell complete incompatibility, yet, the two men developed from the outset what was perhaps the most exemplary bond as existed in the West between senior political and military leaders. Part of their close relationship stemmed from their shared outlook that they were strategic orphans in the Grand Alliance. Curtin, a complete novice in military matters, was awed by MacArthur. MacArthur's private opinion of Curtin was not so high, but he radiated an affinity. Indeed, one of the remarkable paradoxes of MacArthur's career was the stark contrast between his tumultuous relations with senior American officers, particularly naval officers, and his customary harmony with senior foreign political figures in the Philippines, Australia, Japan, and Korea.[13]

It is true that MacArthur would deploy numerically superior forces against the Japanese after 1942. (Indeed, the only top American commander in World War II who actually achieved great victories with inferior or merely equal forces was Nimitz.) But appreciation of the inherent challenges of making war in the Southwest Pacific and MacArthur's very fine logistical margin demonstrates why he could claim to have done more with less than any other American theater commander. It is exactly their appreciation of these factors that explains why Marshall, Churchill, and British Generals Alan Brooke and Bernard Montgomery held MacArthur in high esteem.[14]

━●━

In assessing any leader, it is important to separate the degree to which he deserves credit on his own from the achievements properly due his subordinates. MacArthur's lieutenants present a very diverse picture in this regard.

It was the sad fate of MacArthur's local naval commanders to bear the burden as the surrogates for MacArthur's great bête noire: Admiral Ernest King. Not only did King sharply ration MacArthur's forces afloat, but also he waged an unrelenting campaign of personal vilification. (King ultimately provoked Marshall into a rare outburst when the chief of staff literally thumped the table and declared: "I will not have the meetings of the Joint Chiefs of Staff dominated by hatred [toward MacArthur]"). Consequently, Vice Admiral Leary and (after September 1942) Vice Admiral Arthur S. Carpender, started with a severe handicap. Their extreme caution in using their admittedly few combatant ships did not help their cause.

In October 1943, Vice Admiral Thomas C. Kinkaid became commander of the Seventh Fleet. King did not think Kinkaid "had very many brains," but he worked well with MacArthur. Kinkaid was by a substantial margin the least capable of MacArthur's senior lieutenants. MacArthur was blessed, however, with Rear Admiral Daniel Barbey. One of the few naval officers with genuine interest in amphibious operations, "Uncle Dan" proved extremely resourceful in developing doctrine and equipment. His flexibility in adjusting to rapidly changing operational demands and mounting multiple landings almost concurrently remains extremely impressive. Barbey (eventually a vice admiral) and Halsey were the two senior naval officers MacArthur esteemed.[15]

On July 30, 1942, MacArthur received Major General George Kenney as his third air commander in nine months. MacArthur lashed Kenney with a verbal whip twined from two strands composed of his airmen's sins of incompetence and disloyalty. After this inauspicious beginning, the bantamweight, dynamic, decisive, and cocksure airpower innovator instituted a resurrection of MacArthur's aviation arm that would make it supremely effective. MacArthur warmed to Kenney as to no other subordinate, just as Kenney came to idolize his chief. Kenney's key contribution was as MacArthur's tutor on air power. What fitted Kenney perfectly to that role was that unlike the dominant heavy bomber obsession in the Army Air Forces, he possessed a true breadth of vision across the full spectrum of air power, including reconnaissance, fighters, medium bombers, and air transportation. He exhibited a keen eye for technical innovation and functioned capably as a salesman. There was a direct connection between Kenney's lobbying and the fact that MacArthur's most plentiful tools were his air units. Kenney converted MacArthur from skeptic to zealous true believer in air power. This proved a key to MacArthur's greatest triumphs in World War II, but would betray him in Korea. To a less conspicuous extent, Barbey served a parallel function as MacArthur's mentor on amphibious operations. Thus, these two officers proved more vital to

MacArthur than any of his other staff or commanders. MacArthur demonstrated his sublime confidence in Kenney and Barbey by leaving them alone.

While giving Kenney his due as MacArthur's teacher is just, Kenney received (and was not bashful about claiming) a great deal of credit that really was earned by his stable of talented subordinates. Preeminent in this group was Ennis C. Whitehead, first deputy commander, then commander, of the Fifth Air Force. It really was Whitehead, not Kenney, who formulated plans and tactics for major victories at Bismarck Sea and Wewak. Also important was Paul Wurtsmith, the fighter commander of the Fifth Air Force.[16]

Under the original command arrangements for SWPA, MacArthur's senior ground commander was Australian Thomas A. Blamey, a man consistently underrated by his American contemporaries and seldom accorded his due in American accounts of MacArthur's campaigns. Tall, rotund, and projecting a jovial façade, Blamey's appearance belied the fact that he actually was a tough, competent, well-schooled career soldier with a distinguished staff record beginning in World War I. (He was a general officer at age thirty-four, thus besting MacArthur's record.) Prime Minister Curtin handled well-founded demurs about Blamey's private indiscretions with the comment that he was recruited as a "military leader, not a Sunday School Teacher." Blamey's outstanding qualities were his sophisticated understanding and energetic efforts to master the myriad problems in organizing Australia's armed forces; his rapid grasp of the intertwined air, sea and land elements of the Pacific War; his drive; and his fierce defense of Australian interests. He wore one arresting verbal accolade bestowed by Australian Major General George Rankin: Blamey, declared Rankin, "was ruthless enough to deal with our Allies, the Americans."

Blamey took dual appointments as MacArthur's ground forces commander and as commander of Australian Military Forces, jobs that conflicted in 1942 and 1943, when Australians did most of MacArthur's ground fighting. Blamey possessed shrewd political instincts and kept Curtin's respect even as he created a record that reflected adroit sabotage of any potential rivals to his seat. Perhaps ironically, Australian histories of World War II sometimes castigate Blamey as spinelessly subservient to MacArthur. Blamey did disgrace himself in relieving subordinates on New Guinea to appease MacArthur in 1942 in order to retain his own job, but Blamey proved a generally sound tactician, particularly in 1943, and he successfully rebuffed MacArthur's meddling on many occasions.[17]

In 1944, when American soldiers finally outnumbered Australians, Walter Krueger supplanted Blamey as MacArthur's main ground commander. German-born, like Willoughby, Krueger rose from the ranks. Like MacArthur, he was scholarly about his profession (he translated German military texts), having attended both the army and, important for a commander required to mount repeated amphibious operations, the navy war colleges. He was the oldest American to command a field army and he owed that distinction entirely to MacArthur. Few sentences describing Krueger lack the word "cautious," but he was competent and genuine in his care for his men. While he proved on Luzon that he would stand up to MacArthur's needling, overall, his record in this regard was lamentably uneven.[18]

MacArthur eventually made Robert Eichelberger commander of the Eighth Army. Eichelberger turned the bitter lessons of Buna into a curriculum of tough training that paid great dividends in subsequent campaigns. He acted as MacArthur's "fireman" again at Biak and exhibited in the Philippines considerable dash and ingenuity. MacArthur employed the well-tried method of playing Eichelberger off against Krueger in an attempt to propel each to greater efforts. In the end, MacArthur showered Eichelberger with praise, but never promoted him to four-star rank as he did Krueger. This left Eichelberger bitter and the fount of venomous attacks on his old chief.[19]

+>===<+

How and why the United States ended up pursuing dual advances across the Pacific in World War II has provided grist for endless dispute. Although the "Germany First" strategy was initially proposed in November 1940 by Admiral Harold Stark, the chief of naval operations, its most commonly heralded champion is George C. Marshall. At the surface level, it appears that MacArthur's vehement and incessant dissent from this policy and in favor of concentration on his SWPA for the march to Japan should have provoked equally strident opposition from Marshall and the Joint Chiefs of Staff (JCS). As in so many of MacArthur's controversies, the reality is a much less simple tale.

First of all, MacArthur's otherwise relentless adversary, Ernest King, recognized from the outset that the cornucopia of U.S. material resources permitted simultaneous offensive wars in both the Atlantic and Pacific theaters. He also believed it would be folly to grant the Japanese a long respite to fortify their defenses. Thus, deferring action in the Pacific was foolhardy, and the real question was apportionment: How many assets could be diverted safely to sustain the Pacific War? Accordingly, on the "Germany First" policy, MacArthur had an unexpected ally.

If King proved to be one ally of MacArthur in subverting a pristine "Germany First" strategy, the British inadvertently proved another. As historian

Mark Stoler noted, the conviction that keeping the Soviet Union in the war constituted "*the* key to victory" operated less publicly, but profoundly as the central pillar of U.S. strategy. Without Soviet participation, the war in Europe was not winnable. In the minds of U.S. strategists, a prompt attack into Northwest Europe thus constituted the proper direct method of sustaining the Soviets. A major 1942 European effort would have compelled radical economy of forces in the Pacific. But when the British demonstrated that they were unwilling to mount such an attack until the indefinite future, they triggered a reaction from the JCS. Deferring the major European effort for a year or two created a window in which the forces produced early in the mobilization could be employed elsewhere.

Two factors then drove the JCS to commit many of the forces made available by the deferred European attack to the Pacific. Indeed, historians have long marveled at the seeming paradox that despite the "Germany First" avowed strategy, there were approximately equal U.S. land and air resources deployed to the Pacific through late 1943. One factor was the political decision by Churchill and Roosevelt that Australia and New Zealand would not be permitted to fall. This in turn mandated protection of those nations and their Pacific lines of communication. The Japanese thrust down into the South Pacific, even after Midway, unwittingly had stomped on the sciatic nerve of the Western Alliance: shipping. The shortage of shipping shaped allied strategy into 1944. Japan's push in the South Pacific in 1942 threatened to place an unsustainable burden on shipping resources and compelled a response.

The second, and much less advertised reason, for substantial U.S. investment in the Pacific was that it was viewed as the best alternative to an attack on Northwest Europe to aid the Soviets because it ensured that Japan remained preoccupied in the Pacific. Even while ostensibly complying with President Roosevelt's directive for an early American offensive against Germany, which became the North African campaign in 1942, the JCS, very much including Marshall, quietly diverted a major stream of troops and planes to the Pacific. It was logistics, basically the worldwide shortage of shipping, rather than indifference to the Pacific at the JCS, that kept MacArthur on shorter rations than he craved.20

From the moment command in the Pacific was divided in March 1942 and the prospect of a dual advance emerged, arguments commenced and have never ceased about whether the United States should have confined its effort to one axis of advance and, if so, which one. The strongest point in favor of MacArthur was that the SWPA axis appeared the geographically obvious and superior route for severing Japan's communications with the resource areas in the southern regions, upon which Japan's war economy depended, notably oil. The strongest point in favor the Central Pacific route was that its open expanses permitted the United States to best deploy its naval superiority, particularly its aircraft carriers. It also promised to bring Japan more readily within range of heavy bombers.

But another vital element emerged that favored a two-front advance. The Allied counter-offensive against Japan began in August 1942 at Guadalcanal, and the war ended almost exactly three years later. This three-year span can be divided into two parts. Up to November 1943, MacArthur and Halsey orchestrated only extremely limited geographical advances in the SWPA and South Pacific. A projection of Allied progress as of November 1943 based on the rate of advance in these theaters since August 1942 would have foretold a war stretching out to two decades. But this period ensnared Japan in a terrible attrition battle that radically reduced the combat effectiveness of her air forces and severely weakened her lighter naval forces. This bleeding left Japan's air and sea forces in a debilitated state that permitted the extraordinarily swift advances that marched to Japan's shores in the second part of the Allied counteroffensive.

When the importance of this attrition phase is appreciated, the superiority of the two-front strategy becomes clear. By engaging the air units of the Imperial Navy in the Solomons and the air units of the Imperial Army on New Guinea, as well as naval units in both areas, the Allies greatly increased the rate of attrition. Further, threatening two separate regions overstrained Japan's inadequate shipping resources. Allied aerial and sea dominance effectively negated Japan's potential superiority in ground forces. Even after November 1943, a single-front advance would have bestowed on Japan the advantage of concentrating her inferior resources to block that line of advance.

The dual axis also served to keep Japan off balance and constantly readjusting. For example, the fighting on Guadalcanal drew Japanese priority in the fall of the 1942 and by itself forced termination of the threat to Port Moresby. Moreover, Guadalcanal and later the offensives in the Solomons and Central Pacific absorbed a preponderance of Japan's air power and a vast majority of her naval power. MacArthur never appeared to recognize his tremendous good fortune in having the majority of Japanese air and sea forces kept away from his axis of advance.

All of this retrospective assessment aside, the underlying reason for the two-front advance was the inability of the JCS to agree on one commander for the Pacific. What is interesting is how a policy adopted for the "wrong" reasons proved to generate quite unanticipated profits that exceeded those that would have been produced by a more "rational" approach.

7

Apprenticeship

THE JAPANESE RECAST THEIR COMMANDS AND PLANS AFTER THE LOSS of Guadalcanal and Papua. Lt. Gen. Imamura Hitoshi led the senior Imperial Army headquarters in the South Pacific, the Eighth Area Army. The Eighteenth Army under General Adachi Hatazo became the top command on New Guinea. Imamura devised a scheme for a delaying action in eastern New Guinea while he built up forces to hold western New Guinea. Imamura and Adachi decided to reinforce the Japanese positions at Lae and Salamaua with the 51st Division.

A convoy of eight transports escorted by an equal number of destroyers departed Rabaul on February 28, 1943. The convoy carried about 6,400 soldiers and marines, and masses of supplies. Thanks to Ultra, Kenney was ready—and with Whitehead's new tactics. Instead of ineffectual high-altitude bomb runs, most Allied attack pilots would bore in at mast-top level literally to "skip" bombs into Japanese hulls. Kenney unleashed 330 aircraft over March 1–3 which sank all but four destroyers. This quartet rescued about half the passengers and crews of the sunken vessels and retreated to Rabaul. MacArthur's communiqué christened this event "The Battle of the Bismarck

Sea," and correctly proclaimed a "major disaster" for the Japanese. Japan never again risked a major convoy in this region.*

MacArthur's "Battle of the Bismarck Sea" communiqué grossly overstated Japanese losses (fourteen instead of eight transports, and eight instead of four destroyers). But in this instance, it was not MacArthur's creative hand at fault. The communiqué itself accurately reflected the all-too-typical inflated claims that aviators often registered in the heat of a sprawling and confused battle. In this instance, radio intelligence clearly revealed the exaggeration, and the navy attempted to make MacArthur publicly issue a correction. MacArthur and Kenney bristled at this, justifiably pointing out that American air commanders in Europe issued equally if not more grossly exaggerated claims. The real significance of this episode is that it illustrates the dangerously personal cast of the conflicts between MacArthur and the navy had assumed by this time.

At the end of March, MacArthur received a new directive from the Joint Chiefs of Staff. The product of much dispute, the fresh order conspicuously amended the July 1942 directive by substituting the "ultimate seizure of the Bismarck Archipelago" for the capture of Rabaul as the ultimate goal. The list of other authorized targets provided MacArthur's agenda for 1943. During these exchanges, Marshall rebuffed navy designs to make Nimitz the supreme commander in the Pacific and, failing that, to renege on the provision that MacArthur would command for the last two phases set forth in the July 1942 directive. This episode provided yet another example of how Marshall supported MacArthur despite the latter's paranoia that the chief of staff worked tirelessly to undermine him.[1]

Since MacArthur now held the reins for Tasks Two and Three from the July 1942 directive, this meant Admiral Halsey would come under his command. Consequently, Halsey paid a visit to his new boss in April 1943. Much to the surprise of everyone else—and perhaps to themselves—Halsey recorded: "Five minutes after I reported, I felt as if we were lifelong friends. I have seldom seen a man who makes a quicker, stronger, more favorable impression." Of their relationship, Halsey declared, "Not once did he, my supe-

---

* One unusual bonanza from the battle was the capture from a lifeboat of an alphabetical list of all Japanese Army officers as of October 1942 and their assignments. Soon translated, this list produced extremely valuable intelligence for the rest of the war by permitting correlation of the names disclosed by code breaking with branch assignments, units, and ranks. In 1945, for example, the name of one officer proved a key clue to identifying a Japanese armored unit on Kyushu.

rior officer, ever force his decision on me." MacArthur reciprocated the warm regard and the two strong-willed officers collaborated extremely well.[2]

+>==>=+

A fresh plan, Cartwheel, meshed the new directive from the Joint Chiefs with the available forces. Overall it provided a flexible schedule for about thirteen invasions and captures over eight months. Halsey would advance up the Solomons to southern Bougainville by way of New Georgia. MacArthur's efforts in 1943 essentially sought to secure the Huon Peninsula (defined by the villages of Lae, Salamaua, Finschhafen, and Madang) and air bases on western New Britain. Kavieng, on New Ireland, would be captured, but whether Rabaul would be isolated or assaulted remained open. For his operations, MacArthur secured General Walter C. Krueger to command the Sixth Army, the American field army under MacArthur's command. By rights, American ground forces should have answered to Blamey, but without consulting either the U.S. or Australian governments, and without serious protest from Blamey, MacArthur effectively segregated his ground forces along national lines by command and mission. Blamey's Australians would pursue a campaign on New Guinea into early 1944. Meanwhile, MacArthur designated Krueger's command Alamo Force, now with three American divisions (including one marine) and separate infantry, dismounted cavalry, and parachute infantry regiments. But Krueger's deployable strength numbered much less, as the 32nd Infantry and 1st Marine Divisions required lengthy recuperation.

On the eve of Cartwheel, Japanese forces deployed against MacArthur and Halsey totaled some 123,000 ground troops. About 55,000 of these defended the northern coast of New Guinea in the region MacArthur planned to attack, with approximately 15,000 around Lae-Salamaua and 20,000 in the Madang vicinity. Halsey's first target, New Georgia, contained a garrison of about 10,500 Japanese. In the South East Area, the Japanese deployed 540 aircraft, of which about 390 were operational. On land, sea, and air, MacArthur and Halsey's combined forces heavily outnumbered the Japanese.

Cartwheel commenced with baby steps. In the first real amphibious assault in the Southwest Pacific, Rear Admiral Daniel Barbey's VII Amphibious Force lifted American troops to seize the islands of Woodlark and Kiriwina, east of the Papua tail, on June 30. The islands provided air base sites that proved of limited utility. But the operation proved extremely useful as a template for all of Barbey's subsequent operations. At the same time, a shore-to-shore movement secured Nassau Bay, on the north coast of New Guinea, as a key landing craft staging base for the planned advance on Lae.[3]

Synchronized with MacArthur's largely bloodless seizures of Kiriwina and Woodlark Islands and Nassau Bay was Halsey's June 30 attack on New Georgia, in the middle of the Solomons chain. The ground campaign dragged on to October 6. Roughly 2,500 Japanese died on New Georgia. American losses alone amounted to 1,121 dead and 3,873 wounded ashore. The Imperial Navy inflicted two tactical reverses on the U.S. Navy and both sides recorded heavy air losses, though the Japanese got the worst of it. The allies gained the island, but the real honors of the campaign on land and sea went to the Japanese.[4]

⊹⊱━⊰⊹

After the war, Prime Minister Tojo Hideki stated that the three principal factors in Japan's defeat were the leapfrogging strategy, the depredations of American submarines, and the ability of American carrier forces to remain at sea for extended periods. The next obvious target after New Georgia was Kolombangara. Halsey skipped over that island and instead seized lightly held Vella Lavella in what constituted the first deliberate instance of the leapfrog, or bypassing strategy, in the Pacific—by the Allies, because the Japanese bypassed the Philippines before it was secured to strike the Dutch East Indies.[5]

The concept lacked novelty. A 1940 naval war college study contemplated bypassing the Marshall Islands for a strike directly at Truk in the Carolines. In early 1943, President Roosevelt as well as Admirals King and Nimitz recommended it. Nimitz is sometimes credited with its first allied application in the assault on Attu. Nimitz skipped past Kiska for Attu, however, not from a deliberate application of bypassing strategy, but because he possessed forces for only one operation. One of Halsey's staff officers urged bypassing New Georgia but was overruled. The one unequivocal benefit from the New Georgia episode was to render Halsey highly receptive to the idea of skipping over Kolombangara (which the Japanese were preparing as another New Georgia) and seizing the very lightly held (and euphoniously named) Vella Lavella. And so it was that before the fighting was done on New Georgia, on August 15 Halsey's sailors landed a reinforced regiment of the 25th Infantry Division on southeast Vella Lavella. The Japanese reacted violently by air, but sustained serious losses for no commensurate damage. The follow-up New Zealand 3rd Division drove the last Japanese off Vella Lavella by October 3. In stark contrast to New Georgia, total allied losses came to twenty-six American and thirty-two New Zealanders dead and a combined one hundred forty wounded.[6]

MacArthur's moves to Kiriwina, Woodlark, and Nassau Bay did not distract the Japanese from their intentions to hold Lae and Salamaua as outer defenses for Wewak and Madang. But the breakdown of Japanese logistics following the Bismarck Sea disaster left the defending force of approximately 10,000 men riddled with undernourishment and disease. Recognizing that effective defense required aerial might, Imperial Headquarters dispatched the Fourth Air Army to the Wewak area.

In August 1943, General Blamey moved to Port Moresby to oversee the new offensive on New Guinea. Major General E. F. Herring, however, exercised tactical command under his Australian I Corps headquarters at Dobodura. Their immediate targets were Lae, on the north coast of New Guinea, and the Markham and Ramu Valleys, which lay inland northwest of Lae. The valleys contained sandy level stretches suitable for airfields. The village of Lae provided a port from which a stream of supplies could be hauled by road to the air installations inland. To Blamey goes the credit for an overall scheme of drawing the main Japanese forces down to Salamaua to thwart a feint from Nassau Bay while the real effort struck behind them to cut off the 51st Division.

An attack on Lae presented formidable operational challenges. The terrain precluded an extended overland approach of a major force. But MacArthur lacked enough ships for a major amphibious thrust or enough planes for a large-scale airborne assault on Lae. Consequently, resource limitations and terrain enforced a combined scheme for both an amphibious assault and an air assault followed by the airlift of a division.

MacArthur and Blamey detailed the 3rd Australian division (with the U.S. 162nd Infantry Regiment attached) to fake an advance on Salamaua from Nassau Bay. But Kenney's most skillful subordinate, Ennis Whitehead, conceived the imaginative idea of taking Lae via the proverbial "back door" with an airborne assault at Nadzab, site of a prewar airfield northwest of Lae in the Markham Valley, followed by a march to the village. Meanwhile, Kenney learned from Ultra of the build-up of Japanese airpower on New Guinea and the key role of the airfield complex at Wewak—a location chosen by the Japanese precisely because it was outside the range of escorted allied bombers. Kenney concocted an extremely innovative idea for stretching the range of his fighters so that they could cover bombers raiding at Wewak. New Guinea's extremely inhospitable terrain dictated that both combatants usually confined their control to coastal enclaves, leaving the inland areas a vast no man's land.

Based on the sound selection of another of his subordinates, Paul Wurtsmith, Kenney had "secret" grass airstrips constructed at Tsili Tsili (pronounced "silly, silly") along the Watut River. These served as staging bases for his fighters to project their reach as far west as Wewak. The remarkable ingenuity required to construct the airstrip included cutting trucks into two pieces suitable for loading in a C–47 and then welding the two halves together.[7]

With all in readiness, Kenney struck the four Wewak airfields housing the Fourth Air Army on August 17. Typically, Kenney claimed that the series of strikes extending to the end of the month destroyed 200 Japanese planes. The actual total was about 82 of 120 operational aircraft.[8]

Kenney's raids provoked a momentous change. For eighteen months, MacArthur's naval commanders refused to commit anything larger than a PT boat or landing craft to the waters along the north coast of New Guinea. The sailors pleaded the danger of uncharted rocks and reefs coupled with the peril posed by Japanese airmen. Even as firm a friend of the navy as historian Samuel Eliot Morison expressed exasperation with these arguments, save for the fair point that there was no sound system for assuring support of Kenney's fighters. Once Kenney drubbed Wewak, however, the navy for the first time thrust warships (admittedly just four destroyers) as far up the northern coast of New Guinea as Finschhafen to conduct a bombardment.[9]

When the weather finally aligned the way Kenney desired on September 4, the multipronged attack began. (It was well it did, for fickle weather conditions soon proved that even a one-day delay might have played havoc with the whole operation.) Two brigades of the Australian 9th Division (Maj. Gen. G. F. Wootten) numbering about 7,800 men landed at dawn on September 4 east of Lae beyond Japanese artillery range. A second lift the night of September 5–6 added the division's third brigade, with another 2,400 Aussies. One Australian war diary called the sealift a "long line of ships form[ing] a formidable but inspiring sight." Morison was closer to the truth that the eclectic assembly looked quite "strange to an old seaman's eye." Barbey's VII Amphibious Force contained only destroyer transports (APDs), Landing Ship Tanks (LSTs), Landing Craft Infantry (LCIs) and Landing Craft Tanks (LCTs) while the 2nd Engineer Special Brigade featured only landing craft. No vessel bigger than a destroyer escorted the flotilla. Though the 9th Division already boasted a splendid reputation won in its Mediterranean campaigns, this was its first operation against the Japanese. Moreover, the operation marked the first Australian amphibious operation since Gallipoli in 1915. Fortunately, Lae proved incomparably better executed. Casualties to vigorous Japanese air strikes exceeded those ashore.[10]

September 5 brought one of the greatest military spectacles MacArthur ever witnessed. Thus far in the war, Allied airborne operations had been a disappointment and the whole concept dangled in doubt. MacArthur ordered Col. Kenneth H. Kinsler's 503rd Parachute Infantry Regiment (with a small detachment of stalwart Australian artillerymen) to jump on the airfield at Nadzab. Engineers would improve the crude facility to take a steady stream of C–47s that would ferry up most of the Australian 7th Division (led by Maj. Gen. George A. Vasey). The Australians would then attack down the Markham River Valley to place Lae in a pincers between the 9th Australian Division advancing from the east and the 7th Australian Division from the northwest.

On the morning of September 5, the ninety-six C–47s began takeoff at 0825. The troop carriers formed up and then rendezvoused with their escorting and supporting armada of Kenney's combat types on time to the minute. Altogether the task force numbered 302 aircraft from eight different airfields.

The C–47s rumbled down the Watut Valley and headed right at the Markham River gradually descending to between 400 and 500 feet. Inside each plane, paratroopers stood up, hooked up, and formed a line from the exit door. In perfect coordination, as the C–47s approached Nadzab, six squadrons of B–25 strafers, each with eight nose-mounted 50-caliber machine guns and sixty fragmentation bombs swept over the field to suppress the defenders. Just as the last bombs exploded, a half-dozen A–20s swooped low to dispense smoke to screen the drop zones. Starting at about 1020, eighty-one C–47s emptied out the three battalions of the 503rd in just four and a half minutes. There were three fatalities and thirty-three injuries in the jump; but no Japanese resistance.[11]

Squadrons of Kenney's fighters flew protective circles over the aerial spectacle but there was no Japanese reaction. High above the whole circus cruised three B–17s. These bore MacArthur, Kenney, and senior staff officers. MacArthur admitted to Kenney that he was afraid that he might embarrass himself with air sickness in front the "kids," as he called them. Australian and American engineers improved Nadzab so swiftly that that the following afternoon, a brigade of Vasey's 7th Division began arriving.[12]

The imaginative concept, planning, and execution of the Nadzab operation illustrate the excellence of Kenney and his subordinates. Moreover, MacArthur's successful use of the 503rd Parachute infantry Regiment at Nadzab produced far-ranging effects. The costly and relatively ineffective performance of allied airborne units on Sicily in July 1943 shook the faith of senior army leaders in the whole air assault concept. Eisenhower declared that he could not see the benefit of an airborne division. The Nadzab triumph caused the powerful commander of the Army Ground Forces, Lt. Gen. Leslie J. McNair, to pause in his plan to curtail the program and restrict airborne operations to battalion size. McNair gave the airborne advocates another chance, and an exercise by the 11th Airborne Division convinced McNair to retain the army's airborne divisions. The use of the 82nd and 101st Airborne Divisions proved absolutely critical for the Normandy landings. Thus, MacArthur's successful generalship in the Pacific indirectly contributed an indispensable element to the D-Day assault.[13]

+≻═≺+

"Most Australian soldiers who fought in the South-West Pacific would agree that they would rather face an aroused enemy than an angry Nature," noted the official Australian historian. It was mostly "an angry nature," not the tough but sparse Japanese defenders, that kept Wootten's 9th Australian Division at bay from Lae. A series of water courses checked the advance. The worst of these was the Busu River which formed multiple channels of swiftly swirling water. One battalion alone saw thirteen men drowned trying to cross.[14]

Meanwhile, the lead brigade of Vasey's 7th Division commenced an advance from Nadzab down the Markham Valley toward Lae. Weather, however, halted the airlift between September 10 and 12. When a captured Japanese order revealed Imperial Army plans to withdraw from Lae on September 8, the Australian generals perforce attempted both to speed the advance on Lae and to cut Japanese withdrawal routes to the northeast toward, Sio across the Huon Peninsula. At dawn on September 15, the 9th Division, only a mile and a quarter from Lae, seemed poised to reach easily reach the objective first as the 7th Division was still some seven miles away and meeting much stiffer resistance to boot. But Brigadier Kenneth Eather of the 25th Brigade, 7th Division, pinned the Japanese facing him with two battalions and led his third battalion—literally as a pistol wielding lead scout—into Lae just after noon, ahead of Wootten's 9th Division.[15]

During this campaign, the Australian 7th and 9th Divisions sustained a combined 188 dead and 501 wounded. They inflicted at least 2,200 casualties on the Japanese, largely the 51st Division. The battered Japanese soldiers fought well, but their leaders were out-generaled. Only the delayed advance of the 9th Division inflicted by the flooded Busu River saved the Japanese from annihilation. About 8,000 Japanese attempted to march along an inland retreat route from Lae, over the mountains, with half-rations for ten days. It took twenty-six days, and about 2,000 Japanese died of starvation.[16]

+≔≕+

The fall of Lae and Salamaua, following close upon the heels of defeat in the Central Solomons and expulsion from the Aleutians, convinced Imperial General Headquarters that Japan's defense perimeter must be contracted. Tokyo hailed the new line as the "absolute national defense line to be held by all means." It extended from Western New Guinea through the Carolines to the Marianas. The Southeast Area as well as the Gilberts and Marshall Islands became a "forward wall," or outpost line, ordered to conduct a protracted defense. The Imperial Army staff officers identified a pattern in MacArthur's moves of jumps within the 240–300-mile range of his fighter planes. Each jump required about two months. Thus, the Japanese calculated it would take MacArthur eight to ten months to reach Western New Guinea, time enough for them to convert it to a fortress.

General Imamura and his senior naval counterpart, Admiral Kusaka Jin'ichi, pinned their hopes on holding Bougainville in the Solomons, New Britain and Finschhafen on New Guinea. The 38th Division was at Rabaul, the 65th Brigade guarded New Britain, and on New Guinea, the 51st Division was retreating from Lae-Salamaua, the 20th Division was between Madang and Lae, building a road and the 41st Division held Wewak. With the landing at Lae on September 4, Adachi recognized the threat to Finschhafen, then held by approximately a thousand defenders. Adachi detailed Major General Nakai Matsutaro, the infantry group commander of the 20th Division, to take a regiment from the division to a blocking position on the approaches to Finschhafen at Kaipit. The main body of the 20th Division, however, faced a 200-mile march to get to Finschhafen and only set out on September 10.

Meanwhile, MacArthur analyzed a series of recommendations from Blamey and his American subordinates and settled on a course of action. On September 15, he ordered Blamey to capture Kaipit, at the head of the Markham Valley and Dumpu, about thirty miles south of Bogadjim. Two days later he added Finschhafen to Blamey's objectives.[17]

In a daring move, an Australian independent (commando) company seized Kaipit on September 19. Kenney flew in two brigades of the 7th Division, and one secured Dumpu by October 6. The 7th Division then fought an epic struggle against Nakai's men along the Finisterre Mountains to February

1944. The now well-experienced VII Amphibious Force picked up a brigade of Wootten's 9th Division at Lae and landed it eighty-two miles further north at Finschhafen on September 22.

After seizing Finschhafen, the Australians turned to the task of defeating about 4,000 Japanese defenders on the Sattelberg heights, overlooking their beachhead. Wootten shrewdly deduced that it was better to permit the Japanese to come to him, which they proceeded to do. Starting on October 16, the Japanese struck by land and sea. The vicious fighting around the Sattelberg Heights extended into December. Wootten then captured Sio by January 15.[18]

+====+

While MacArthur's Australians moved on Finschhafen and Sio, Halsey closed in on Rabaul. After conducting feints in the Treasury Islands and on Choiseul to reinforce Japanese expectations of the next American move, Halsey landed the 3rd Marine Division at Empress Augusta Bay, nearly midway up the western side of Bougainville, on November 1. This operation completely surprised the Japanese and bypassed stronger Japanese forces at the southern end of Bougainville. Engineers soon prepped air bases from which allied fighters could range over Rabaul. Between October 1943 and February 1944, flyers from Halsey's and MacArthur's commands, aided by timely strikes by Nimitz's fast carriers, inflicted horrendous attrition on Japanese air units at Rabaul in furious air battles. Japan committed her refitting carrier air groups which sustained crippling losses. Finally, Japanese aviation could no longer bear the attrition and was withdrawn. A massive Japanese counterattack on the perimeter at Empress Augusta Bay was crushed in March 1944.[19]

Simultaneously, MacArthur envisioned operations to seize positions along the New Britain coast which formed the eastern edge of the Vitiaz-Dampier Straits, as necessary protection to the right flank of his advance. After much discussion and debate, an army regiment (112th Cavalry, fighting as infantry) seized Arawe (intended as a PT boat base) and then the 1st Marine Division secured Cape Gloucester (an airfield location) between mid-December 1943 and March 1944. The Marines encountered sharp fighting in totally miserable conditions of mud and rain. These operations proved to mark the last instance of the cautious approach instilled by two years of tough fighting with the Japanese in three dimensions. Prospectively, both operations appeared prudent; in retrospect, they were not necessary.

On January 2, 1944, with very short notice reflecting the now tremendous efficiency of MacArthur's forces, the 126th Regimental Combat Team (of the 32d Infantry Division) landed at Saidor. Not only did this bypass strong Japanese forces seventy-five miles east at Sio, it also served to divide the Japanese Eighteenth Army in two, with one-half around Sio and the remainder clustered at Wewak and Madang. Imamura faced a key decision: Attack Saidor or withdraw forces at Sio back to Madang? He chose the former, a fateful decision. The isolated Japanese embarked on an agonized inland retreat over mountains on extremely sparse rations, moving at night to avoid air observation, and chilled to the bone by nocturnal temperature dips. Starvation, disease, and exhaustion cumulatively just about halved the 20,000-strong ranks of desperate Imperial Army soldiers before they reached what the Japanese believed was surely MacArthur's next target: Madang.[20]

The MacArthur family, Fort Selden, 1884. From the left, Douglas, Arthur, Arthur III, and Mary Pinkney Hardy MacArthur ("Pinky").

General Pershing decorates MacArthur. Note MacArthur's nonregulation cap, part of his signature look Pershing detested.

(left) *MacArthur pre–World War II in Manila with his key staff officers, T.J. Davis (left) and Dwight Eisenhower (right).*

(below) *MacArthur in 1943 with (from left) Rear Admiral Daniel Barbey, Lt. Gen. George Kenney, and Lt. General Walter Krueger.*

MacArthur with Australian General Thomas A. Blamey.

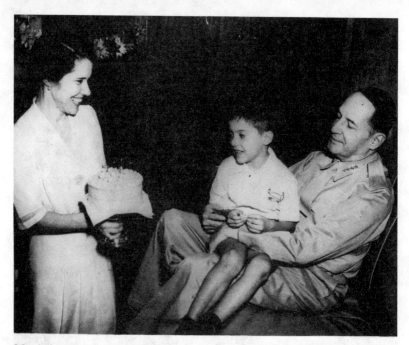

MacArthur with second wife Jean on son Arthur IV's sixth birthday, February 21, 1944.

(right) *This picture was taken eight days after the prior photograph: MacArthur with corpse of Japanese solider on Los Negros, rebutting the "Dugout Doug" canard.*

Pearl Harbor conference July 1944. President Roosevelt's appearance shocked MacArthur. Admiral Chester Nimitz, MacArthur rival Pacific theater commander, is on the right.

The most famous photograph of MacArthur in the United States, his "return" to the Philippines at Leyte October 20, 1944.

One of the greatest moments of MacArthur's life, the surrender ceremony on the Missouri, September 2, 1945. The officers to MacArthur's immediate rear are Lieutenant Generals Jonathan Wainwright (front) and Arthur Percival (British). Their presence reflects MacArthur's masterful handling of symbolism.

(left) *The most famous photograph of MacArthur in Japan, his first meeting with Hirohito. Japanese officials attempted to suppress publication of an image that conveyed MacArthur's towering dominance.*

(right) *MacArthur in Korea with his miracle worker, Lt. General Mathew Ridgway (immediately behind MacArthur).*

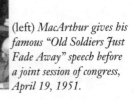

(left) *MacArthur gives his famous "Old Soldiers Just Fade Away" speech before a joint session of congress, April 19, 1951.*

The record setting ticket tape parade in New York City, April 20, 1951.

8

Breakthrough

BY JANUARY 1944, MACARTHUR'S RECORD IN TWENTY MONTHS OF theater command had graduated from dubious to respectable, but remained far from the stuff of legend. By the metric of his scant 300-mile advance, roughly one fifth of the way along the northern coast of New Guinea, Tokyo disappeared below a twenty-one-year distant horizon. Meanwhile, his rival Nimitz had just orchestrated a 2,000-mile leap in the Central Pacific through the Gilberts, in November 1943, to the Marshall Islands, in January 1944. Moreover, in December 1943 the JCS refused to approve any of MacArthur's projected operations beyond securing Mindanao, thus implying his relegation to a strategic backwater capped off at the equator.

Once again, as in early 1941, just as the comet of MacArthur's career seemed about to fizzle out, events—he probably saw them as destiny—intervened. More specifically, there was an extraordinarily tiny scene in the vast theater of the global war that exerted extraordinary leverage. During the agonized retreat of the Japanese 20th Division from the Huon Gulf area, the division radio platoon found that they could no longer manhandle the heavy steel chest with the division's complete cryptographic library, including codebooks.

Dampness and danger precluded burning the material. The bedraggled, exhausted Japanese buried the steel chest by a streambed near Sio. When Australian troops reached Sio, their fear of booby traps prompted a young Australian engineer to sweep the area with a mine detector. He located the steel chest, and an anonymous intelligence officer recognized its priceless contents. While Central Bureau had managed its first solutions of Imperial Army messages in June 1943, it could not achieve a sufficient quantity of timely break-ins to provide useful information. With this treasure trove, MacArthur's code breakers leaped from solving several hundred messages per month to solving twenty thousand per month.[1]

Central Bureau's newfound ability to produce Imperial Army Ultra afforded the essential catalyst for MacArthur's daring new timetable. Before the coup, MacArthur enjoyed only a dim understanding of Japanese army deployments. This induced caution, hence his current plan called for an elementary hundred-mile jump to Hansa Bay. The Japanese easily anticipated this move and positioned their forces accordingly. The ability to read Imperial Army messages cleared away the usual "fog of war" and suddenly revealed to MacArthur the whole military chess board. Ultra not only delivered the precise deployment of major Japanese formations, but also the actual thinking of Japanese commanders. While the three division's of Adachi's Eighteenth Army desperately prepared for another slugging bout with MacArthur's Australians and Americans around Wewak and Hansa Bay, Ultra revealed a 375-mile gap between those forces and the next major Japanese formation, the 36th Division, at Sarmi. Almost midway between the Imperial Army concentrations were Aitape and Hollandia, occupied mainly by service and air units. Willoughby (in one of his redeeming moments) mooted a plan to bypass Hansa Bay and leap for Hollandia. The chief of the G–3 (operations) planning section, Brig. Gen. Bonner Fellers enthusiastically concurred, but Feller's cautious boss, Maj. Gen. Steven Chamberlain, the G–3, vetoed that scheme. Fellers used the bypass technique at the staff level and brought the plan to MacArthur. In a remarkable parallel to the Cote de Chatillon in World War I, MacArthur secured his greatest World War II triumph by making someone else's plan his own. Chamberlain fired Fellers for his insubordination, but MacArthur rewarded Fellers by making him his military secretary.

The overture to the bold leap, however, required securing the flanks of the advance and finally disposing of Rabaul. Here too, Ultra played a role, but a very different one. In January and February 1944, Kenney's airmen reported that not only did they meet no aerial resistance, but also they clamored that few if any Japanese remained on Los Negros in the Admiralties. Willoughby,

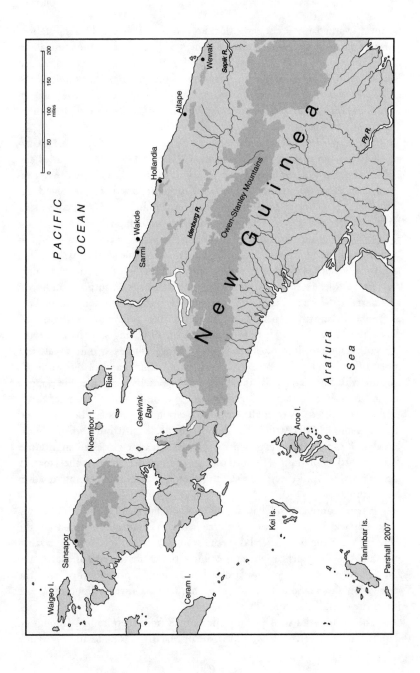

however, warned quite correctly that Los Negros in fact held a substantial Japanese garrison (3,250 estimated, versus 3,646 actual, based, of course, on radio intelligence). On the evening of February 24, Kenney convinced MacArthur to dispatch forthwith a "reconnaissance in force" to Los Negros to exploit the opening. A successful venture would speed up the timetable of SWPA advance by a month and keep MacArthur in the race with Nimitz. MacArthur set the attack for February 29.

The assault force comprised a thousand-man detachment of the 1st Cavalry Division under Brig. Gen. William C. Chase. MacArthur boarded the cruiser *Phoenix* to accompany the expedition. En route he learned that a reconnaissance team prudently inserted by Krueger reported that the island was "lousy with Japs." But MacArthur pressed on, whiling time away, conversing freely with the sailors and amiably signing many autographs.

As historian Edward Drea drolly noted, the Japanese commander on Los Negros, Col. Ezaki Yoshio, "knowing that Americans never do anything in a small way" disposed his men to meet a major landing in the north at the magnificent Seeadler Harbor. Instead, the cavalrymen staged a surprise landing at an unexpected eastern beach and occupied the airfield two hours later. That afternoon MacArthur personally inspected the lodgment with Chase. MacArthur casually strode through the area, dispelling any basis for the "Dugout Doug" calumny. After passing many minutes within small-arms range of assembling Japanese defenders, MacArthur marched out onto the runway with hundreds of Japanese just on the other side. Sniper fire popped around him, but he remained utterly cool and disdainful. [2] His aide, Roger Egeberg, admitted his own almost overpowering urge to hug the earth, and later questioned MacArthur about the episode. MacArthur explained that based on his vast combat experience in World War I, he possessed an intuitive feel for battle situations. His intuition at Los Negros was that the Japanese were gathering for a counterattack, and therefore would not be interested in MacArthur.[3]

Having commended Chase for his efforts so far, warned of the impending counterattack and promised reinforcements, MacArthur returned to the *Phoenix*. Over the next several days the gradually expanding band of cavalrymen and Seabees repelled ferocious counterattacks. By the end of March, the last defenders were being hunted down, as American planes settled onto the newly won airfield. Seeadler Harbor became a vast, and vastly important, base for future operations.[4]

The Admiralties stroke won plaudits even from skeptics in Washington. The JCS now perceived newfound virtue in MacArthur's plans and on March

12 authorized the big vault to Hollandia. MacArthur correctly appreciated that the Admiralties operation effectively ended the campaign against Rabaul, and he dropped his prior unwise insistence on seizing strongly held Kavieng. Beyond the tangible rewards, both proximate and remote, of the Admiralties operation was a huge intangible benefit: The episode convinced MacArthur of the accuracy of Ultra. It had been right when Kenney's airmen, photographs and other intelligence means were wrong. Moreover, it undoubtedly swayed the JCS to authorize the bold bolt because they, like MacArthur, could see the chess board and recognize it as a smashing blow against Japanese weakness.[5]

But Ultra's contributions continued. Intercepts permitted submarines and airmen to exact a heavy toll of Japanese supply and reinforcement convoys. Further, Ultra provided Kenney with detailed insight into Japanese air strength and deployment as the Imperial Army massed its planes at Hollandia. The Japanese were confident that the base was beyond Allied fighter plane range, and could defend itself against unescorted bombers. But new models of the P–38 fighter plane sported additional fuel capacity, and Kenney carefully restricted their employment to deny the Japanese awareness of their enhanced range. When all was ready, Kenney struck on March 30 and 31 and April 3. His aviators turned most of the 131 operational Japanese aircraft into charred ruins on the ground.

MacArthur's largest landings to date took place on April 22. Krueger deployed about 50,000 troops. To Hollandia went the Reckless Task Force (the two-division I Corps, led by Lt. Gen. Eichelberger). Since MacArthur's subordinates were not privy to the Ultra secret, they were as surprised as the troops at the lack of opposition. Terrain proved the greater obstacle. Hollandia's Japanese garrison of about 15,000 comprised almost all service and air units. Only about a thousand survived a westward retreat. Hollandia became a huge base hosting 140,000 men, but the terrain proved recalcitrant to titillations by engineers to establish a bomber base.

Nimitz's fast carriers supported the initial landings; however, Nimitz refused to permit them to be tethered for more than a few days. Consequently, MacArthur also targeted the airfields at Aitape, about 125 miles to the southwest of Hollandia. Brig. Gen. Jens Doe Persecution Task force (two regimental combat teams) seized it. Kenney moved fighters forward to those fields to cover the area.[6]

MacArthur's use of Ultra in the opening months of 1944 is instructive. He boldly chose to disregard the Ultra warning that Los Negros packed a much greater garrison than his airmen argued. The operation proved a triumph. Hollandia proved still more stunning and reflected complete reliance on Ultra. Even with the ability to see Japanese dispositions and intentions, it required a daring commander, not a plodder, to authorize the huge leap outside the normal effective range of his airpower. It is impossible to see a Krueger, an Eichelberger, or for that matter, an Omar Bradley, taking such a risk. As Edward Drea, the leading student of MacArthur's use of radio intelligence, aptly sums it up: "Hollandia culminated two years of dreadful attrition warfare fought in reeking jungles and displayed MacArthur's supreme moment of generalship in the Pacific. Besides imagination, courage, decisiveness, and the martial virtues, great soldiers also need luck. Ultra supplied MacArthur luck . . ."[7]

+ーⴷー+

After Hollandia, Ultra's forewarning of Japanese plans to fortify a series of locations in Western New Guinea energized MacArthur to push his forces relentlessly and sometimes recklessly toward the Philippines. But Ultra also showed that, contrary to MacArthur's expectation, Adachi refused to let his army simply die quietly in Eastern New Guinea. The Japanese general commenced marching his 60,000 men westward toward Aitape.

Within hours of discerning success at Hollandia on April 22, MacArthur proposed an immediate strike westward to Wakde-Sarmi. Rather than staging new forces from far in the rear, MacArthur envisioned picking up the just-landed 41st Infantry Division from Hollandia and thrusting it ashore some 140 miles further along the New Guinea coast. Admiral Barbey favored the move; Krueger stood noncommittal. But Eichelberger, fearful of a Japanese counterattack at Hollandia, vigorously opposed the scheme. Eichelberger won the immediate argument, but this display of caution MacArthur never forgot or forgave. MacArthur would never recommend Eichelberger for a fourth star.[8]

A change in Japanese codes clouded Ultra's vision coincident with the actual Hollandia landing. Radio Intelligence located the major Japanese formation next facing MacArthur, the 36th Division, at Sarmi. The island of Biak, to the northwest of Sarmi, with a strategically positioned airfield, appeared weakly held. Intercepted traffic demonstrated the rebound of Japanese airpower in Western New Guinea. Code breaking also permitted another submarine ambush of reinforcement convoys. Knowledge of heavy losses among Imperial Army reinforcements and consequent disarray in Japanese plans mobilized MacArthur to insist on a landing on the island of Wakde, close by Sarmi, to secure advanced fighter bases on May 17. This would be followed a mere ten days later by a landing on Biak to obtain advanced bomber bases.

This time, Willoughby flashed caution. He warned that, for the first time, the Imperial Navy posed a very dangerous threat to MacArthur's naval components because Biak sat within striking distance of major Japanese naval forces. But MacArthur was now obsessed with the need for speed to reach the Philippines. Further, radio intelligence permitted MacArthur to see the glittering rewards for striking before the Japanese air and land forces regained their equilibrium, and to judge the threat of Japanese sea power as acceptable.[9]

On May 17, the 163rd Regimental Combat Team landed without initial opposition at Wakde. The American good fortune stemmed from the aggressive reaction of Japanese commanders hurling about half the prior garrison eastward to attack Hollandia. The American invaders dealt with Wakde's defenders, but since high ground on the nearby New Guinea shore dominated Wadke's airfield and adjacent Maffin Bay (a major future staging point), Krueger authorized further operations by the separate 158th Regimental Combat Team to clear this terrain and thwart what Ultra warned was a Japanese counterattack. But Ultra disclosed only one of three separate converging regimental-size Japanese columns. Consequently, the fighting there lurched into a perilous phase, as the unexpected Japanese units made their presence known.[10]

Just as fighting around Wakde surged, MacArthur's advance encountered a stern challenge. When Maj. Gen. Horace Fuller's 41st Division (styled the Hurricane Task Force) splashed ashore on Biak on May 27, they faced not only well-dug-in Japanese with ample firepower, but innervating equatorial heat and humidity, scrub foliage and abrasive coral. In a replay of Kokoda, Willoughby underestimated the strength of Biak's defenders by about half. For decades thereafter, American historians also accorded accolades to the Japanese commander on Biak, Col. Kuzume Naoyuki, for abandoning beach defense for an astute deployment of his 12,350 men on rugged high ground overlooking the invaders key prize: land for a bomber field. It turns out that the landing caught the chief of staff of the Second Area Army on Biak, Lt. Gen. Numata Takazo, who stayed just long enough to order a conventional Japanese defense. Kuzume only resorted to the defense in depth by force of circumstances after Numata's plan failed. MacArthur believed that the slow American progress reflected wanting leadership. Moreover, he felt pressured to establish American airpower on Biak to keep his promise to support Nimitz's landing in the Marianas on June 15.

MacArthur subjected Krueger to relentless prodding. Krueger sent his chief of staff, George Decker, to Biak. Decker accurately described Fuller's very real woes and Krueger declared his satisfaction. Fuller requested reinforcements to deal with a fresh infusion of Japanese strength, but Krueger wrongly doubted Fuller's report. In another echo of the 1942 campaign, Krueger sent Eichelberger forward to take charge. Fuller demanded to be relieved, and was replaced by Doe. Demonstrating that certain reprehensible habits lingered, MacArthur announced Biak secured on June 3. Even with Eichelberger's energy and reinforcements, the struggle continued until August 20. Biak cost some 2,400 American battle casualties and another 7,400 non-battle casualties. About 4,700 Japanese died and 220 were captured.[11]

The protracted Biak campaign afforded one of the clearest illustrations of the benefits of the two-pronged American advance. Just as Willoughby warned, this time the Imperial Navy schemed to administer MacArthur a crushing blow in the Kon Operation. First, airmen gathered in Western New Guinea, only to have their ranks ravaged by scrub typhus. Then the Imperial Navy scheduled three reinforcement efforts. The first turned back on detection by American search planes and erroneous news of the presence of American carriers. An Allied cruiser-destroyer task force rebuffed the second during the night of June 8–9. Then the Japanese assembled a reinforcement unit featuring the *Yamato* and *Musashi,* the two biggest battleships in the world, mounting 18.1-inch guns, far outclassing MacArthur's naval forces. But just as this third overpowering effort commenced, Nimitz landed in the Marianas. The Japanese hurriedly abandoned the Kon Operation, and hence Biak, and diverted these powerful units to confront the Central Pacific drive.[12]

When Biak failed to provide quickly a heavy bomber base, MacArthur ordered a landing at Noemfoor Island, about sixty miles west of Biak, as an alternative. Under pressure for speed both to hasten the advance along the New Guinea coast and to act before Japanese reinforcements arrived, Krueger designated as assault beaches near the airfield the area his scouts warned him were well defended. The Cyclone Task Force (158th Infantry Regiment with reinforcements to a total of 13,500 men) landed on July 2 behind a very intense air and sea bombardment that stunned and scattered the defenders. Willoughby's estimate placed only about 1,750 defenders on the island. When a prisoner stated that the actual garrison numbered 4,500, American officers, well aware of the underestimates at Wakde-Sarmi and Biak, immediately summoned reinforcements. Transport planes dropped about 1,500 men of the 503rd Parachute Infantry Regiment onto Noemfoor's rocky terrain, resulting in 128 injuries, none caused by Japanese fire. Engineers readied an airfield quickly. By the time the last defenders perished in August, the final bill was about 70 American and 2,000 Japanese dead.[13]

MacArthur's long campaign on New Guinea reached its terminus with the landing at Sansapor, on the Vogelkop Peninsula, on July 30. Ultra again provided MacArthur a relatively clear picture of Japanese dispositions. It disclosed about 15,000 Japanese at Manokwari, 120 miles east of Sansapor, and 12,500 at Sarong, about sixty miles to the west. Further, Ultra told MacArthur that the Japanese expected him to land at Sarong. Armed with this knowledge, MacArthur sent the Typhoon Task Force of about 7,300 men of the 6th Infantry Division to overwhelm a few dozen Japanese at Sansapor. While a shield of high mountains around the American enclave, coupled with American airpower and PT boats, snuffed out any Japanese countermeasures, engineers emplaced an airfield that could support the next hop to Halmahera in the Palau Islands on the path to the Philippines.[14]

In an August 1944 message to Marshall, MacArthur proclaimed that the bypassed Japanese garrisons on New Guinea "represent no menace to current or future operations." Unfortunately, while the bypassed Japanese could now play no strategic role, they retained tactical menace so long as their commanders persevered. The epitome of perseverance was General Adachi of the Eighteenth Army, a hard-drinking poet and exemplary samurai. After the landings at Hollandia and Aitape, Adachi placed his 60,000 men on the march to the latter. It took him almost the exact same one hundred days to creep the 280 miles from Madang to Aitape that it took MacArthur to complete his 1,100-mile gallop along the New Guinea coast from Hollandia to Sansapor.[15]

Allied intelligence produced numerous symptoms of Adachi's resolute march: not the least of these was the ability of Australian radio intercept operators to track the daily advances of Adachi's main transmitter. While Adachi's plan won applause from his superiors, the Eighteenth Army's soldiers endured horrendous hardships from air attack, miserable terrain, ever more stingy rations, and ambush by disease. Meanwhile, another major break into Imperial Army codes (stemming from documents salvaged off of Aitape, ironically) in late May generated a cornucopia of detail about Adachi's intentions and capabilities. But Willoughby tainted his assessments with his trademark superimposition of his own operational vision. He deduced that the "correct" Japanese target was Hollandia, not Aitape; hence he left a dense cloud of ambiguity around projections of when, if ever, Adachi would attack Aitape.

But Allied mastery of Japanese messages was not complete. A missed message postponing an attack on the covering position American forces had established along the Driniumor River east of Aitape triggered a false alarm on June

29. Further mischief entered the equation from the highest levels. On June 12, the JCS queried MacArthur about the prospect of bypassing the Philippines in favor of Formosa; the cited virtue of this scheme was that it would speed up the timetable of ending the war. MacArthur reacted violently to even the thought of bypassing the Philippines, but he recognized that he needed to free up as many forces as possible, as quickly as possible, to maintain his momentum and justify liberating the Philippines and redeeming his promise. The 32nd Infantry Division defending Aitape along the Driniumor was one of the formations he needed. Consequently, he applied pressure on Krueger to crush Adachi as soon as possible.

Two more false alarms on July 4 and July 9–10 occurred. Willoughby again offered his view that the attack might yet be delayed during July 10. "That night," commended Edward Drea, "ten thousand howling Japanese burst across the shallow Driniumor River." For the next month, the Americans grappled with Adachi's warriors in the unforgiving jungle. When it was over, American casualties totaled about 3,000 including 440 killed. About 10,000 Japanese died at the Driniumor or on the march. Adachi's Eighteenth Army was spent.[16]

<hr />

Coincident with MacArthur's most admirable achievements as a commander transpired a murky episode that affords another timeless warning to senior officers of the American armed forces. The adulation MacArthur garnered in the early weeks of the war, founded in large part on his own self-promotion through his highly suspect communiqués, lessened but never abated. Its enduring legacy manifested itself as late as March 1945, when public opinion surveyors asked a sample of the American people who was the greatest U.S. general of the war. MacArthur towered above all the others as the pick of 43 percent. Trailing MacArthur were Eisenhower (31 percent) and Patton (17 percent).[17]

MacArthur's prominent national standing and his known political leanings attracted the attention of some Republican leaders. These men found the strong showing of their party in the 1942 Congressional elections as a sign that Roosevelt was beatable with the right candidate. The two dominant figures in the GOP were Wendell Willkie, the 1940 nominee, and the up-and-coming governor of New York, Thomas Dewey. Neither, however, was as conservative as a large segment of the party. Had nature taken its proper course, MacArthur should have issued an unequivocal statement that his only goal was to finish the war and that he would not participate in any fashion in politics. But nature did not take its course.

The godfather of the MacArthur presidential candidacy in 1944 was Michigan Senator Arthur H. Vandenberg. He headed a loose confederation that he called his "cabinet." It included General Robert Wood, a MacArthur West Point classmate, head of Sears & Roebuck, and former leader of the America First movement. Wood provided funds. A few other senior Republican figures became involved, but the effort boasted a formidable battery of press lords, including Frank Gannett (head of the Gannett chain), Roy Howard (of the Scripps-Howard chain), Joseph M. Patterson (*New York Daily News*), Cissy Patterson (*Washington Times-Herald*), Col. Robert McCormick (*Chicago Tribune*) and William Randolph Hearst (several papers, including the *San Francisco Examiner*). Conspicuously absent was Henry Luce of the *Time-Fortune* empire.

Willoughby met with Vandenberg in June 1943 for a "long talk," which had patent political overtones. Thereafter, MacArthur himself rigorously avoided blatant and direct political communication with Vandenberg or his allies, but prominent members of his staff, like Sutherland, Willoughby, his personal aide Lloyd A. Lehrbras, and Lt. Col. Philip La Follette, all entered a network of links to Vandenberg's nascent movement on MacArthur's behalf.

Quite outside of Vandenberg's "cabinet" sprouted a large network of "MacArthur Clubs" that sprang up spontaneously to promote MacArthur for president. To Vandenberg's distress, a good deal of very radical flotsam and jetsam on the far right, despairing of the prospects for one of their own, also drifted toward the MacArthur candidacy, although at no time did MacArthur reflect their overall views. But Vandenberg realistically apprised the situation and knew that since MacArthur could not openly campaign for the nomination, and since Willkie and Dewey were well ahead in securing the nomination, only a deadlock at the convention could open the path to a dark-horse nomination for MacArthur.

The prospect of a MacArthur challenge did not escape administration notice. In April 1943, Secretary of War Stimson publicly restated a regulation of long pedigree that prohibited serving officers from holding any public office they had not held prior to entering active service. This was interpreted, accurately, as aimed at dampening any prospects for MacArthur. Then in January 1944, the liberal *American Mercury* magazine published the first really detailed criticism of MacArthur's leadership since the war began. The article violated no security provisions and in retrospect was a reasonable assessment of MacArthur's performance, especially as a corrective to the fanciful tales that were then all too abundant. But the War Department officials placed the article on a recommended list for reading materials to be carried by army libraries worldwide. The transparent political overtones of this directive compelled an embarrassed Marshall and Stimson to reverse hastily the action.

A number of MacArthur loyalists later insisted, as did the general, in his memoirs, that he never really was interested in running for president and that he did not take any action to further such an adventure. This is just not so. MacArthur indiscreetly talked of his ambitions and aims on a few occasions, notably to Eichelberger. Moreover, it is simply incredible that so many members of his staff participated in the effort without his encouragement. There is a mass of damning circumstantial evidence of MacArthur's real intentions: The inflated communiqués served not simply to flatter his ego but to build his image; he far outstripped any other commander in his willingness to send greetings upon request to civic organizations, thus accumulating political chips; and he evaded public contact with Mrs. Roosevelt during her trip to the South Pacific in 1943, which played well to the rabid Roosevelt haters, an important constituency in the Republican nomination process.

The embarrassing dénouement of the effort perhaps explains why MacArthur took pains to deny he was ever really interested in the presidency. The April 4, 1944, Wisconsin primary proved decisive. Contending for twenty-four delegates were Thomas Dewey, Harold Stassen (the popular former governor of adjacent Minnesota, who like MacArthur was on active duty), MacArthur and Wendall Willkie. That is the order in which they finished, but Dewey secured fifteen of the delegates (with two uncommitted leaning his way); Stassen, four; MacArthur, three; and Willkie, none. This finished Willkie as an electoral figure. Vandenberg recognized that the primary proved Dewey was unstoppable, and that, therefore, MacArthur's chances were nil. But the sad tale dribbled onward. Facing only a political unknown, MacArthur swept the Illinois primary. Then a Nebraska congressman released two letters from MacArthur reflecting agreement with the congressman's vehement denunciation of administration policies as well as failure to disavow the congressman's entreaties that MacArthur run for president. This forced MacArthur to issue a statement saying that "I am not a candidate for the office nor do I seek it." This, however, was correctly interpreted as a failure to exclude a draft and thus not a complete rejection of political ambitions for a general conducting active operations. Finally, on April 30 MacArthur announced that he would not accept a nomination. This effectively ended the episode, but unfortunately did not cure MacArthur of political aspirations.[18]

MacArthur possessed an extremely keen intellect capable of mastering many subjects. He clearly entertained political ambitions, but his gyrations in practical politics revealed a striking and uncharacteristic ineptitude in this area. The explanation for this dichotomy may be that his exulted evaluation of his performance and sense of destiny persuaded him that the presidency would be handed to him on a platter by a grateful public. Therefore, he need not master or practice what he looked down upon as the sordid day-to-day ways of politics. His lengthy sojourn away from the United States also no doubt contributed to his startling misapprehensions about the attitudes of ordinary Americans. Finally, he grossly failed to grasp that he could not mount a serious campaign from far away and without a massive investment of time— time he could not spare from his military responsibilities.

9

Return and Redemption

THE BARREL-CHESTED HEAVY CRUISER *BALTIMORE*, PROUDLY FLYING the president's flag, nudged gently up to a dock at the Pearl Harbor Navy Yard on July 26, 1944. Some twenty-six flag officers in stiff and dazzling whites formed ranks to pay respects to the commander in chief. At the command of "Right Face" two of the flag officers, long unpracticed in close-order drill, swiveled left, prompting laughs from the assembled sailors and marines. The admirals and generals then trooped aboard to greet the president. Shortly after, an impressive car pulled up and out sprang General Douglas MacArthur, looking one or two decades younger than his age, in his trademark heavily braided cap, khakis and aviator jacket.

Just anointed by his party for an unprecedented fourth term, Franklin Roosevelt's trip to Honolulu reverberated with obvious political overtones. Of the JCS, only Admiral Leahy accompanied the president, who claimed his sole purpose was to get the first-hand views of his Pacific commanders on strategy. A few months later, Roosevelt regaled historian Samuel Eliot Morison with the key scene. "Douglas, where do we go from here?" asked Roosevelt. And MacArthur replied: "Leyte, Mr. President, and then Luzon." Many accounts, including those of respected historians, hold that this meeting set the American course in the Pacific for the liberation of the Philippines.[1]

This makes for a vibrant, romantic history of larger-than-life figures shaping the nation's destiny in a short exchange of banter. Alas, as Morison figured out, it is not true.

After the JCS authorized the seizure of the Marianas early in 1944, they wrestled ferociously for months over further Pacific strategy. Admiral King advocated that U.S. forces bypass the Philippines and seize Formosa. MacArthur, of course, championed the liberation of the Philippines. The notion that this contest was settled in Honolulu is belied by the records of the JCS documenting two more months of debate with no hint of any presidential order. The first crack in the impasse appeared only when a frustrated Admiral Nimitz pointed out in early September that the JCS must issue a directive because the last authorized operation was about to transpire.

From this point, events accelerated from worm's wiggle to incandescent flash. The still-deadlocked JCS issued authorization on September 9 for MacArthur to land on Mindanao on November 15, Leyte on December 15, and then U.S. forces would either secure Manila by February 20, 1945, or Formosa and Amoy on the China coast by March 1, 1945. This directive lasted a little over a hundred hours. When Admiral William F. Halsey completed the missions of his South Pacific command, Nimitz advanced him to alternating leadership of the key striking elements of the Pacific Fleet. The ships remained the same, but under Admiral Raymond Spruance they were designated the Fifth Fleet and under Halsey they were the Third Fleet. Halsey's Third Fleet operations debuted in late August. By September 12 his carrier flyers had ravaged Japanese airfields along the approaches to the Philippines and as far as the Visayas without encountering significant opposition. On September 13, Halsey daringly proposed dropping preliminary operations, taking the forces allocated for those operations, and plunging directly to Leyte. Nimitz concurred.

Halsey's message found MacArthur at sea under radio silence. He originally targeted the island of Halmahera for his next jump after Sansapor, but the Japanese easily recognized Halmahera's suitability as an airfield stepping-stone between New Guinea and the most southern Philippine Island of Mindanao. Radio intelligence warned MacArthur of a major build-up on Halmahera, so he wisely veered his attack instead to lightly defended Morotai. Thus, Halsey's recommendation found MacArthur incommunicado en route to Morotai. Well knowing his commander's mind, Sutherland in MacArthur's name immediately concurred with Halsey's Leyte scheme. Within ninety minutes of receipt of the signals by the JCS on September 15, they relayed their approval. MacArthur landed the same day on Morotai and the island quickly fell. Engineers readied an airfield by early October.[2]

Halsey's proposal, however, housed a basic flaw. He equated the lack of resistance to a lack of defenders. But the Japanese merely chose to preserve their forces for a great decisive battle they called the Sho Operation. It comprised four variants, but Tokyo's lucid reading of American intentions is reflected by the fact that Sho 1 covered defense of the Philippines. Loss of the Philippines meant loss of access to the resource areas to the south, particularly oil. Without oil, the fleet would be useless. Thus, the Imperial Navy prepared to fling all its major forces to the battle. The Imperial Army meanwhile rushed air and ground reinforcements to the Philippines.[3]

In the months preceding the landing on Leyte, a torrent of Ultra decrypts delineated the frantic Japanese preparations to defend the Philippines. This included a retooled command structure, with Lieutenant General Yamashita Tomoyuki, "the Tiger of Malaya," and one of Japan's most illustrious generals, appointed to head the new Fourteenth Area Army, charged with overall defense of the islands. Ultra identified most of the Imperial Army ground and air formations. Leyte, for example, far from being unprotected, housed some 21,000 Japanese (including one infantry division). The enumeration of Japanese air power was particularly impressive, with estimates off by a mere twenty planes of the nearly 700 the Japanese massed to support their soldiers. Japanese defenders would have been still more numerous and well-equipped save for the tremendous execution by American submarines Ultra coached to deadly rendezvous with Japanese reinforcement convoys. Japanese divisions lost significant elements altogether, or mustered only survivors without their equipment or supplies. But ironically, for once in the Pacific War, Ultra's ability to locate Imperial Army units and intentions outstripped its ability to perform the same service with regard to the Imperial Navy.[4]

✦━━✦

On October 20, Krueger's Sixth Army landed with the X and XXIV Corps abreast on Leyte's eastern shores. That afternoon, Douglas MacArthur dramatically returned. When his landing craft grounded off shore, a photographer snapped a soon-famous image of MacArthur, his face inscribed with a stern "sense of destiny," sloshing purposefully through knee-deep water to shore. Later stories that MacArthur staged the landing, or the photograph, are entirely lacking in foundation. MacArthur inspected the 24th Infantry Division lodgment, where the stiffest Japanese resistance had been encountered and small arms and mortars still contested the assault. MacArthur then stepped up to a signal corps microphone and broadcast a radio address, announcing his return and calling Filipinos to rise up and support their liberation. These hours represented a transcendent moment in MacArthur's life.[5]

The Americans aimed to secure Leyte as a pad for airfields to support MacArthur's capture of Luzon. MacArthur's land-based air power, save heavy bombers at Morotai, could not reach Leyte. Consequently, the navy's carriers afforded initial aerial protection until the engineers developed the necessary airfield infrastructure. In preliminary planning, however, MacArthur's engineers warned that the soil and the weather might very well defeat the airfield development program—and hence the whole purpose of the operation. As it happened, unrelenting rain and soupy soils rendered it impossible to install the planned air power on Leyte.

But the Japanese saved MacArthur from threatening humiliation by committing even more egregious errors. Yamashita shrewdly intended to mount his main defense on Luzon, where the density of his forces, the terrain, and his best possible air support offered the most promising opportunity to stall MacArthur's advance. Field Marshal Count Terauchi Hisaichi, commander of the Southern Army, overruled Yamashita and demanded a decisive battle on Leyte.[6]

Terauchi's vision harmonized with the Imperial Navy's plans. Almost all the remaining major warships in the Imperial Navy fought in the Battle of Leyte Gulf (October 23–25). Halsey's Third and Kinkaid's Seventh Fleets crushed them. But the emperor's sailors proclaimed the results a great victory that left the American navy in extremis and MacArthur stranded. The emboldened Japanese sailed a series of reinforcement convoys to Leyte, delivering at least 38,000 men. Ultra enumerated hundreds of Japanese aircraft flocking into the Philippines from virtually every corner of the empire and the Home Islands.[7]

And the Japanese found a remedy for qualitative air inferiority: the kamikaze. Starting just before the Battle of Leyte Gulf and continuing to near the end of the campaign, Imperial Navy and Army pilots crashed their planes into American ships, sinking relatively few, but damaging many, including about a third of Halsey's carriers. The suicide onslaught disrupted MacArthur's air support and left the American beachhead exposed to repeated attacks. One key result of this experience was that MacArthur resolved never again to mount a landing beyond range of land-based fighter cover, an operational principal that the Japanese recognized.[8]

Willoughby believed that the "correct" Japanese strategy was to evacuate Leyte and make their stand on Luzon. For days, as the Japanese soldiers swarmed into Leyte's west side, Willoughby persisted in misinterpreting Japanese intentions. Ultra entirely missed the arrival of the crack Japanese 1st Division, a unit that Krueger later acknowledged extended the campaign more than any other. As the calendar showed November, the evidence became overwhelming: the Japanese, bolstered by false assessments of the American situation, intended to make Leyte the site of the decisive battle in the Philippines. Krueger would later be much chided for his caution, but the intelligence picture before Krueger, coupled with the lack of air cover and horrible weather, warranted prudence.[9]

MacArthur experienced first-hand the loss of air superiority. He moved his headquarters into a private house in Leyte's capital city of Tacloban, an ordinary structure without any reinforcement. With almost clockwork regularity, the Japanese raided Tacloban, particularly at twilight. Bombs exploded all around MacArthur's headquarters (one destroyed the Filipino house next door) and bullets punctured its walls. The roar of Japanese aircraft swooping overhead, the scream of falling bombs and their nearby detonations punctuated his dinners with staff officers. MacArthur's only concession to these events was an occasional conversational pause when the racket peaked; then he then picked up, once the din subsided. One night he found an unexploded American antiaircraft shell in his bedroom. After having it defused, he presented it to William Marquat, his antiaircraft commander, the next morning, remarking: "Bill, ask your gunners to raise their sights just a little bit higher."[10]

Extremely difficult fighting against tenacious Japanese warriors dragged on in Leyte's sodden mountains. During November and December, Ultra regularly forewarned of Japanese reinforcement convoys, and American flyers blasted twenty-four cargo ships of about 130,000 tons with thousands of soldiers, to the bottom, as well as thirteen escort vessels. What finally brought the campaign to a belated close was a brilliant amphibious landing by the 77th Infantry Division at Ormoc on December 7, thus closing Leyte's back door. Yet again MacArthur prematurely announced the fighting effectively over on Leyte. Eichelberger's Eighth Army assumed responsibility for Leyte on December 26, but continued vigorous operations against the Japanese into May 1945. Eventually, nine American divisions fought on Leyte. Casualties ashore came to 15,584, including 3,593 killed. At least 48,790 Japanese defenders perished, the equivalent of more than five divisions. These units disproportionately comprised the most formidable ones in the Philippines. Leyte proved far more costly in time and casualties than MacArthur anticipated, and capturing it never benefited American air power to the extent he intended. But vastly offsetting these deficits was the fact that the Japanese ruined their best chance to at least check MacArthur for significantly longer on Luzon. And they lost their fleet.[11]

+———+

After Nimitz belatedly convinced King that Formosa was impractical, on October 3 the JCS at long last settled on Luzon as the next step after Leyte. The protracted fighting on Leyte compelled postponement of the Luzon operation to January 9. Moreover, Leyte's deficiencies as an airfield location compelled an intermediate operation. On December 15, MacArthur landed two regimental combat teams on Mindoro Island ("none too pleasant a place," remarked the army historian), midway between Leyte and Luzon. These troops swiftly pushed the thousand-man Japanese garrison away from ground that the engineers rapidly converted to air bases to support the Luzon assault. (Mindoro was one of a few operations in the Pacific in which American casualties at sea and in the air far outstripped losses ashore. Total casualties numbered 475 killed and 385 wounded, but only 20 and 71, respectively, were ashore.) The Japanese correctly interpreted the move as signaling that Luzon came next.[12]

The intelligence officer of the Sixth Army, Col. Horton V. White, and Willoughby worked from much the same data, but reached radically divergent conclusions about Japanese strength on Luzon. Willoughby projected the defenders at only 172,000. White pronounced the garrison numbered 234,000. The actual number was 287,000. When Krueger's chief of staff, Brig. Gen. Clyde Eddleman, briefed MacArthur on White's numbers, MacArthur rejected them as "bunk." MacArthur was not about to let intimidating intelligence data deflect him from his goal of liberating Manila. Immediately after this scene, however, MacArthur took Eddleman to a private room and told him there were three great intelligence officers in history and "mine is not one of them." This vignette illustrates how MacArthur's command techniques included routinely playing his subordinates off against each other, giving each man the sense of MacArthur's special trust.[13]

Luzon demonstrated that MacArthur's main subordinates would confront him even on matters close to his heart. The protracted Leyte campaign provoked strong cautionary warnings successively from Sutherland on ground force deficiencies and from Kenney for aviation deficits. Then Kinkaid forcefully argued for delay, citing the kamikaze peril to troop-laden transports traversing the center of the Philippines. Faced with almost unanimous and cogent opposition from his subordinates, MacArthur postponed the date of the landing by two weeks.[14]

On December 16, 1944, Congress passed and President Roosevelt signed legislation authorizing promotion of seven officers to five-star rank. The law bestowed an order of seniority, carefully alternating between the navy and the army (except for Arnold): William Leahy (the president's chief of staff), George C. Marshall, Ernest J. King, Douglas MacArthur, Chester W. Nimitz, Dwight D. Eisenhower and Henry H. Arnold (chief of the Army Air Forces). The official title for the army officers was general of the army. Later William F. Halsey (1945) and Omar N. Bradley (1951) would be raised to five-star rank, making a total of nine officers honored for their World War II service with the nation's highest military rank.[15]

Meanwhile, Yamashita skillfully played his losing hand. He realized it would be folly to fight on the Luzon Plain against overwhelming American mobility and firepower. He sought instead to tie down American forces for as long as possible by drawing them into a protracted fight in the mountains. While Yamashita vacillated about whether to turn Manila into an oriental Stalingrad, one of his subordinates, Rear Admiral Iwabuchi Sanji, did not. Iwabuchi resolved to defend Manila to the end with his sailors. Not only did radio intelligence fail to detect Iwabuchi's decision, but the revelation that Yamashita pulled his headquarters from the city convinced MacArthur that the Japanese would not fight for Manila.

Krueger's Sixth Army landed at Lingayen Gulf on January 9, 1945. Two divisions of the XIV Corps formed the right flank of the army and the two divisions of the I Corps formed the left flank. Yamashita deployed his forces in rugged terrain astride the Luzon Plain. He remained with about 150,000 men of the Shobu Group on Krueger's left, or eastern, flank. Another 30,000 soldiers of the Kembu Group waited on Krueger's right in the environs of Clark Field and Bataan, while yet another 80,000 defenders comprising the Shimbu Group stood east and south of Manila.[16]

From the moment of the Luzon landing, a fabled and heated conflict ignited between MacArthur and his field commander. MacArthur burned to liberate Manila swiftly, preferably by his birthday on January 26. Beyond the issues of political symbolism and prestige, MacArthur pursued the sound strategic objective of seizing the Clark Field complex (by now actually about fifteen air bases) so that Kenney could advance his air power not only to support the Luzon operation, but also the upcoming Iwo Jima invasion on February 19. Krueger aimed to defeat Yamashita while keeping his casualties low. Radio intelligence served to sharpen, not bridge, this difference. MacArthur believed Willoughby's low estimate of overall Japanese strength and that they would not fight for Manila—or at least he was not about to pay heed to intelligence to the contrary. Krueger believed his intelligence officer White; hence Krueger knew the Japanese were vastly more numerous than Willoughby reported and that they would fight for Manila. With Yamashita's main body on his left flank, Krueger reasoned it would be foolhardy to press on to Manila until an additional two divisions and one regiment joined him in late January.

As early as three days after the landing, MacArthur met with Krueger to urge a lightning thrust to Manila. The fiery exchange failed to budge Krueger. Then an intercepted diplomatic message from Japan's foreign minister seemed to confirm Krueger's fears that the Japanese intended to counterattack his extended flank. MacArthur remained unmoved. He waged a campaign of unsubtle carrots and sticks. He beckoned the possibility of promotion to four stars. Krueger refused to change his stance. MacArthur sent his staff to drop very blunt hints that Krueger might be relieved. Krueger refused to change his stance.[17]

When Krueger received his reinforcements, he pushed more aggressively toward Manila, particularly now that White reassured him that the Japanese did not intend to fall on his flank. MacArthur then added the 11th Airborne Division, which landed on January 28 to the west of Manila—and under command of rival Eichelberger's Eighth Army. But Ultra's portrait of Japanese forces and dispositions remained clouded. The Sixth Army faced a disconcerting series of false identifications and then missed identifications of Japanese units, although Willoughby's gross underestimate became increasingly obvious to everyone. On February 1, the Imperial Army adopted a new code book and Ultra temporarily went dark. The next day, Krueger created a race to Manila between columns of the 37th Infantry Division and the 1st Cavalry Division (the "cavalry" title remained an honorific, as it fought as infantry).

Totally exasperated by Krueger's caution, MacArthur resorted to humiliation. He moved his theater headquarters twenty-five miles nearer Manila than Krueger's Sixth Army Headquarters, and MacArthur began making jeep forays to the very tip of the advance. In one of these, he literally drove into the line of fire between an American and Japanese unit. In just two days, a flying column of the 1st Cavalry Division reached Manila and liberated civilian internees and prisoners of war. MacArthur arrived soon after for an overwhelmingly emotional reunion with the starved skeletal figures of a handful of the men he left behind in March 1942.[18]

Admiral Iwabuchi ultimately gathered about 26,000 men and set to turning the old city in Manila and the modern buildings into a fortress. As the battle began, the doomed Japanese began to systematically exterminate Filipino males and abuse and rape Filipino women on a huge scale. MacArthur again displayed his now quixotic sense of warfare limitations. He forbade the use of American planes in support of the riflemen clearing Manila block by block. His local commanders made up for this deficit with liberal application of artillery firepower. An estimated 100,000 Filipinos perished in the Battle of Manila which continued until February 25, when Iwabuchi committed suicide. One study reports that American fire caused as much as 40 percent of the deaths. The Filipinos vented their outrage not at the Americans who forestalled still greater slaughters, but at the Japanese who made Manila second only to Warsaw as the most devastated allied capital in the war.[19]

The capture of Manila coincided with the emergence of a searing issue: collaboration. That the prewar elite collaborated wholesale could not be disputed. If conduct alone stood as the criterion, then a purge of just about the entire elite would be in order—but this constituted almost the whole body of trained leaders in the Philippines. Dismissing them all promised tremendous practical problems affecting the population's well-being. For those prepared to look beyond conduct to motivation, a much more complex set of issues emerged. The alleged collaborators could argue that they really acted only in the interest of the Philippine people. Once an examination of individual cases began, culpability often became a murky issue.

During the war, MacArthur issued decrees requiring that alleged collaborators be held captive for disposition after the war. This threw the tough questions back on President Sergio Osmena (Quezon died just before MacArthur returned to the Philippines). With the prospect that even his own sons might be collaborators, Osmena vacillated and failed to develop a policy while in exile. Then excruciating moral and practical collaboration issues coalesced around one special case: Manuel Roxas. A gifted Filipino politician who had known MacArthur since at least the 1920s, Roxas served as a lieutenant colonel on MacArthur's staff when the war began. He had helped persuade Quezon to go into exile and remained behind—he also knew of Quezon's payment to MacArthur. After capture by the Japanese and a razor-thin escape from execution, Roxas served in the collaborationist government. Both Quezon and MacArthur favored Roxas over Osmena. When Roxas reached American lines, MacArthur immediately acted to set a precedent of judging Roxas by motivation, not conduct. Once this example was set, it proved difficult if not impossible to go back to any other. Ultimately, Roxas became president of the Philippines. There is good reason to question MacArthur's actions which clearly interposed into civilian matters nominally beyond his proper scrutiny. And as with so many other issues involving the Philippines, MacArthur acted not simply to further the interests of the United States over those of the Philippines, but to throw his weight behind Filipino elites he personally favored. [20]

The capture of Manila by no means marked the end of the campaign on Luzon. The XIV Corps (two divisions and a regiment) cleared southern Luzon. MacArthur sent just parts of two other divisions to take vital water supply facilities for Manila away from the 30,000-strong Kembu Group. Through gross incompetence, however, MacArthur's headquarters initially sent them after the wrong dam. In fierce fighting, the commander of the 1st Cavalry Division was wounded and Maj. Gen. Edwin D. Patrick of the 6th Division was killed. Then Hall's XI Corps took charge, but only prevailed after each of the original assault divisions was replaced. By late June, with the Manila water supply secure, the tattered survivors of the Kembu Group thereafter devoted themselves to seeking food.[21]

One brilliant episode during the Luzon campaign merits particular mention. To MacArthur and many of his old "Bataan Gang," Corregidor harbored enormous sentimental value. As the army historian remarked, they "fervently" wished to recapture it "and if could be done dramatically—by means of a parachute drop, for instance—so much the better." On February 16, the 503rd Parachute Infantry Regiment executed a stunningly successful parachute drop onto the tiny topside area of Corregidor—the transport planes were only over the drop zone for six seconds. Two infantry battalions followed by amphibious assault. Willoughby placed only 850 Japanese on "the Rock." The day after the assault, a decrypt revealed at least 3,000 Japanese encamped on Corregidor—just about exactly the number of American attackers. The paratroopers exploited the enormous tactical advantage of fighting down from high ground rather than up from low ground. The combat was savage and climaxed with several massive suicidal detonations of explosives by the last Japanese. The defenders actually numbered 4,500 (including about 1,000 laborers), of whom only 20 survived to become prisoners. American losses were 1,005, including 210 killed. On March 2, MacArthur returned to Corregidor as he had left, by PT boat, just nine days less than three years after his departure, for an emotional flag raising ceremony.[22]

10

Regression, Invasion, and Surrender

MACARTHUR'S LEGITIMATE CLAIM TO HIGH STATURE AS A
commander rests on the pillars of his mastery of modern air and amphibious
warfare coupled with the audacious execution of a bypass strategy. He inno-
vated none of these. Rather, he adopted them after an arduous apprenticeship
under tutors like George Kenney, Daniel Barbey, William F. Halsey, Jr., and
harsh experience. This combination enabled him to achieve remarkable advances at relatively low cost from February 1944 to about March 1945. Therefore, MacArthur's wholesale abandonment of the bypass strategy in the spring
and summer of 1945 constitutes one of the greatest paradoxes of his career.

The first manifestation of this came on Luzon. Once Krueger secured the
Clark Field complex, Manila, and areas required for staging an invasion of
Japan, further offensive operations promised little strategic advantage. But
having underestimated yet again Japanese strength, Krueger permitted a
painfully difficult advance to continue against Yamashita's Shobu Group
across the mountainous jungle reaches of northeast Luzon. (Having started at
Buna, the 32nd Infantry Division fought its last campaign there. Ironically,
while MacArthur told Eichelberger that the 32nd "had never been any good,"

when Yamashita was asked in a post-war interview to identify the best U.S. unit he encountered, he picked the 32nd.) The struggle against Yamashita would eventually require four U.S divisions and the notable contribution of Col. Russell W. Volckmann's 18,000-strong guerilla unit. (MacArthur declared them the equal of a regular division.) At the time of surrender in mid-August, the Shobu Group still had about 65,000 of its original 150,000 men. Nonetheless, Yamashita was still tying down three infantry divisions, a separate regiment, and several tank battalions.[1]

Still more striking were the operations beyond Luzon. The JCS had approved only Leyte, Mindoro, and Luzon, but, as early as September 1944, MacArthur envisioned liberating all the Philippines. Even before his forces reached Manila, MacArthur issued orders for seizure of the remainder of the central and southern Philippines, notwithstanding the absence of any clear warrant for such actions by Washington. Eight of these operations were already on the books before the JCS provided official authorization, but the JCS registered no rebuke to MacArthur. This episode forms the other bookend—with the failure in 1942 to bring MacArthur to heel—of the abdication of responsibility by Macarthur's superiors of their duty to enforce subordination.[2]

MacArthur's reasons for this campaign were multifaceted and at least some carried strategic heft. First and most cogent, the whole purpose of taking any soil in the Philippines was to sever Japanese communications with the southern resource area. Complete interdiction of Japanese sea lanes mandated airfields more westerly than those around Clark Field and Mindoro. Such westerly airfields would also permit land-based aircraft to support other projected operations into the East Indies. Thus, operations on Palawan and Zamboanga possessed legitimate strategic purpose. The need for base areas for up to thirty divisions staging for the invasion of Japan also carried merit as a reason to take, for example, Cebu City (the second-largest city in the islands, with a good harbor) and its surrounding environs.

Once beyond these rationales, however, MacArthur's reasoning becomes debatable. Closely intertwined and weighty humanitarian and personal reasons existed to support such actions. American prisoners of war were believed to be languishing on some islands, possibly subject to massacre by the Japanese (as happened horrifically on Palawan, where the Japanese herded over 150 prisoners into an air raid shelter and then incinerated all but 9 of them). MacArthur bore personal, not just command, responsibility for their fate. Moreover, the repeatedly demonstrated capacity of some Japanese to exact terrible vengeance on the Filipino population provided reason to free every possible Filipino—the slaughters in Manila placing an exclamation point behind this factor. Beyond these reasons was the prospect that these islands contained an electorate that likely favored precisely those Filipino politicians MacArthur supported. While the liberation of Leyte, Mindoro, and Luzon served to restore much of the enormous amount of American prestige squandered in the debacle of 1941–42, permitting the Japanese to retain the remaining islands would remain a blot on American (and MacArthur's) honor.[3]

As early as February 6, MacArthur directed seizure of Palawan and its very useful airfield sites. A week later he added the Zamboanga Peninsula and Sulu Archipelago. Then, at the end of June, MacArthur relieved the Sixth Army and I Corps of responsibility for combat operations so that they could concentrate on preparations for the invasion of Japan. At the same time, the Eighth Army took responsibility for cleansing the entire archipelago of Japanese. The Eighth Army had five infantry divisions and the separate 503rd Parachute Infantry Regiment. The Seventh Fleet and two special army engineer brigades with landing craft provided sea lift, and the Thirteenth Air Force, air support. Very powerful guerilla units, particularly on Panay and Mindanao, enormously eased Eichelberger's task. But there was a huge trade off: MacArthur shifted three divisions from Sixth Army to Eighth Army that Krueger desperately needed to complete all his missions in minimum time and with minimum casualties.

The Eighth Army cleared the Southern Philippines in a series of fifty-two landings, involving forces ranging from a company to a two-division corps. The major components of these operations were: Palawan (February 28); Zamboanga (March 10); Sulu Archipelago (March 16); Panay (March 18); Cebu (March 27); Negros (April 2); Bohol (April 11); Eastern Mindanao (April 22); and Western Mindanao (April 30). Overall, Eichelberger's operations highlighted the American perfection of amphibious warfare and generally sophisticated tactics. In several instances, however, Japanese forces were pursued far more vigorously than circumstances warranted, resulting in unnecessary casualties.[4]

During the second Philippine campaign, about 450,000 Japanese fought ashore. Their combat elements formed nine divisions and the equivalent of six more. When the surrender came on August 15, there were still about 115,000 live Japanese (including civilians). They demanded the attention of the equivalent of nearly five American divisions (of the equivalent of sixteen committed on Luzon and the southern Philippines) and approximately 118,000 Filipino guerillas. Excluding losses on Leyte, MacArthur's command suffered almost 47,000 battle casualties, including about 10,380 dead. Nonbattle losses, primarily sickness, numbered over 93,400, including 260 dead. At least 1,100 Filipino guerillas died on Luzon alone.[5]

By the fall of 1944, Australians replaced the six American divisions containing Japanese forces on New Guinea, New Britain, and the northern Solomons to free them for other operations. Beginning in March 1945, however, the Australians shifted from merely containing the Japanese as they "withered on the vine" to actively seeking the destruction of the bypassed Japanese forces. Blamey's justification for the operations included the fallacious notion that these units still constituted a threat, and the valid point that passivity was bad for the morale of the Australian units. But he also discerned that MacArthur himself had abandoned the bypass strategy in the Philippines in favor of liberating the whole archipelago for political reasons. Blamey believed Australian interests were served in similar fashion by clearing the Japanese from all Australian territory.

The now supremely skilled Australian "diggers" sliced through and around the Japanese Seventeenth Army on Bougainville and the Eighteenth Army on New Guinea, effectively destroying both. A prudently less ambitious offensive cleared the Japanese from western New Britain, but did not challenge the 90,000 Japanese at Rabaul. In these operations, about 991 Australians died in battle. Japanese losses came to approximately 18,500 battle deaths and another 23,000 who perished of starvation or disease.[6]

In February 1945, MacArthur began planning to use the I Australian Corps (the veteran 6th, 7th and 9th Australian Divisions) to seize Northern Borneo. MacArthur reasoned that that this would provide oil for Allied operations within ninety days of a landing. The Army-Navy Petroleum Board in Washington declared this proposition egregiously in error; this body estimated it would take a year. In March, MacArthur revealed to Prime Minister Curtin a still more ambitious expansion of operations to retake Java. "My purpose in projecting this campaign," wrote MacArthur, "is to restore the Netherlands East Indies authorities to their seat of government as has been done within Australian and United States Territory . . ."

The JCS acceded to MacArthur's schemes in the Netherlands East Indies despite their glaringly obvious defects. The Australian I Corps (less the 6th Division) duly landed a brigade of the 9th Division at Tarakan on northeastern Borneo on May 1. On June 10, two brigades of the 9th Division assaulted Brunei Bay on northwestern Borneo. The Japanese thoroughly prepared the next target, Balikpapan, so MacArthur ordered a devastating sixteen-day preliminary bombardment. The 7th Division landed on July 1 and sustained very light losses. In these unnecessary Borneo operations, Australians lost at least 569 men killed; Japanese dead numbered around 4,800.[7]

Lingering at war's end was MacArthur's astonishing intention to land the Australian I Corps on Java, a very well-defended and huge island. This operation might have been one of the great bloodbaths of the Pacific War. David Horner, however, a skilled Australian historian, concluded persuasively that a fundamental shift in the attitude of the Australian government in 1945, coupled to stiffening opposition of the JCS, would have stopped MacArthur from invading Java.[8]

But it will not do to lay all the blame at MacArthur's doorstep. In retrospect, it remains simply amazing the that the American government, the Australian government, the JCS, and Australia's senior military leadership all acquiesced in this series of operations that contributed nothing essential to the defeat of Japan. Further, the proposal to retake all of the Netherlands East Indies to restore Dutch colonial administration apparently elicited nothing like the degree of crucial scrutiny it should have, given its tremendous foreign policy implications.

In April 1945, the Joint Chiefs ordered a new Pacific command structure. Once again, and for the same reasons as in March 1942, the army and navy could not agree on a single supreme commander. Instead of separate theaters with unified commanders for each, the new scheme provided for united commands by service. MacArthur thus became commander in chief of all army ground, service and air forces (except the Twentieth Air Force with the B–29 strategic bombers). Nimitz became commander in chief of all naval forces.[9]

The services remained sundered in their visions of how to end the war with Japan. Ultimately, a political, not a military question, divided them: what factor would undermine the will of the American people to see the war through to the national objective of unconditional surrender? The army, led by Marshall, believed the critical factor was time. Therefore the army argued that only an invasion of the home islands could end the war within a span tolerable to the American people. MacArthur, who stood to command the greatest amphibious operation of all time, adamantly agreed with this view. The navy, led by King, held that the crucial factor was casualties. Decades of study had convinced naval leadership that invading the home islands was certain to produce unacceptable casualties. The navy therefore advocated an alternate strategy of bombardment and blockade. This strategy ultimately aimed to force Japan's surrender by killing or threatening to kill tens or hundreds of thousands by aerial bombardment and millions by starvation. (After the war naval and some air officers declared that they would have ended the war without atomic bombs. They may have been correct, but the bombardment and blockade strategy they backed involved killing vastly more Japanese noncombatants than did the atomic bombs.)

This conflict resulted only in an unstable compromise. In May 1945, the JCS ordered the first of a two-part invasion of Japan, Operation Olympic. The target date was November 1, 1945 (designated X-Day). This would seize air and sea bases on Kyushu, the southernmost home island, to support Operation Coronet, a landing in the Tokyo region, tentatively set for March 1946. But Admiral King sent a memorandum to his colleagues making it clear that he was not agreeing actually to execute Olympic; he only approved issuing the order to make the option of invasion available in November. He expected the JCS would return to the question of whether it was prudent in August or September.[10]

MacArthur commanded the land forces and Nimitz the naval forces for Operation Olympic. MacArthur designated Krueger's Sixth Army to direct the actual maneuvers ashore. Krueger would have 693,295 men divided among four corps comprised of fourteen divisions, two separate regimental combat teams, and massive support units. One division and a regimental combat team would seize offshore islands along the approaches on X–1. Then on X-Day, one army corps would land on southeastern Kyushu at Miyazaki, and a second at Ariake Bay. Simultaneously, three marine divisions forming a third corps would land at Kushikino, on the southwestern side of Kyushu. A fourth army corps constituted a reserve as well as the 11th Airborne Division.[11]

The Americans predicated all of these plans on the estimate that on X-Day the Japanese would garrison Kyushu with only six field divisions, and only three of these would be in the targeted southern part of the island. Intelligence estimates figured that the Japanese might eventually send as many as eight to ten divisions to Kyushu, and a total of 350,000 men, but these would arrive piecemeal. Estimates also optimistically calculated that Japanese air strength would total 2,500 to 3,000 planes in all of the Home Islands.[12]

Olympic provides the classic example of the problem of a one-axis advance: the Japanese experienced no difficulty in correctly calculating where, when, and in what strength the United States would strike. Senior Japanese officers in January 1945 shrewdly determined that the Americans would invade, not simply blockade and bombard. Further, Imperial Army and Navy leaders readily deduced that their adversary would seize Okinawa in order to secure air bases within fighter plane range of Kyushu—a hallmark feature of MacArthur's campaigns. Simple examination of topographical maps told the Japanese where the actual Kyushu landings would fall. The Japanese embarked on a huge build-up on Kyushu (as well as in front of Tokyo) and waited, confident that they would either be able to defeat the initial invasion or inflict such losses that the Americans would negotiate an end to the war far more acceptable to Japan than unconditional surrender.[13]

In one of its most important but least-known achievements, from mid-July to the end of the war, radio intelligence unveiled the stunning assembly of Japanese forces in the homeland in general and the even more perturbing evidence of massing Japanese formations at the proposed landing areas on Kyushu. By war's end, intelligence identified thirteen of the fourteen field divisions (nine in the southern half of the island) and five of the eleven brigades on Kyushu. The final revised estimate of August 20 credited the Japanese with all fourteen field divisions and an aggregate of 625,000 troops on Kyushu—the actual total approached 900,000.[14]

The portrait of Japanese air power varied only between dark and bleak among the various intelligence centers. By the surrender date the newly created Joint Army-Navy Committee on the Japanese Air Forces estimated Japanese air strength in the homeland at 5,911.[15] Nimitz's intelligence center calculated by August 13 that the Japanese had 10,290 aircraft available for homeland defense.[16] The actual total floated around 10,700.[17]

To his credit, Willoughby bluntly warned that further unchecked increase of Japanese strength on Kyushu threatened "to grow to [the] point where we attack on a ratio of one (1) to one (1) which is not the recipe for victory."[18] At the JCS, the secretariat assimilated the radically altered situation and began an agonizing reappraisal of Olympic. Planners turned to alternatives, notably a landing on Northern Honshu.

While the JCS staff temporized about directly soliciting the views of the theater commanders, Marshall and King did not. On August 7, Marshall asked MacArthur for his personal assessment of the situation. MacArthur replied, essentially, that he did not believe the intelligence! He urged that Olympic go forward. Admiral King now intervened to play his trump card. Since May, King knew in confidence that Nimitz had withdrawn his prior support for at least Olympic. Now on August 9, King ordered Nimitz to make his views known to Washington and MacArthur. But Nimitz paused before igniting what was sure to be a major confrontation with the army and MacArthur when, for the first time, evidence appeared that a Japanese surrender might be at hand.[19]

The complete secrecy surrounding radio intelligence assured that this startling story, overturning prior conventional wisdom about the proposed invasion of Japan, remained unknown during MacArthur's lifetime. Further complicating the picture is the 1990s revelation that the Soviet Union was poised to invade Hokkaido, the northernmost main Japanese home island, just as the war ended. The most likely upshot of these events is probably that Truman would have withdrawn his support for Olympic in the face of the new intelligence and adamant navy opposition to the enterprise. Meanwhile, if the Soviets landed on Hokkaido, it is quite possible that a landing on Northern Honshu might have provided an alternative to Olympic that the army and navy, as well as MacArthur, would have supported.[20]

MacArthur did his reputation no good by indulging in two deceptions in later years. Curiously, one became an article of faith with the right, and the other with the left. In the 1950s, MacArthur claimed that the concessions to Stalin at the Yalta Conference to obtain Soviet entry into the war were unnecessary, as was Soviet entry itself. The reality is that MacArthur told not one, but two different War Department representatives in February 1945 and the Secretary of the Navy in March 1945 that he favored getting the Soviets in at the earliest date possible after Germany's defeat. He again reiterated this belief in a message outlining his strategic views in June 1945.[21]

The willingness of MacArthur to dissimulate postwar about his actual beliefs in 1945 also extended to the issue of his confidence in the proximity of Japan's surrender before it occurred and the use of atomic bombs. In June 1945, MacArthur talked with Hap Arnold, the Chief of Staff of the Army Air Forces. According to Arnold's notes, MacArthur "believes that bombing can do a lot to end the war but in final analysis doughboys will have to march into Tokyo." Moreover, MacArthur's vehement insistence to Marshall on the viability of Olympic as late as August 9 (*after* Hiroshima and Nagasaki) completely contradicts any suggestion that he believed Japan's surrender was or had been imminent. At no time prior to Japan's surrender did he register to his superiors any qualms about the atomic bombs. It was only postwar when MacArthur (and his acolytes) fabricated tales in line with the Hoover-style conservative critique (later adopted by the left) that Japan had been about to surrender when the atomic bombs were used unnecessarily.[22]

⊢►══◄⊣

On August 15, Emperor Hirohito in an unprecedented broadcast announced the termination of the war—he did not say that Japan surrendered. That same day, Truman formally notified MacArthur that he would be the supreme commander for the occupation. Japanese officers arrived to work out the details of the surrender and occupation. They warned of revolt among some units, including those at Atsugi, an airfield near Tokyo, where the initial occupation forces would land; MacArthur accommodated them by postponing his arrival by three days. MacArthur arrived at Atsugi on August 30, at a time when only about a thousand or so Americans were present, with hundreds of thousands of Japanese soldiers nearby. Winston Churchill declared: "Of all the amazing deeds of bravery during the war, I regard MacArthur's personal landing at Atsugi as the greatest of the lot." MacArthur was convinced that the emperor's announcement on August 15 would insure compliance with the surrender, but the fact was that between August 10 and at least the 17th, many Japanese commands, particularly those overseas, teetered very near revolt.[23]

The surrender ceremony stands as one of the great moments of MacArthur's career. He deftly combined theatrical grandeur, deep symbolism, and, most importantly, magnanimity that contrast sharply to the almost furtive, inglorious, midnight-shadowed assembly during which Germany's representatives capitulated.

In deference to the president, the battleship *Missouri,* named for his home state and Halsey's flagship, provided the scene. Ranks of flag officers of the U.S. and Allied nations formed an "L" with the table upon which the instruments of surrender rested facing the base of the "L." Unlike in Europe, however, not just high brass participated. On every deck, platform, and turret within sight on the *Missouri,* the enlisted men representing their peers who made the victory possible clustered in whites to witness the moment.

The *Missouri* flew the flag that had waved at the U.S. Capitol on December 7, 1941, as a destroyer delivered the Japanese delegation at 0900 on September 2. When Japan's representatives reached their place, MacArthur appeared. Standing on either side and just to his rear were Lt. Gen. Jonathan Wainwright, who surrendered at Corregidor, and Lt. Gen. Arthur E. Percival, who surrendered Singapore. Their visibly wasted appearance wordlessly exemplified the worst face of Japan's war. MacArthur then spoke perhaps the most memorable speech of his career.

> We are gathered here, representatives of the major warring powers, to conclude a solemn agreement whereby peace may be restored. The issues, involving divergent ideals and ideologies, have been determined on the battlefields of the world and hence are not for our discussion or debate. Nor is it for us here to meet, representing as we do

a majority of the people of the earth, in a spirit of distrust, malice or hatred. But rather it is for us, both victors and vanquished, to rise to that higher dignity which alone befits the sacred purposes we are about to service, committing all our people unreservedly to faithful compliance with the understanding they are here formally to assume.

It is my earnest hope, and indeed the hope of all mankind, that from this solemn occasion a better world shall emerge out of the blood and carnage of the past—a world dedicated to the dignity of man and the fulfillment of his most cherished wish for freedom, tolerance and justice.[24]

One member of the Japanese delegation, Kase Toshikazu, an English-speaking Foreign Ministry official, found to his profound surprise and relief that MacArthur totally eschewed any humiliation to the Japanese participants or nation. Instead, Kase declared that MacArthur's words transformed *Missouri's* deck "into an altar of peace." After the Japanese signed, the leaden skies parted as if on divine cue. In the fresh sunlight, a massive flypast of four hundred B–29s and fifteen hundred carrier planes provided a deafening final hymn over the proceedings.[25]

One of the mainstays of MacArthur's reputation as a commander in World War II is the tenet that his skillful direction saved his Southwest Pacific forces from the allegedly heavy casualties sustained in the parallel efforts in the Central Pacific under Admiral Nimitz. General Marshall and many army officers believed this. It was a fixture in the barrage of publicity accorded MacArthur by his fervent admirers then and afterwards. Even critics usually fail to dispute this claim, but the reality is quite different.[26]

It is important to remember in this controversy that the argument centers on casualties in campaigns ashore. There was no reasonable dispute that the great bulk of the U.S. Navy's losses, totaling 57,149 casualties, including 29,270 deaths in the Pacific, stemmed from combat that crushed the Imperial Japanese Navy and Japan's merchant marine.[27] With the exception of losses among U.S. Navy medical personnel assigned to marine units and an extremely tiny fraction of other casualties ashore, the navy's casualties would have occurred regardless of whether the United States pursued a single or dual advance in the Pacific.

Another confounding issue involves losses among prisoners of war. It is unjust to charge MacArthur personally with the terrible savagery of the Japanese that resulted in massive deaths among Americans held prisoner. Accordingly, POW losses are set apart from other losses. Finally, unlike Nimitz, MacArthur's forces in land battles included very large contributions from allied nations, particularly the Philippines and Australia. The exigencies of the war render it impossible to provide more than an estimate of Filipino losses.

With these caveats in mind, the following two tables present first U.S. casualties, and then allied casualties in the two theaters in ground campaigns.

To place these numbers in context, the United States Army calculated that overall it sustained 160,276 total battle casualties, including 55,145 deaths, in the Pacific area campaigns. Of these losses, no fewer than 11,163 of the deaths occurred among 27,181 prisoners of war—or almost exactly one in five of all deaths. By comparison, U.S. Army losses in European/Mediterranean Area campaigns numbered 749,832 total battle casualties, including 174,090 deaths. Of these casualties, 90,597 Americans were captured, of whom just 1,074 died.[31] The navy and Marine Corps sustained a total of 127,294 casualties in the Pacific, including 48,426 deaths.[32] Thus, the combined sum of all American service battle casualties in the Pacific (excluding the

Table 1   Battle Casualties Among U.S. Servicemen in Ground Campaigns Under MacArthur and Nimitz[28]

| | MacArthur | | Nimitz | |
Service	Total Casualties	Deaths Among Casualties	Total Casualties	Deaths Among Casualties
United States Army (Including Army Air Forces)	112,331	37,227	36,131	10,265
Marine Corps	5,276	1,880	70,007	17,802
Naval Medical Personnel	107	30	2,743	628
POW Deaths	–	11,159	–	143
Totals (including POW deaths)	117,714	50,296	108,881	28,838
Total Deaths (NOT Including POW deaths)	–	39,137	–	28,695

Table 2 Battle Casualties Among Allied Servicemen in Ground Campaigns Under MacArthur and Nimitz[29]

	MacArthur		Nimitz	
Service	Total Casualties	Deaths Among Casualties	Total Casualties	Deaths Among Casualties
Canada	–	–	25	21
Australian	18,547	6,631	–	–
New Zealand	400	222	–	–
Republic of the Philippines (Estimate, including prisoners of war)	60,000	10,000	–	–
Republic of the Philippines (Estimated deaths, not including prisoners of war)	–	2,500	–	–
Total Allied Casualties (including Filipino prisoners of war)	78,947	16,853	25	21
Total Allied Deaths (Not including Filipino prisoners of war)	–	9,353	–	–

Table 3 Grand Total of Pacific Battle Casualties in Ground Campaigns: MacArthur Verses Nimitz[30]

	MacArthur		Nimitz	
Service	Total Casualties	Deaths Among Casualties	Total Casualties	Deaths Among Casualties
Totals (including POW deaths)	196,661	67,149	108,906	28,859
Total Deaths (NOT including POW deaths)	–	48,490	–	28,716

merchant marine) was 287,570, with 103,571 deaths—just about one in three of this total stemmed from campaigns in the Philippines.

Examination of these figures demonstrates that whether or not losses among prisoners of war are counted, MacArthur sustained greater battle losses in his ground campaigns than did the forces under Nimitz. The disparity is more marked if prisoners of war losses are counted, and still large if they are excluded.

Several factors explain this result. First, MacArthur's casualties in the Kokoda-Buna-Gona (Papua) campaign on New Guinea in the second half of 1942 until early 1943 resulted in higher losses ashore numerically and proportionally than army and marine losses in the contemporary campaign on Guadalcanal.[33] Second, casualties in the recapture of the Philippines nearly balanced losses at Iwo Jima and Okinawa. Third, and most important, MacArthur's supporters generally managed to overlook or to omit from consideration losses among allied forces, particularly Australian troops, who carried the heaviest burdens on New Guinea, and Filipinos who died under MacArthur's command.

While this examination illustrates that the claim that MacArthur's numerical losses were lower than Nimitz's is without foundation, as painful as the actual losses were, proportionally losses under both commanders were remarkably small given the scope of the campaigns and the ferocity of the warriors the American commanders faced. One measure of this is the comparison with Japanese losses. According to one set of figures, the Imperial Army alone sustained 485,717 deaths facing U.S. forces and the Imperial Navy 414,879 deaths, the overwhelming majority against U.S. forces. The combined total is thus 900,596 fatalities.[34] Thus, for every American who died fighting Japan, about nine Japanese perished.

11

Shogun in Khaki

A STORY EXEMPLIFIES THE AURA OF MACARTHUR'S RULE OVER JAPAN. The American officer in charge of setting up MacArthur's office in the Dai Ichi building, just across the moat south of the Imperial Palace, delivered a carpet to the Japanese building manager. The carpet proved too large for the room. The building manager expected instructions to cut the carpet to fit the room. Instead, the American officer told him the carpet was MacArthur's personal property and therefore he must move a wall so the room fit the carpet. The message was clear: conventional boundaries did not apply to MacArthur.[1]

Throughout his reign, MacArthur resided in the American embassy compound—a five-minute drive from his office. Except for visits to Manila in 1946 and Seoul in 1948, his routine virtually never varied: two round trips per day between his residence and office, seven days a week, holidays not exempted. Astonishingly, he never roamed outside the immediate Tokyo area for a first hand-look at the country he ruled. He treated visiting dignitaries and guests to luncheons, but rarely dinner. He did dine occasionally with Brig. Gen. Elliot Thorpe, his counterintelligence chief. As he oversaw a web of informers, mail openers and wire tappers, Thorpe fascinated MacArthur with "interesting tidbits of what really was going on behind the façade of propriety." Overall, however, MacArthur maintained almost complete isolation from mid- or lower-level staff and sharply restricted the access of everyone else except his chief of staff and aide. There was one peculiar exception to his isolation: he personally opened all mail addressed to him. Further, unless a mere pro forma response sufficed, he drafted replies. Thus, virtually anyone could get a message to MacArthur—and a reply—simply by writing him a letter.[2]

MacArthur held two major commands in Tokyo. The first constituted his continuing American theater command over forces in the Western Pacific, eventually designated the Far Eastern Command. The second nominally represented an international command as the Supreme Commander Allied Powers (SCAP), in which MacArthur answered to the Far Eastern commission (FEC), an eleven-member allied body ostensibly overseeing the occupation. MacArthur unified both commands as General Headquarters (GHQ), replicating his wartime staff arrangement, complete with the same cast of senior officers.

To this apparatus MacArthur would eventually append thirteen special staff sections. These generally paralleled the structure of the Japanese government and reflected his careful analysis of Washington's directives. While this sprawling headquarters at peak numbered 5,000, MacArthur effectively retained control by funneling everything through a handful of officers of proven loyalty. Of the special staff sections, one stood preeminent: government. The capable Maj. Gen. Courtney Whitney headed a small but brilliant staff. A wealthy prewar Manila lawyer, Whitney joined MacArthur in 1943 and ran the guerilla effort and then civil affairs in the Philippines. He also morphed into the role of MacArthur's closest friend.

Of the other sections, just two require comment. Willoughby continued as chief of foreign intelligence and greatly enhanced his power by bureaucratically capturing domestic intelligence as well. He was obsessed with communists and radicals, both within Japan and within GHQ. MacArthur made the witty, hard-working, and trusted Maj. Gen. William Marquat head of the economic section. Marquat projected the persona of a football coach. He knew plenty about antiaircraft defense, but little of the substance of his new domain. Amazingly, even a tough-grading Japanese scholar called Marquat "surprisingly effective," for Marquat shrewdly picked sound policy advice from his subordinates.[3]

The American occupation of Japan extended for six and a half years and touched almost every aspect of Japanese life. The documents from this era form an archipelago scattered through American and Japanese archives that defeats the industry of any single historian. Most accounts place political, economic, and cultural aspects at center stage. Indisputably, these are vital and fascinating topics with rich lessons, but they are the wrong place to start in forming judgment of MacArthur's achievements. The first thing that must be understood about the occupation of Japan is MacArthur's role in forestalling a demographic catastrophe that would have trivialized every other aspect.

In October 1945, the JCS expressly forbade MacArthur from "gratuitous" use of U.S. supplies for relief. As to Japan's economy, Washington charged MacArthur only to eliminate war industries. In the fall of 1945, roughly 40 percent of Japan's urban reaches were charred rubble and as many as 15 million of Japan's 72 million inhabitants were homeless. With the repatriation of overseas Japanese servicemen and civilians, the jobless numbered about ten million. Rampant inflation and black market activities ravaged the feeble economy. The Tokyo Chamber of Commerce estimated that with 100 as the index for retail prices as of 1930, the index reached 304 by mid-1945 and soared to 13,009 by July 1948.

Most threatening of all, about ten million Japanese perched at the very precipice of starvation. The sharp decline in domestic rice production and fishing, the elimination of imports, which previously provided about 20 percent of Japan's food needs, and the siphoning of food stuffs into a black market raised the very real specter of famine. The cities depopulated radically (Tokyo by about half), as desperate Japanese sought refuge in rural areas. The official food ration would plunge to a mere 1,042 calories per day in Tokyo by the spring of 1946, and actually averaged 800 calories per day because the ration was not always delivered.

MacArthur immediately violated the letter of his orders and directed his command to provide sustenance to the Japanese so long as it did not impair the feeding of occupation forces. He distributed about 3.5 million tons of food stockpiled for the invasion of Japan. The most desperate times arrived with the approach of the end of the November 1, 1945 to October 31, 1946 "Rice Year." In anticipation of looming catastrophic shortages, MacArthur transmitted a powerful plea to Washington stressing the moral obligation of the United States for the welfare of the Japanese, which he pointedly compared to the situation of American prisoners of war in Japanese hands. He emphasized the importance of preventing famine for securing enduring political reform and peace. Later commentators often cite the final flourish in his message—pointed warnings of potential unrest ("Give me bread or give me bullets")—as indicating his main reason for feeding the Japanese was to maintain a peaceful occupation, but any perusal of the whole dispatch reveals that moral obligation and long-term political transformation constituted his central thrust. American supplies proved vital in very narrowly averting a famine by September 1946 that would have killed millions and had terrible developmental effects on a generation of Japanese children. Even so, Japanese scholars estimate that the debilitated state of many Japanese due to malnutrition contributed to what probably numbered in the thousands of deaths.

A desperately close margin between food supplies and needs continued for the first three years of the occupation. The general nutritional value of national food supplies did not reach the level for a healthy life until 1949. No Japanese who lived through the period ever forgot the daily gnawing concern for food. One Japanese man who passed through these years as a teenager later declared that MacArthur's successful effort to secure American food supplies constituted "the general's most noble and perhaps the most important achievement during the occupation." While well-publicized efforts at democratization and demilitarization are often cited as the reason why most Japanese viewed MacArthur and the occupation as well intended and successful, even while recognizing defects, the more visceral reason was that they recognized that without MacArthur's efforts, millions of them would have perished.[4]

But famine was not the only one horseman of the apocalypse stalking Japan as the occupation began. Japan's medical and sanitation systems nearly collapsed in the final months of the war. Malnutrition weakened the resistance of vast swaths of the population. With an influx of repatriated Japanese from overseas bearing diseases, the initial months of the occupation found Japan poised for devastating epidemics. A favorite of MacArthur's, Col. Crawford Sams, spearheaded the occupation medical effort, an apolitical element in which American and Japanese cooperation reached a pinnacle. The dynamic and authoritarian Sams organized antiepidemic campaigns of unparalleled size. The first crisis was a typhus outbreak sweeping through the Korean population in Japan as they headed for repatriation ports. Sams mobilized 80,000 U.S. and Japanese medical personnel in 800 centers to disinfect people (a half million in four days) and treat water.

Cholera was imported in 1946. Sams again sprang into action and vaccinated 35 million Japanese to forestall the epidemic. Between 1946 and 1949, Sams spearheaded assaults that drove rates for smallpox, typhoid, paratyphoid, diphtheria, and dysentery down by 79 to 90 percent. The death rate from tuberculosis fell by 40 percent. Nor did Sams neglect the infrastructure of Japan's medical system. Major components like the Japanese Medical Association and Red Cross were reorganized, vast training systems created, a network of local clinics instituted, and a school lunch program to improve child nutrition initiated. Overall, the annual death rate in Japan plummeted from 18.7 per thousand in 1933–40 to 8.1 in 1950–51. Sams estimated reasonably that without public health efforts and reforms, some three million Japanese would have needlessly died between 1945 and 1952, a toll greater than that of the war.[5]

Had famine and disease ravaged Japan, killing millions, both the moral authority for and the practical ability of the United States to implement reforms would have been destroyed. MacArthur's achievements in these spheres were absolutely central, not simply incidental, to the success of the occupation.

+‑‑‑+

Japan's march of conquest resulted in at least 17 million dead, the vast majority Asian noncombatants. The victors and victims demanded war crimes trials as in Europe. About 5,700 alleged Japanese war criminals were divided into three classes. Charges of essentially masterminding aggression were leveled against twenty-eight Class A defendants. These men were tried in Tokyo before the International Military Tribunal for the Far East (IMTFE). The remainder fell into Class B (ordinary war crimes) and Class C (crimes against humanity). These defendants faced trial at the venue of the alleged crimes not only in Japan, but all across Asia. Of the Japanese tried as Class B and C war criminals by the courts of the allied nations, exclusive of the Soviet Union, some 4,405 were convicted and there were 904 executions and 475 life sentences. Despite limited access to Japanese, the Soviets tried approximately 10,000 and executed 3,000.

MacArthur took personal interest in the trials of the two Japanese generals he fought in the Philippines. General Yamashita was not and could not have been charged with ordering or authorizing the very large-scale massacres of Filipino civilians in 1944–45. He was instead tried beginning in October 1945 on tenuous charges of command responsibility. He was tried before five American officers without legal background in Manila, the epicenter of Japanese atrocities. Not surprisingly, the panel on December 7 delivered a sentence of death by the humiliating method of hanging. Appeals to the Philippine and United States Supreme Courts and President Truman were all rejected. Yamashita was hanged on December 23.

The trial of General Homma began in January 1946. Again a panel of five American officers without legal background conducted the trial. The charges centered on Homma's responsibility for the Bataan Death March.

Whatever the defects of the judicial proceedings, the fact is that unlike Yamashita, a colorable case for responsibility existed against Homma. His headquarters was near the route and he traveled on it personally. There is little doubt that he knew of the events, and it is clear that he did nothing about it. Homma was convicted but received the more honorable death by firing squad in April 1946. MacArthur's role in these events constitutes one of the very lowest points of his career, although responsibility extends beyond MacArthur to other officials, including the United States Supreme Court.

Sir William Webb, the chief judge of the IMTFE, made it clear that despite his friendship with MacArthur, he would not brook MacArthur's meddling. During a two-and-a-half-year trial, two defendants died and one was declared insane. In November 1948 the panel ordered seven defendants hanged, sixteen to serve life sentences and two to serve lesser sentences. Many Japanese expected MacArthur to commute some of the sentences, but he did not. The IMTFE failed in its central purpose of convincing the Japanese people that justice had been done. Instead, it left the distinct flavor of "victor's justice." What had started as anger at many of the senior officials for Japan's fate turned to pity.[6]

The single biggest war crime legal issue was the disposition of the emperor. The American public and Congress demanded his trial; many expected his execution. MacArthur was initially ordered not to do anything to the emperor without Washington's approval. Within MacArthur's staff, opinion divided as to whether Hirohito should be tried or whether he would better be exploited to further the goals of the occupation reforms.

On November 30, the JCS directed MacArthur that the emperor was not immune from trial and ordered him to assemble evidence necessary to enable Washington officials to decide on trial. MacArthur replied at length on January 25, 1946. He claimed to have reviewed the evidence and found that up to the end of the war, Hirohito's role had been ministerial and confined to the advice of his counselors. MacArthur predicted a "tremendous convulsion" in Japan if word of his trial was announced, with "chaos" requiring up to a million-man occupation force, which he well knew was impossible. He added, "Destroy [Hirohito] and the nation will disintegrate." The message transparently contained gross exaggerations, but senior military and civilian officials were intimidated into acquiescence.

This outcome proved a mixed blessing. The failure to hold Hirohito accountable, while lesser figures who performed all their acts in his name were tried and in thousands of cases executed, undermined the very lessons the trials were supposed to instill. The failure provided an opening that would be exploited by Japanese ultraconservatives for decades to come to obscure or deny Japan's responsibility for some truly horrendous actions. On the other hand, the emperor proved an extremely pliable and useful tool in implementing the occupation reforms that fundamentally changed Japan from a feudalistic and aggressive militaristic state into a flawed but peaceful and democratic country.[7]

We know now something shielded by secrecy for decades from MacArthur's critics and supporters: an intercept from the Imperial Navy in August 1945 provided American officials with indisputable evidence that the emperor's intervention had been the key step to Japan's surrender. This evidence, and the prospect of his usefulness in implementing reforms in circumstances in which Japanese cooperation was essential, made the initial decision not to try the emperor as a war criminal defensible. Perhaps hindsight suggests that an opportunity was missed to achieve a more equitable outcome by retaining Hirohito through approximately 1948 and then insisting on his abdication in favor of the crown prince and public assumption of war responsibility.[8]

✦━━━✦

The first two tasks of the occupation beyond survival of the Japanese people involved demilitarization and repatriation. In general, these proceeded efficiently. About 6.4 million Japanese servicemen returned to civilian life. American troops would track down caches of arms sequestered by die-hards for several years, but generally they soon disposed of the last arsenal of the Imperial Army. The remnants of the Imperial Navy performed repatriation duties before being scuttled or transferred as reparations, the smaller types being handed over to the Japanese for fishing or other civilian uses. One sour note was Washington's orders to destroy five Japanese cyclotrons.[9]

More traumatic was repatriation that witnessed some eight million people uprooted. About 6.6 million of these were Japanese, about half were servicemen. More than a million Koreans and Chinese forced laborers were returned to their homelands. But not everyone returned promptly—or at all. Estimates of the number of Japanese nationals captured by the Soviets in Manchuria, Korea, Sakhalin and the Kurils range from "roughly 1.7 million" to 2.7 million. Of these, approximately 700,000 were shipped to labor camps, producing at least 60,000 documented deaths. All told, somewhere between 300,000 and 500,000 Japanese perished or remained "missing" in Soviet hands. One estimate indicates that 66,000 military and 177,000 civilians died just in the first winter of 1945–46 in Manchuria. While the inhumanity of the Soviets stands out, the British detained about 113,500 Japanese, the Chinese about 100,000 and the United States about 70,000 for labor work rather than promptly repatriating them as the Potsdam Proclamation promised. Moreover, the Soviets occupied the southern islands of the Kurils that were both historically and legally Japanese. The combination of the massive numbers of abused or missing Japanese plus seizure of the Kurils saddled the communists in Japan with a serious burden that undercut their appeal.[10]

†⊨══•══⊨†

MacArthur mythology maintained that the vast reform program implemented during the occupation spurted from the fountainhead of MacArthur's brow. The reality is that Washington supplied three directives that charted the basic course of the occupation. Two of these, the Potsdam Proclamation and an August 29 document entitled "United States Initial Post-Surrender Policy for Japan," provided broad goals, while a November 3 Pentagon dispatch titled "Basic Directive for Post-Surrender Military Government in Japan Proper" set very specific objectives. This trio made it clear that while ostensibly the occupation would be an allied effort, in reality it would be effectively controlled and dominated by the United States and hence MacArthur as SCAP. Washington's grand design aimed for democratization of Japan both politically and economically.[11]

Two other basic policies set in Washington shaped the occupation. First, Washington declared that Japan's surrender was unconditional, and hence MacArthur did not have to negotiate basic reforms. But qualifying that edit was the further order that, unlike in Germany, MacArthur should exercise indirect rule by working through existing Japanese governmental structures. It further was as obvious to MacArthur as to Washington that the American people were not prepared to sustain a huge occupying army to impose American reforms at bayonet point. The U.S. Army shrank from 8.3 million men to about 1.3 million by the end of 1946. Accordingly, MacArthur's and America's success in its vast ambitions depended fundamentally on gaining the cooperation of the Japanese.[12]

Americans high and low worked independently to gain that cooperation, and the average Japanese judged the occupation more by the example set by GIs than MacArthur's efforts. While the conduct of American troops remained far from spotless throughout the occupation, Soviet and Imperial

Japanese examples assured that it appeared a model of decorum. Americans proved patronizing, but as an Australian noted, the average GI outshined his Aussie counterpart by his free distribution of candy, gum, and cigarettes, and "a sentimentalism that makes them much easier and more friendly in manner to the Japanese."[13]

Meanwhile, MacArthur wisely rejected suggestions that he order the emperor to report. Instead he met with the emperor on September 27 upon the latter's request. The event captured two faces of MacArthur that illustrate how he could both repel and attract. MacArthur later reported falsely that the emperor announced that he accepted full responsibility for the war. The exchange more likely consisted of mutual congratulations on how successfully the bloodless occupation so far had progressed. But before the session, MacArthur bid the emperor stand next to him for a photograph. The image revealed a diminutive, exhausted, and nervous-looking emperor, appearing nearly strangled in a severe, formal, tight-fitting coat and tie, standing next to the towering, relaxed American pro counsel dressed casually in an open-necked khaki shirt and pants. Japanese officials immediately recognized the stunning message the photograph conveyed of Japan's and the emperor's status and tried to suppress it. But American officials insisted on its publication. Much like the stagecraft of the surrender ceremony, MacArthur brilliantly contrived a means of conveying a message to the Japanese people more potent than a million words: he was supreme, but not vengeful.[14]

The critical political phase of the occupation commenced with a series of thunderclaps. On October 4, SCAP ordered what became known as the Japanese Bill of Rights, or Magna Charta, abrogating all legal restrictions on freedom of thought, speech, assembly, and the press as well as all legal mandates creating discrimination based on creed, race, nationality and political views. Those previously in custody for prior transgressions under these legal restrictions were to be released and the police apparatus that enforced them was to be dissolved. Prime Minister Higashikuni Naruhiko and his cabinet resigned the next day en masse in silent protest. Higashikuni was replaced as Prime Minister by Baron Shidehara Kijuro.

On October 11, MacArthur summoned Shidehara and read him a list of Five Great Reforms he demanded the Japanese government enact swiftly. These included the emancipation of women, encouragement of union organization, abolition of child labor, education reform, and democratization of economic institutions and immediate and "vigorous" action on housing, food, and clothing for the population. Interestingly and tellingly, Washington provided the items on the list, but MacArthur made emancipation of women first. This action represented no sudden or recent conversion. MacArthur had spoken in favor of emancipation of women with journalist William Allen White while on occupation duty in Germany in 1919; now twenty-six years later he commanded it. One could easily, and probably correctly, read into this a link to MacArthur's high regard for strong women like his mother and his second wife Jean.

December 15, Shinto was displaced from its position as a state religion. Accompanying this measure was a declaration effectively removing the divine status of the emperor. On January 1, Hirohito appeared to disavow his divine status in a Rescript (an imperial proclamation). The effect of this rescript was also a clear message to the Japanese people that they should follow his example of working with and not against MacArthur. In reality, the rescript's clever phrases renounced a Western concept of a divine figure, but nowhere did Hirohito deny the ancestral myth of Imperial descent from the Sun goddess. The emperor also managed to reiterate the concept that Emperor Meiji had "bestowed" democracy on the people and thus he remained the seat of sovereign power.[15]

Having already banned ultranationalist and militaristic organizations and teachings, on January 4, 1946, MacArthur announced a vast purge of ultranationalist and militarists from public life. In stark contrast to the approach to collaborationists in the Philippines, this purge worked by categories, not by individual cases. It disqualified 90 percent of the Diet (Japan's legislature) from reelection and barred virtually all public servants who held positions between July 1937 and September 1945. Two following waves of purges in 1946 and 1947 yanked thousands from positions in bureaucracy, commerce, industry, and the press. In total, about 210,787 persons were banned. (In Germany, in the American zone, such policies banned 418,307 individuals. Proportionally, the ratio was 0.3 percent of Japanese and 2.5 percent of Germans in American jurisdiction.) Although in his memoirs MacArthur alleged his doubts about the program, the reality was that he resisted a proposal for relaxation of the purge from the National Security Council in 1948.[16]

Without a doubt, the centerpiece of occupation political reform was the new constitution. In accordance with guidance from Washington, MacArthur demanded the Japanese revise their national charter, but the conservatives and liberals deadlocked. Worse yet, even the liberals appeared prepared to leave sovereignty in the emperor, not the people. MacArthur decided to disregard explicit orders from Washington not to intervene. On February 3, 1946, he directed Whitney to "prepare a draft constitution." MacArthur personally itemized its three key elements: (1) the emperor would be head of state, but the people sovereign and the emperor's powers flowing from the constitution; (2) Japan would renounce the sovereign right to wage war "even for preserving its own security"; and (3) abolition of the Japan's feudal system. In one astonishing week of frenzied work, unencumbered by deep knowledge of Japanese political history, twenty-four Americans in Whitney's government section wrote a new constitution. Not only did it accomplish MacArthur's three basic points, but also it abolished nobility, provided for a government structure on the parliamentary model with an independent judiciary, and extended freedoms beyond even the American model. This foreign import shocked members of Japan's political establishment. They did not find it meritorious, but they believed it would end the occupation early, protect the imperial institution and preclude a still more unpalatable charter if other nations were to have a hand in the process.

Two features remain controversial. First, it made the emperor head of state, but stripped away his substantive powers. The emperor's continued existence, even as a figurehead, proved the secure anchorage for the conventional centrism and conservatism in the coming decades. Second, despite his later attempts to claim that the idea originated with Japanese officials, MacArthur himself was the author of the concept in the famous Article IX renouncing war and armed forces. MacArthur's original concept would have denied Japan even the right of self-defense, but the final version and the Japanese interpretations of that version provided for "self-defense" and endless debate over the scope of that term.[17]

Not all political goals were achieved during the occupation, nor was MacArthur instrumental in all successes. American reformers tried to reverse Japan's centralization of power move it into local hands. These efforts proved evanescent. Far more successful was reform of Japan's judiciary. The success of these revisions, however, owed next to nothing to MacArthur or his senior staff and almost everything to the wisdom of Alfred C. Oppler, an American judge, a refugee from Germany, who blended persuasion with a shrewd choice of measures with Japanese roots.[18]

12

Triumphs and Challenges

AMERICAN PLANNING BEFORE THE OCCUPATION IDENTIFIED THE root causes of Japan's imperialist aggression to be an underdeveloped national economy and unequal income distribution that provided Japan with an unfair advantage in its export drive. The virtual serfdom of most Japanese farmers propelled droves into urban areas, where they became an unending source of cheap and docile labor that permitted the great industrial combines to lower export prices artificially. Under the banner of economic democratization, SCAP attacked each of these three areas.[1]

Of the economic reforms, the most far ranging was land reform. When MacArthur arrived in Japan, seven out of ten Japanese farmers were tenants in a system MacArthur condemned without exaggeration as virtual slavery. Under orders from MacArthur, the Japanese government adduced a scheme that touched only about a third of the tenants. Thereafter, U.S. and Japanese agricultural experts hammered out a law passed in October 1946—with critical expansion of coverage by an Australian, MacMahon Ball. Absentee landlordism was abolished. The government purchased the lands of noncultivators and resold it to farmers on favorable long terms. The decentralized implementation proved a bonus of practical experience in democracy. By December 1949, cultivators owned 89 percent of farmland in Japan, more than reversing the 1945 ratio. There is no dispute that MacArthur's personal interest and support proved vital to the program. Takemae Eiji, the great Japanese scholar of the occupation period, acclaimed land reform as "a peaceful agrarian revolution that swept aside pre-modern social relations and transformed the Japanese countryside."[2]

The second front of economic democratization was the labor movement. SCAP authorities, with MacArthur's explicit support, pressed to revitalize the labor movement. Union ranks soared astronomically from a miniscule 707 members in October 1945 to 6.6 million in June 1949. MacArthur, however, drew a line over an impending general strike in 1946. The critical issue from his perspective was the huge numbers of unionized workers in the railway, communications, and other public service sectors. Disruption of the rail system literally threatened the lives of millions of Japanese because of its vital role in food distribution. At MacArthur's direction, the Japanese government enacted restrictions on collective bargaining and strikes by public service workers.[3]

In contrast to triumphs in land reform and unionization, the third prong of economic democratization, dismantling of the huge Zaibatsu, obtained only modest success. From the 1850s, approximately fifteen families allied as the Zaibatsu (literally "financial clique or combines") seized a stranglehold over the Japanese economy with an intricately veiled network of tentacles in holding companies, interlocking directorates, and financial arrangements. They were estimated to effectively control up to 75 percent of Japan's financial, industrial, and commercial activities. Many Westerners reviled them as partners with Japan's militarists in fomenting aggression.

The attempt to dismantle the Zaibatsu provides a complex and melancholy story. While the Zaibatsu skillfully and collectively resisted efforts to abolish them, their opponents proved inept and divided. Japan's enfeebled economy powerfully enforced restraint for concern that Zaibatsu dissolution would depress productivity. Within SCAP, factions even among the reformers clashed on how to attack the Zaibatsu and how far to go. Moreover, the Japanese socialist government that held office during a critical period contemplated nationalization and thus found such massive economic concentration potentially handy for implementing state control.

The course of events serves to demonstrate how important MacArthur's role was in the occupation. As Takemae observed, MacArthur "harbored a deep distrust of big finance," but initially displayed no enthusiasm for tackling the Zaibatsu. Stung by criticism, and likely with political considerations in mind, in 1947 MacArthur backed legislation that promised a monumental uprooting of the Zaibatsu and a "purge" that affected 2,200 business leaders. Ultimately, the reform surge liquidated two of the four great Zaibatsu combines, Mitsui and Mitsubishi, each of which spawned about 2,000 firms. But this produced a vehement counterattack from business groups in the United States fearful that capitalism in Japan would be destroyed. The Zaibatsu's cagy delaying maneuvers paid off when Washington dictated a change of direction.[4]

Americans identified ultranationalism and glorification of war as key contributors to Japan's aggression. Education, religion, and information propagated these notions and SCAP therefore launched a full-scale attack in all of these areas, with the breathtaking goal of altering fundamentally Japan's culture. American efforts to alter Japan's education system, comprised of 18 million students and 400,000 teachers, addressed both structure and content. The prewar system segregated students by gender and only required six years of formal schooling. Japanese reformers designed a new coeducational "6–3–3" formula (six years primary, three of middle school, and three of high school, with the first two parts mandatory). In a reverse of many other episodes in the occupation, the Japanese reformers then circumvented domestic opposition by having their American counterparts present it as a U.S. proposal. On the other hand, the attempt to decentralize Japan's education failed. The assault on elitism, particularly the dominance of Tokyo Imperial University and the "old boy" system of university appointments, enjoyed only mixed success.

Liberal Japanese educators supported the effort to modify content so enthusiastically that SCAP abandoned formal decrees. In what proved an enduring reform, rewritten Japanese textbooks eschewed ultranationalist and militaristic content and advanced democratic principles. At the classroom level, the reform tide introduced more problem-solving elements amidst the traditional heavy emphasis on rote learning. A clash between proponents of maintaining or abandoning complex Chinese-derived written characters in favor of a Latin script was settled in a compromise that simplified the characters. In the course of these reforms, about 24 percent of Japan's teachers resigned or were purged.[5]

Curiously, even as his own rule achieved widely acclaimed success with its political and economic reforms, MacArthur privately insisted that occupation periods almost invariably were later judged by history as dark spots in the history of the occupier and the occupied. He argued that keeping the occupation brief would be essential to confounding that record. As early as 1947, he called for a peace treaty and end to the occupation. It is possible his motives were pure; it is probable that politics played a role because a last realistic opportunity for the presidency beckoned. By 1948, the woeful public regard for Truman and encouragement from Republican politicians persuaded MacArthur to mount a bid for the White House. Much rose-tinged analysis of polls and news and urgings of allies from the 1944 effort prompted MacArthur to announce publicly in March 1948 that he was seeking nomination—something he did not do in 1944.

One of the interesting ironies of the abortive effort was the fact that among some conservatives, MacArthur's economic reforms in Japan were deemed socialistic. His campaign lacked funds, organization, and endorsements. It came to an ignominious end in April 1948 in the Wisconsin primary, where Harold Stassen won 19 delegates to MacArthur's 8. At the Republican convention, MacArthur's perfunctory nomination was poignantly seconded by Jonathan Wainwright, who had become a fast friend since his liberation, despite MacArthur's wretched treatment of him in 1942.[6]

+≡≡≡+

The primacy of Europe, followed by the Mediterranean region, in Washington's calculations continued without interruption into the postwar period. Certainly, the tertiary status of Japan in the galaxy of issues confronting American leaders after September 1945 constituted one important reason for MacArthur's considerable discretionary authority over the details and timing of the occupation reforms. By 1947, however, the clashes with the Soviet Union congealed into what became known as the Cold War. With the collapsing position of the Nationalist Chinese all too clear, Japan emerged as the obvious outer Pacific rampart for the Long Peace.

This new outlook prompted review of American policies in Japan to strengthen it, and to secure it from external and internal threats. A practical manifestation of the policy shift came with an appropriation by Congress in June 1948 of $530 million worth of economic assistance to Japan. George Kennan, the father of "containment," later assessed that his second-greatest achievement in public service after the Marshall Plan was a parallel program for Japan. His views appeared in NSC 13/2 "Report by the National Security Council on Recommendations with Respect to United States Policy Towards Japan" of October 1948. It stands with the "United States Initial Post Surrender Policy" of September 1945 as one of the two most important directives guiding the occupation.[7]

The essence of the new policy was: curtailing new reforms to permit assimilation of those already implemented, strengthening Japan by reviving its economy (an objective "second only to U.S. security interests"), tapering off the purge and war crimes trails, building understanding between the American and the Japanese people, reducing the SCAP presence (it fell from 3,500 to 2,000 between 1948 and 1950), and augmenting the internal police forces to guard against subversion.

Bureaucratically, at this same time MacArthur lost maneuvering room. Previously, Washington disarray and his status as not only a national commander, but also as an international commander, opened overlapping jurisdictional tiers he could skip between in order to fend off measures he opposed. The reorganization of the American national security structures resulted in a common front, and the Washington-dictated negation of MacArthur's international responsibilities left him no scope to challenge the new policy guidance in general or in particular.[8]

Some historians branded the ensuing events as a "reverse course," arguing, to varying degrees, that they marked the abandonment of the idealistic early aims of the occupation. Japanese historian Takamae more accurately captures this passage as "a change of emphasis, a course adjustment or shifting of gears, not a volte-face." Overall, by 1947, the occupation had achieved the vast majority of its original objectives, with Zaibatsu decentralization the one conspicuous shortfall. The new marching orders from Washington mandated little or no change in core areas such as legal and political reform, land redistribution, women's rights, and health and welfare guarantees. Washington's new directives confined their impact primarily to the economy and to the political space afforded the communists.[9]

The purge that blacklisted almost 220,000 Japanese, about 80 percent of them former officers in the armed forces, was dismantled from the autumn of 1948; eventually, almost all were restored their rights. Escalating violence inspired by communists peaked after May Day 1950, with unprecedented attacks on American service personnel. MacArthur retaliated by purging members of the central committee of the communist party and communist journalists.

Given Japan's devastated economy, from the start MacArthur resisted reparations. The threat of reparations undoubtedly served as a severe check on Japanese economic recovery because of reluctance to invest in capital items that might be seized as reparations. In May 1949, the United States unilaterally renounced reparations claims and left other nations to seek bilateral accords. Coincident with NSC 13/2, Prime Minister Yoshida Shigeru's party won an absolute majority in the Diet and thus the Japanese government joined SCAP in emphasizing pragmatism, not further adventures in idealism.[10]

The face of the economic course change was Joseph Dodge, an American banker. His "impact on the Japanese during the occupation was second only to that of MacArthur," according to one occupation official. Fresh from currency reform duties in Germany, Dodge arrived in Japan in February 1949 and implemented an economic stabilization plan ordered by Washington, over MacArthur's objection, in December 1948. This plan aimed overall to cut the costs of the occupation, revive Japan's economy, and resuscitate the ability of Japanese companies to compete internationally.

What became known as the Dodge Plan featured a draconian array of policies designed to stamp out inflation, stabilize the currency, balance Japan's budget, end government subsidies of Japanese industry, and reorient companies from domestic to foreign markets. The winners in this system were big enterprises, usually of Zaibatsu lineage. The losers were small- and medium-sized enterprises, many of which went bankrupt, militant labor elements, and initially a major swath of the population. Under the impact of these measures, by June 1950 industrial production fell to one-third of its 1931 level and investment to one-half of the 1949 level. This was labeled fairly the "stabilization depression."

What finally jump-started the languishing Japanese economy on the path to economic superpower status was the massive inflow of U.S. military procurement dollars during the Korean War. This totaled $184 million just in the last half of 1950 and reached $824 million in 1952. The index of Japanese manufacturing rested at about one-third of the 1934–36 average at the start of the Korean War. By the end of 1950, it was up to 94 percent and reached 171 percent by mid-1953.[11]

MacArthur overall displayed remarkable tolerance for communists early in the occupation and continued to downplay their significance as late as 1948–49. But the changing direction of the occupation generated a series of legal measures that combined both liberal and conservative aspects and were billed as an effort to increase democratization and accountability that provided a platform for attacking radical union leadership, particularly communists. Further, under the Dodge Plan, the industrial and public sectors both implemented massive layoffs, employed usually to rid the work force of radicals and break the hold of communists.[12]

Prime Minister Yoshida Shigeru won a major victory in January 1949 and formed a strong government. The radical left wing prepared to challenge the government. Yoshida took a series of actions to defang the communists. He purged a left-wing member of the upper house, provoking major demonstrations. In April, a new law empowered him to outlaw "subversive organizations." Yoshida then mounted a purge of major left-wing subversive or "anti-democratic" organizations. Many historians dispense heavy criticism of this purge. Its putative authority derived solely from SCAP's 1946 purge instructions, which had targeted the right, not the left. The criticism, however, runs afoul of the issue of the underlying principle: if the basic tactics were acceptable for employment against "rightists," then there was no principled basis for opposition to the same tactics being deployed against "leftists." This episode found ready support from Willoughby, who had pursued "subversives" throughout the occupation and now found his outlook shared by a much wider segment of American and Japanese officials.[13]

The extremely sensitive issue of Japanese rearmament illustrated the limits of Washington's success in mustering Japan as a full-fledged ally in the Cold War. From 1948, policy papers in Washington looked to reconstituting Japanese armed forces. There were a number of obstacles to this. The first was Article IX, the "peace" provision in the Japanese constitution. Not far behind this stood MacArthur's opposition. Only a few days before the outbreak of the Korean War, MacArthur belatedly altered his position when he saw the prospect of trading rearmament of Japan for an early peace treaty and the end to the occupation. Another problem was that even conservative Prime Minister Yoshida regarded revival of Japan's armed forces as an anathema.[14]

Had North Korea not attacked its neighbor in June 1950, it is not clear as to when or to what extent Japan might have rearmed on its own. But when all of the Eighth Army's tactical troops moved to Korea, Japan was left virtually defenseless on the ground. On July 8, the same day MacArthur became the United Nations commander in Korea, he directed Prime Minister Yoshida to create a 75,000-man National Police Reserve to augment the existing 125,000-man national police force. This "police reserve force," however, was trained and organized as company-size units of light infantry. They possessed few heavy weapons and a handful of tanks (called "special vehicles"). Meanwhile, Willoughby had clandestinely supported a number of talented former Imperial Army officers, who maintained lists of other former officers, who in turn could become a new general staff and form the nucleus of a revived army. MacArthur, however, vetoed Willoughby's effort to merge his project into the recreated ground force.[15]

━┥══╪━

Even with the vast scope and success of the occupation reform program, there remained significant philosophical quandaries and areas of unfinished business.

Perhaps the biggest contradiction was MacArthur's authoritarian methods to impose democratic ends. But as Takemae concludes: "This was unavoidable and necessary, for in the absence of an army of occupation, GHQ and progressive Japanese could never have broken, even momentarily, the stranglehold of the immensely powerful and tenacious Old Order, with its ingrained habits of thought, entrenched political interests and steely grip on the machinery of state. Without the goad of an Allied military presence, Japan's postwar transformation could not have begun."[16] Thus, the occupation of Japan stands as an obvious rebuff to simplistic slogans about how "you can't impose democracy with bayonets" or, one might add, by edicts.

The occupation also depended on censorship, in daily contradiction to the professed goal of democratization. SCAP authorities zealously prohibited Japan's media from publishing items critical of MacArthur. (The other strongly forbidden topic was the atomic bombs.) Foreign correspondents, including Americans, who breached this barrier found themselves isolated and in seventeen cases, expelled. At the same time, SCAP achieved some success in elevating the quality of leading Japanese newspapers and put a dent in the truly sensationalistic ethos that existed before the occupation commenced.

Beyond these theoretical contradictions, there were some pragmatic shortfalls. In order to secure military bases, the U.S. occupation severed Iwo Jima and Okinawa from Tokyo's control and largely exempted them from political reforms. Occupation authorities also failed to breach the long-standing high discriminatory walls isolating minority groups, notably the indigenous natives, and particularly the Koreans. Despite the overall stellar achievements in health and welfare, there were two terrible blots on the U.S. record in this sphere. The Imperial Army created the infamous Unit 731, under Lt. Gen. Ishi Shiro, to study chemical and biological warfare. The Japanese offset their lack of resources with the ruthless resort to human experimentation that killed at least 3,000. The findings of these horrific trials represented a treasure trove of knowledge U.S. officials viewed as invaluable in the budding Cold War. Ishi shrewdly bartered his grisly findings for immunity from war crimes trials. Sams as well as MacArthur participated in this, but the moving force was Washington.

Washington mandated what became the Atomic Bomb Casualty Commission to study the human effects of the atomic bombs. While ostensibly a joint American-Japanese effort, American officials dominated the organization. They used this dominance to classify the study results, denying much information to the Japanese, and particularly any useful findings that may have contributed to treatment of the atomic bomb victims (the *hibakusha*). The authoritarian behavior of the examiners and the official *ukase* barring treatment of the victims generated much merited ill-will.

But perhaps the most important institution that largely escaped even a swipe at serious reform was Japan's bureaucracy. Indeed, historian John Dower persuasively argues that the core of what became labeled the "Japanese model" of development originated before 1945, and that the occupation nurtured it by its centralization while cleansing it of its link to militarism.[17]

One of MacArthur's adventures outside the scope of his orders proved highly quixotic. MacArthur perceived that many Japanese languished in a spiritual vacuum after defeat; he therefore launched a crusade to fill that vacuum with Christianity. MacArthur was not a regular churchgoer himself, but he was conversant with the Bible. Mostly, however, the effort stemmed from his ethnocentric American outlook and his philosophical conviction that democracy and Christianity were mutually supporting. He deployed enormous official and nonofficial efforts into missionaries, bibles, and countless public and official acts designed to facilitate the spread of Christianity. By 1948, however, even MacArthur realized his efforts had failed, although he probably did not know that the numbers of Christians in Japan remained very nearly the same as in 1941.[18]

Finally, we come back to the emperor. After their initial September 1945 session, MacArthur rejected invitations for a reciprocal meeting at the Imperial Palace and thereafter the emperor always came to MacArthur. The evidence seems clear that they genuinely shared a mutual regard. In the emperor's case, he had much to be thankful for in MacArthur's rejection of war crimes trials or abdication. There is no doubt the emperor was an asset in selling the occupation, and he began a series of unprecedented visits around the nation that enormously boosted his popularity.[19]

As with virtually all other aspects of his life and career, MacArthur's achievements in the occupation of Japan incite controversy. Indeed, at least one historian goes so far as to question whether MacArthur really was significant. [20]

On the contrary, MacArthur's achievements were real and critical. But exactly what they were and how he achieved them must be correctly identified. Contrary to claims of some of his strongest supporters, Washington, not MacArthur, devised virtually all objectives of the occupation. But MacArthur was immensely more than a mere rubber stamping functionary. He was more like the conductor of a very peculiar orchestra—an orchestra he largely had to inspire rather than command. A great composer handed him a brilliant score. But this score by itself amounted to no more than inert ink on parchment with few markings for tempo or emphasis. Thus, the ultimate success required a great deal of careful input by the conductor. Moreover, the eventual performance contained critical sections composed by the conductor (for example, constitutional reform and thwarting a famine). Likewise other sections, like reparations, eventually disappeared from the performance despite the fact that the composer provided them.

The conductor analogy is further useful in highlighting the importance of two of MacArthur's fortes: style and symbolism. Whether it was the rhetorical content of the surrender ceremony, the deliberately distant mystique of MacArthur's presence, or the incredibly powerful message sent by MacArthur's pose in the September 1945 photograph with the emperor, he conveyed supremacy, high ideals, and magnanimity. His aura was immense power wielded wisely and with restraint for the everlasting good of the Japanese people. His record in Japan also illustrates the quandary his habitual insubordination raises. Arguably, his two greatest feats, the food crisis and the constitution, both followed his direct violation of Washington's orders. Thus, it is not possible to align his record as the "good" MacArthur who obeys orders and the "bad" MacArthur who violates them.

13

Korea Triumph

THE FATE OF KOREA CAREENED FAINTLY ACROSS AMERICAN POLICY counsels from August 1945 to June 1950. When the end of Japan's thirty-five years of savage colonial rule appeared imminent, hasty expediency prompted two key American decisions. First, officers selected the 38th Parallel from a map as the arbitrary dividing line between prospective Soviet and American occupation zones. Second, the crude dictates of shipping space and availability rather than suitability selected Lt. Gen. John Hodge's XXIV Corps as the American occupation force. Hodge, an effective combat leader, as an occupation commander found ways to alienate Koreans of all political persuasions.

In the Soviet zone, Kim Il-Sung, with modest but real credentials as a guerilla leader, ascended to leadership over a communist reign. In the south, after a United Nations-supervised election, Syngman Rhee, an aging nationalist leader of authoritarian proclivities, became president of the Republic of Korea (ROK). Both leaders denounced their rival as illegitimate; both announced their intention to unite the country, by arms if necessary. The ultimate difference proved to be that Washington denied Rhee the wherewithal to attack the north whereas the Soviets bestowed on Kim a formidable arsenal, and the Chinese released 50,000 to 70,000 trained Korean soldiers from the Chinese Peoples Liberation Army (PLA) to the Korean People's Army (KPA) which permitted his attack on the south.

Kim Il-Sung initially backed a communist-dominated insurgency that started a guerilla war in April 1948, the best date to choose as the onset of the Korean War. Both sides complemented the insurgency with frequent border skirmishes. Rhee's government, struggling economically and politically, nonetheless slowly gained the upper hand over the insurgency. Between late 1949 and January 1950, Kim Il Sung secured the approval of Stalin for a conventional attack that he promised would overrun South Korea before the United States could intervene. Although harboring reservations about potential U.S. action, China's leader Mao Zedong concurred.[1]

In January 1950, Secretary of State Dean Acheson defined an American perimeter that appeared to exclude Korea. Actually, Acheson stated that the United States would not unilaterally intervene if South Korea was attacked, but many missed this nuance. MacArthur made conspicuous public declarations of an intention to defend Korea—another example of his penchant for announcing U.S. policy without official sanction. During internal policy debates, however, MacArthur fell in with those who believed that defending Korea was beyond existing American military capabilities. Truman's containment policy remained heavy on concept and light on means. The defense budget for Fiscal Year 1950 totaled only $13.5 billion. This money purchased an army of just ten incomplete divisions (two in Germany and four in Japan). MacArthur's Eighth Army, at 87,000 troops (under 27,000 in combat units), was radically under strength. The Air Force overall possessed forty-eight groups, but its centerpiece Strategic Air Command wielded only a very limited nuclear capability. MacArthur's Far Eastern Air Force comprised 34,000 men and 1,172 aircraft, about half fighters and bombers. Taxed with worldwide commitments, the navy could spare only 18 of its 238 combatant ships for the Western Pacific.[2]

The KPA struck in a multipronged attack in the morning of June 25, with seven infantry divisions, about 225 tanks, and support by 180 aircraft. The ROK army not only was outnumbered at the points of attack, its American patrons assured it lacked tanks, antitank weapons, aircraft and more than token artillery. Although Willoughby had warned of such an event, typically he had hedged and had even given contradictory projections that negated any claim to foresight. But the other U.S. intelligence agencies, including the CIA and State Department, did no better.[3]

The KPA overwhelmed the South Korean Army, whose effective strength fell from 98,000 to a mere 24,000 in four days. The initial reports reaching

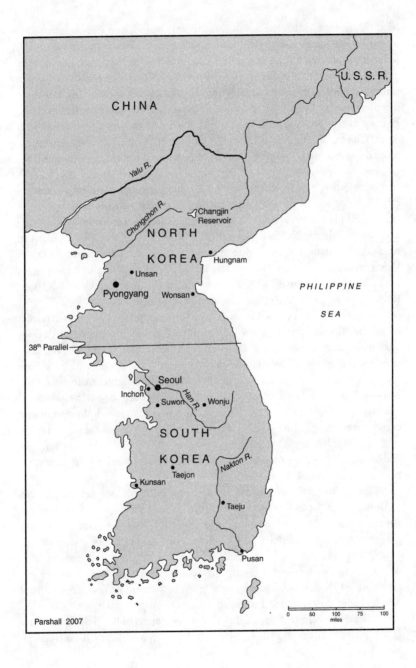

MacArthur stressed that the South Korean army would soon run out of ammunition. Characteristically, without waiting for Washington's approval, MacArthur ordered a ship loaded with ammunition for Korea and directed the air force and navy to escort it. He also ordered his air commander to attack across the border. In each instance, official sanction followed swiftly, but these instances immediately illustrated what to expect with MacArthur in command. Equally as troubling, during real-time teletype conversational exchanges with Army Chief of Staff General J. Lawton Collins in Washington, MacArthur exhibited the effrontery to refuse to even respond to temporizing questions from Collins.[4]

MacArthur flew to Korea on June 29. He personally witnessed the shattered state of the ROK Army and claimed later that he immediately devised the overall plan he followed thereafter. American ground forces would delay and finally halt the North Korean advance and then an amphibious end run would crush them. He sent a dispatch to Washington urging commitment of U.S. ground troops—for Truman had already authorized use of air and navy forces and was maneuvering swiftly and effectively to secure United Nations (UN) approval of the use of force against North Korea.[5]

When the UN approved of the use of force against North Korea, Truman asked the JCS to recommend a UN commander. Despite MacArthur's huge current burdens of command, the need for a figure who displayed "vast concern for the opinions and sensitivities of others" in the words of New York Times correspondent James Reston and a certifiable record of insubordination—freshly exhibited over the past few days—the JCS presented MacArthur's name to Truman. (One interesting but now wholly speculative exercise is to imagine the possible outcomes had the JCS instead suggested inserting a combat proven leader like Generals Maxwell Taylor or Matthew Ridgeway as UN commander.) Truman duly nominated MacArthur's appointment on July 8.[6]

During July and into August, the vigorous KPA advance defeated American units from Japan MacArthur was forced to commit piecemeal. Initially, American soldiers lacked weapons to defeat KPA tanks and some units displayed serious deficiencies in training, morale and discipline. While MacArthur bore some responsibility for this, the larger share stemmed from Truman's policy of stringent control of defense spending. The American and surviving ROK forces withdrew to a perimeter around Pusan in southeast Korea. There they withstood repeated assaults through September.

MacArthur stripped one Eighth Army division to bulk up the other three (1st Cavalry, 24th and 25th Infantry) and the separate 29th Infantry Regiment he sent to Korea. The JCS met his pleas for reinforcements by eventually bringing the Eighth Army units up to full strength (including the 7th Infantry Division) and adding two army divisions (2nd and 3rd Infantry), the 1st Marine Division and the 5th Infantry and 187th Airborne Infantry Regiments. The Eighth Army remained woefully deficient in artillery by World War II standards and possessed only about one-third of the needed service troops. In addition, sixteen other UN nations, mainly the UK and Commonwealth, contributed combat forces.[7]

Two episodes during this period illustrate the mythology verses the reality of MacArthur's penchant for reshaping national policy. First, the JCS ordered extensive strategic bombing in North Korea, including the port of Rashin, only seventeen miles from the Soviet border. Illustrating that paranoid thoughts were not confined to MacArthur, diplomat George Kennan in his memoirs quite wrongly charged that MacArthur ordered the raid in hopes of expanding the war. In reality, not only was Rashin a JCS target, but also MacArthur actually urged that the B–29s' effort aim at tactical, not strategic, targets.

Second, in August, MacArthur accepted an invitation for comments to be read at a U.S. veterans' convention. He eschewed safe topics for a plea for American support for Chiang Kai-shek, blatantly trespassing into foreign policy. Truman rightly viewed this as a direct challenge and later claimed he momentarily contemplated relieving MacArthur. Instead, he ordered MacArthur to retract publicly the statement, which MacArthur ultimately did. Truman's wrath stemmed not from the views themselves, which Macarthur had circulated earlier, but from the fact that MacArthur went public. MacArthur took no heed of the fact that after a decade of his provocations to Washington, Truman had *publicly* enforced his subordination.[8]

As early as July 2 MacArthur began concrete plans to destroy the KPA with an amphibious envelopment at Inchon, just west of Seoul. MacArthur mooted the concept to the JCS on July 13. This plan came naturally to MacArthur, based upon his numerous successes with just such maneuvers in World War II. Eurocentric officers like Omar Bradley and Collins dominated the JCS. Their reference point for deep amphibious envelopments was not MacArthur's brilliant triumph of Hollandia on New Guinea in April 1944, but the near fiasco of Anzio, Italy, in January 1944, an operation mounted to permit the quick seizure of Rome, and the destruction of the German armies defending it, that turned into a stalemate that lurched very near a catastrophic defeat. Even the designated commanders for what came to be called Operation Chromite urged MacArthur to target Posung-Myon, about twenty miles south of Inchon. As one navy staff officer quipped: "We drew up a list of every conceivable and natural handicap and Inchon had 'em all."

The 1st Marine Division and the army's 7th Infantry Division became the X Corps under the ambitious Major General Edward Almond. MacArthur blatantly favored Almond by subordinating X Corps directly to himself, not General Walton Walker's Eighth Army.

On August 23, MacArthur delivered one of the greatest oratorical performances of his life before Army Chief of Staff Collins, the Chief of Naval Operations Forrest P. Sherman, and a contingent of other senior officers. After nine briefers presented the decidedly problematic details of Chromite, MacArthur rose and spoke for forty-five minutes. He brilliantly turned the arguments about the incredible hydrographic and tactical challenges of Inchon—the approach by a narrow twisting channel, easily mined or commanded by shore batteries, a thirty-one-foot tidal cycle that would leave the initially landing force marooned overnight—to his favor by pointing out that these very facts would guarantee surprise because no enemy general would believe any sane commander would attack Inchon. He added the barb: "I seem to have more confidence in the Navy than the Navy has in itself." Several listeners later recorded that he finished with the comments: "I realize that Inchon is a 5000 to 1 gamble, but I am used to taking such odds. We shall land at Inchon and I shall crush them."

On September 15, with MacArthur present, the 1st Marine Division landed at Inchon. As MacArthur predicted, the operation proved a transcendent success—the single most brilliant of MacArthur's career. The Eighth Army and X Corps linked up on September 27 and the next day Seoul was secured after heavy fighting. The North Korean army sustained huge losses and would never again be able to field more than a corps-sized fighting force.[9]

⊬═══⊬

Advancing UN troops discovered at least 8,300 Korean and 485 American victims of North Korean massacres—and vengeful South Koreans retaliated in kind against their northern countrymen. This exacerbated the incendiary issue of whether MacArthur should cross the 38th Parallel, and if so, for what purpose. MacArthur and Rhee enjoyed the enormous advantage of a clear, shared purpose: unify Korea by force under Rhee. They further wielded the practical advantage of exploiting the power vacuum behind advancing UN forces. By contrast, the American and foreign challengers to this vision stood divided in purpose and on the outside looking in. UN resolutions dating from 1947 theoretically sanctioned unification of Korea, but the prospect of actual unification under Rhee provoked second thoughts, particularly sparked by fears of Chinese intervention. As MacArthur recognized, Truman's waffling over whether he required UN sanction for operations across the border only lightly veiled the real concern which centered on the nervous attitudes of key European allies, like Britain, or important UN members like India. The UN manufactured a compromise resolution setting goals of Korean reconciliation and neutralization of the nation; but the UN failed to mobilize any political presence to enforce its writ before the issue became moot.

On September 26, the JCS authorized MacArthur to operate throughout North Korea, provided no "major" Soviet or Chinese forces entered North Korea. The JCS cautioned that such operations were not an occupation and that only South Korean units were to be used in the Soviet and Chinese border areas. But on the 28th, George Marshall, now Secretary of Defense, in an extraordinarily ill-advised personal message told MacArthur: "We want you to feel unhampered strategically and tactically to proceed north of the 38th Parallel." He added that Rhee's authority should remain confined to the south.

The grossly overconfident MacArthur followed the Inchon triumph with markedly maladroit generalship. He ordered Almond's X Corps withdrawn from Inchon and landed on Korea's east coast, a time-wasting, logistical nightmare that handicapped the advance of Walker's Eighth Army and proved useless when South Korean troops secured the proposed landing sites. Largely because of MacArthur's favoritism for Almond, he maintained the tactical oddity of keeping X Corps separate from the Eighth Army as the former advanced to the east of the mountainous spine of the Korean peninsula and the latter to the west. Finally, rather than halting American forces at the natural narrow "waist" of North Korea, he permitted them to rush headlong into the vicinity of the border. The JCS abided what one of them would later characterize as the first clear violation of their direct order not to permit non-ROK troops to venture to the international borders.

Truman directed a meeting with MacArthur and accepted MacArthur's date of October 15 and site of Wake Island. Many weighty military and political issues concerning the apparent end of hostilities in Korea afforded ample basis for the conference, but the circumstances reeked with politics. The event proved even thicker with mythology. In accounts appearing in a book, a play, and a television program in the 1970s, Truman's and MacArthur's planes arrived simultaneously over Wake. Protocol required that MacArthur land first to greet the president, but Truman had to order MacArthur to land and then insist that MacArthur present himself. The reality is that MacArthur's plane arrived the night before and he personally and warmly greeted Truman the next morning. The fact that the myth found an eagerly accepting audience illustrates how MacArthur's detractors could be no more rigorous in their version of history than his supporters.

As for the substance of the conference, both principals were sublimely confident that the Korean War was locked on course for a speedy and safe landing. Thus, it is not surprising that the transcript reflected a wide but extremely shallow skating over an array of issues, many related to postwar rehabilitation. When MacArthur was questioned about the prospect of Soviet or Chinese intervention, he replied that had they come in during the first two months, it would have been decisive. Now he assessed the risk as "very little" and assured Truman that dominating U.S. airpower guaranteed that if Chinese "tried to get down to Pyongyang, there would be the greatest slaughter." D. Clayton James' assessment cannot be improved upon: "The most astonishing fact about this most-quoted portion of the Wake talks is that this was the whole extent of the conferees' probe into the enormous implications that the current [UN] offensive might have for decision makers in Peking and Moscow: one question by Truman, a single response by MacArthur, and absolutely no follow-up questions, challenges or further mention!"[10]

14

Korea Defeat

GIVEN A GREAT PAUCITY OF RELIABLE INFORMATION, FOR OVER FORTY years historians generally assumed that the crossing of the 38th Parallel by U.S. forces triggered Chinese entry into the Korean War. Since 1994, new revelations establish that the original impetus for China's plans and intentions to enter the war was Truman's decision to send U.S. soldiers to Korea in July 1950. This move prompted Mao to foresee the prospect that U.S. forces might not only check the North Korean attack, but also reverse the tide and sweep up to the Chinese border. He ordered the PLA to begin troop deployments and logistical preparations for combat on the Korean peninsula. Mao aimed for military readiness in August 1950, well before Inchon. Thus, while the final decision to commit Chinese forces coincided with the crossing of the 38th Parallel, that event was one step in a process with much deeper roots.

Mao personally drafted, but did not send, a lengthy telegram to Stalin on October 2 that captures his goals, means, and concerns. Mao clearly expected the conflict to remain non-nuclear and at most regional. He emphasized that the preeminent strategic goal was not defense of China's borders, but the triumph of the revolutionary cause throughout the whole Far East. He confidently expected his numerically superior armies to annihilate MacArthur's command and seize all of Korea. He asked Stalin to make good manifest Chinese deficits in air support, heavy equipment, and artillery. Mao expected that China could endure direct attacks on the mainland by American air and sea forces. He acknowledged the possibility that the failure to destroy MacArthur's command might result in a Korean stalemate seriously detrimental to China's domestic situation, but he graded that prospect as only a worst-case scenario. But Mao chose to send a different telegram. While he was resolved on entering the war with defense of China's borders subsidiary to the prospect of far wider spread of communism, other Chinese leaders remained dubious. Mao's rewritten telegram to Stalin reflected Chinese indecision about intervention and that their choice hung on Soviet support, particularly in the air. Stalin made and then reneged on a promise of air cover over Korea. The Chinese leadership paused, but then plunged ahead.[1]

On October 3, Chinese diplomats sent a message through the Indian government that China would confront a U.S. entry into North Korea, but not an advance by South Koreans. Intelligence indicated a massing of as many as 300,000 to 450,000 Chinese troops in Manchuria. Washington and MacArthur both discounted the warning as a bluff and the troop movements as defensive. When the first 260,000 Chinese 'volunteers' entered North Korea between October 19 and 22, both Willoughby and Washington failed to detect them.[2]

It took MacArthur five days after the first Chinese prisoners of war were taken on October 26 to concede that Chinese communists units that had entered Korea around mid month. On November 4, MacArthur expressed doubt about full scale Chinese intervention, but only two days later he asked for authority to bomb bridges over the Yalu to halt massive infusion of Chinese communist forces. On November 7, MacArthur reported that he could not ascertain the total strength of the Chinese forces, but they were sufficient to seize the initiative in the west. By now the JCS believed five or six Chinese armies were in Korea, but in keeping with traditional deference to the field commander, they merely asked MacArthur whether he should halt his advance; they did not order him to do so.

On November 9, MacArthur informed the JCS that he would send the Eighth Army forward on November 24 to discover the strength of the Chinese. On that later date, he launched what he publicly predicted would be the 'home by Chistmas' final offensive to occupy North Korea. The next night, about 180,000 Chinese soldiers struck Walker's Eighth Army. Two days later, perhaps 120,000 Chinese attacked Almond's X Corps. The Eighth Army, driven back amid many scenes of confusion and chaos and sustaining heavy casualties, lost Seoul. The X Corps was evacuated through Hungnam, after the brilliant fighting withdrawal of the 1st Marine Division from the Chosin Reservoir that inflicted terrible casualties on its Chinese adversaries. In December 1950, Walker was killed in a vehicle accident and replaced by Lt. Gen. Mathew Ridgway. In the following weeks, Ridgway produced perhaps the greatest performance of the twentieth century by an American field army commander. He displayed the skill and charisma to resurrect the Eighth Army from its nadir and the cold nerve to recognize that Chinese forces were overextended, seriously short of supplies, and vulnerable to limited counterpunches. During these same weeks, MacArthur immolated his position and inflicted devastation on his career and reputation.

On November 28 MacArthur informed Washington that 'We face an entirely new war.' His initial plan reflected his shock: withdraw Eighth Army to a Pusan bridgehead and X Corps to Hungnam. He reversed his earlier position and requested Nationalist Chinese troops. Washington approved the former but vetoed the latter. When Collins arrived on December 6, a shaken MacArthur argued that unless he was sent reinforcements or freed of restrictions on his actions, Korea should be evacuated. Collins did not believe the situation so dire.[3]

In Washington, Truman and his advisers readjusted American aims. They agreed that the situation was much closer to global war with the Soviets and that therefore no more forces would be sent to Korea. A paper prepared by the National Security Council (NSC–68) in April 1950 had called for a huge American armament program to deal with the new realities of a Communist China and the Soviet detonation of an atomic bomb in August 1949. Chinese intervention did what nothing else had: it secured Truman's endorsement of the program that affected the American posture in the Cold War for the next four decades. Defense spending quadrupled from $13.5 billion for fiscal year 1950 to $52 billion for the following year. In talks with British Prime Minister Clement R. Atlee (prompted by Truman's loose public language implying he was handing over atomic weapons for MacArthur to use as he saw fit), Truman agreed to drop the objective of liberation of North Korea for containment. But nobody bothered to tell MacArthur this.[4]

Without a doubt, Chinese intervention and the defeat of his plan sent the aging MacArthur intellectually and emotionally reeling. All his life he had been blessed with the ability to sleep well no matter what the situation. Now, he could not sleep. From the first days after Chinese intervention,

MacArthur embarked on a path of private predictions of catastrophe, insisting that he must evacuate his forces from Korea, coupled with public justification of his own actions that incorporated a gradual crescendo of excuses and explanations, all designed to lay the blame on others, and particularly his superiors in Washington. On December 5, a seething Truman issued orders ostensibly to all executive branch officials (he still did not single out MacArthur) directing that they clear all statements about foreign policy through the State Department.[5]

The JCS bluntly informed MacArthur that he could expect no reinforcements and that the restrictions on his actions, particularly with regard to striking directly at China, would remain in effect. MacArthur reacted by insisting that the only two available options were withdrawal from Korea, or expansion of the war. For the latter, he advocated employing Nationalist Chinese troops, plus a naval blockade of China, coupled with a naval and air bombardment program against the mainland.

MacArthur's proposals are often depicted as verging on the deranged. But contemporary message traffic shows that Ridgway—always pictured as rock solid in the crisis—on his own initiative endorsed the proposal to bring in Nationalist Chinese forces. Ridgway further demanded to know on January 6 whether his mission was the evacuation of UN forces or holding on in Korea. The JCS actually agreed with MacArthur's set of proposals about employing Nationalist Chinese forces and measures directly against China, but only if the situation deteriorated further. Fortunately, in mid-January Ridgway's rejuvenated Eighth Army launched limited counteroffensives that convinced the JCS and Truman that Korea could be held under current circumstances. This refutation of MacArthur's military judgment, following upon the defeat initially inflicted upon his forces, finally broke MacArthur's Inchon spell over his superiors.[6]

Ridgway's miracle turnaround of the Eighth Army reversed the tide in Korea and proceeded to gain momentum—achievements wholly Ridgway's, without MacArthur's contribution. Starting from late January, Ridgway launched a series of local offensives designed not at terrain objectives but at inflicting unsustainable casualties on Communist Chinese forces. American (with some allied help) and ROK units at first cautiously probed and then absorbed or gave ground before counterattacks, always subjecting the Chinese to terrible losses. But by March the supposedly 'inexhaustible' Chinese Communist forces could not stop the Eighth Army's advance. On March 15, Ridgway secured Seoul permanently and pressed on to the 38th Parallel. There MacArthur authorized him to secure tactically commanding ground across the international border, but not to proclaim this publicly. The only cloud over the relationship was MacArthur's claims that he had ordered Ridgway's offensives when no such order was given.[7]

The final countdown to dismissal started in February. Despite Truman's ban on military officers discussing political matters without State Department clearance, MacArthur issued public statements in February and March, castigating the idea of accepting a stalemate on the 38th Parallel and condemning the restrictions on his forces granting the Chinese communists 'sanctuaries.' Events moved to a climax when the JCS advised MacArthur on March 20 that Truman was about to initiate a move to a reach a political and military settlement. On March 24, MacArthur issued a communiqué that widely exceeded his past record of direct challenges to his superiors. The communiqué taunted the Chinese Communists as lacking the industrial wherewithal to support air and sea forces or to provide their ground forces with first-class firepower. He called upon China's leaders to admit publicly defeat in Korea and approach him as supplicants for a settlement. He clearly aimed with this communiqué to sabotage Truman's diplomacy. Moreover, his larger purpose was to force, by his martyrdom if necessary, a fundamental reorientation of American foreign policy to embrace Chiang and give priority to Asia, not Europe.

Truman later claimed that he resolved to relieve MacArthur that very day; he only temporized about the timing. Amazingly, however, the immediate response was merely a tepid message 'reminding' MacArthur about the prior directive on officials commenting on foreign policy, which suggests more hesitancy. But almost immediately a second brazen incident of insubordination appeared to provide another justification. Republican House Minority Leader Joseph Martin had written MacArthur on March 8. Martin included a copy of a February speech proposing America give strategic priority to Asia over Europe. Further he proposed a formal alliance with Chiang and U.S. support for a Nationalist invasion of the mainland.

On April 5, Martin released MacArthur's response and read it on the floor of the House. MacArthur's letter correctly reported that he had made his views well known to Washington, but he did not request that Martin keep his comments in confidence. MacArthur maintained that the critical arena was now Asia, not Europe, and that he only advocated the nation's historic policy of meeting force 'with maximum counterforce.' Therefore, he endorsed a Nationalist attack on the mainland as consistent with that tradition. In his most famous phrase, MacArthur declared that a military, not a diplomatic, settlement was the manner to end the Korean conflict and that '[t]here is no substitute for victory.'

Acheson supported MacArthur's dismissal, but wisely advised Truman to act only with the concurrence of the JCS. That body wavered for nearly three days, primarily because it could not agree that MacArthur had violated a specific current JCS directive. The JCS did not doubt that MacArthur was clearly out of sympathy with government policy, but found the only clear-cut evidence of insubordination related to Truman's December 1950 letter.

On April 9, after the JCS and his other senior advisers unanimously concurred that MacArthur must go, Truman announced that he had made his mind up on March 24. Ridgway would replace MacArthur. Truman directed Secretary of the Army Frank Pace, then in the Far East, to deliver the relief order personally to MacArthur at noon, April 12, in Tokyo. The actual delivery of the message went awry. When Truman learned the *Chicago Tribune* was about to publish the story, the announcement was made at a 1:00 AM press conference at the White House. MacArthur learned of his relief by public radio broadcast. He commented in his memoirs: 'No office boy, nor charwoman, no servant of any sort would have been dismissed with such callous disregard for the ordinary decencies.' The circumstances did no credit to Truman. MacArthur, on the other hand, displayed the unruffled dignity and grace of an aristocrat in the mundane details of his relief and departure.[8]

It required decades of time, new evidence, and new perspectives to identify correctly the significance of Korea. Defeat in Korea provided an ignominious end to MacArthur's military career. He cannot fairly be saddled with total blame for the surprise of Chinese entry. Washington clearly shared heavy responsibility, but sought with great success to foist the primary onus on MacArthur. From late October, both Washington and MacArthur knew Chinese troops were in Korea. By early November, the JCS feared the Chinese were present in great numbers, but refused to order MacArthur to go to the defensive. MacArthur for the last time rejected intelligence that conflicted with his vision of a triumphant roll back of communism in Asia. That failure led directly to MacArthur's huge responsibility for the vulnerable posture of most UN troops when the Chinese launched their main effort in November. The masterful handling of the 1st Marine Division showed that the Chinese could be dealt devastating blows with careful tactics and resolution. MacArthur's handling of the crisis of Chinese intervention ranks next to the Papua campaign of 1942 as a low point of his generalship.[9]

But Korea shaped far more than MacArthur's reputation. The insatiable costs of the heavy militarization of the Cold War incited by Chinese intervention proved in the long run the undoing of the Soviet Union. In the short run, China obtained restoration of status as a major power by driving UN forces back to the 38th Parallel. But this came at the cost of loss of the greatest opportunity to reclaim Taiwan and a price of hundreds of thousands of battlefield dead to instill the painful lesson that the United States was not, in Mao's dismissive phrase, a 'paper tiger.' Moreover, Mao ruthlessly exploited the war to justify unleashing terror in China to suppress 'reactionaries' that jailed over two million and resulted in 700,000 executions. He then used his newly burnished power to lead China into the successive stupendous catastrophes of the Great Leap Forward and the Great Proletarian Cultural Revolution. Thus, we can see now that MacArthur's Korean failure is far overshadowed by those of Stalin and Mao. Finally, MacArthur's leadership from July to September 1950 defeated the effort to seize South Korea by naked aggression. This may well have been the key event of the Cold War. With the exception of the April 1975 offensive by North Vietnam, never again would a communist country attempt such a blatant action that might have proved a trigger for World War III. Completely obscured for years by later events, MacArthur's Korean campaign through Inchon may have been one of the most important of his career.

⊹═⊱═⊰⊹

A great storm followed MacArthur's relief, with public opinion initially strongly in MacArthur's camp—66 to 25 percent by one Gallup Poll. The Japanese Diet and ROK National Assembly issued resolutions of praise. Hirohito paid him a farewell visit, the first time an emperor paid a visit to a foreigner without an official position. On April 19 MacArthur spoke before a joint session of Congress. In a thirty-seven-minute oration his deep, powerful, resonant voice captured most of his audience of millions via television and radio, even those who noted the logical defects or even perils of his message. He swept his audience along on a mighty emotional tide as he pled his case that for vital principles he had sacrificed his career. His core message was consistent: parity if not primacy for the Pacific over Europe; mischaracterizing the strategic choices as between his for victory and Truman's for appeasement; demands for further actions against China, though he was careful to disavow any aim to engage in a ground war on Chinese soil. He concluded with lines he said came from a barracks ballad popular fifty-two years earlier, when he entered service: 'Old soldiers never die, they just fade away.'[10]

Senate hearings followed. For three days MacArthur gave a dazzling performance in terms of presence. One remarkable point he made was that there was no unitary communist conspiracy orchestrated from Moscow: the Soviet Union and China each had their own interests to pursue. Feckless meandering questions eventually dulled public interest, but, more important, Administration witnesses undermined MacArthur's credibility. The JCS witnesses devastated MacArthur's arguments about how his plans for blockade, bombardment, and use of Chinese nationalist troops would secure victory. While only Collins appeared to charge frank insubordination (sending U.S. troops up to the Yalu), the others justified MacArthur's relief on the basis that he was completely out of sympathy with the policies of the government.

MacArthur worked strenuously against the Truman administration and urged president-elect Eisenhower to take sterner measurers against China to end the Korean War. He gained a measure of vindication on both fronts when Truman declined to run for reelection and Eisenhower's statecraft that ended the war included warnings of escalation. In 1952, MacArthur became chairman of the board of Remington Rand (Speery Rand from 1956). He continued to deploy his keen intellect in active participation in the management of the electronic giants.

His public life ended in two interesting episodes. In 1961, a shaken President John F. Kennedy paid MacArthur what was intended to be a pro forma call after the Bay of Pigs disaster. MacArthur so impressed the young president that he was invited to the White House for a subsequent meeting. MacArthur emphatically counseled that the United States must avoid a war on the Asian continent and that Kennedy would be wiser to devote more time to domestic issues. Then in 1962, MacArthur received the Sylvanus Thayer Award, the highest honor West Point could bestow. His speech there was vintage Victorian MacArthur, unbelievably moving to his friends and intolerably bathetic to his ranks of critics.

He died on April 11, 1964 and was buried at a MacArthur Memorial and Archive in Norfolk, Virginia—on April 13, thirteen years to the day after his relief by Truman. He unwisely decided to write memoirs published coincidently with his death. They detracted from, rather than added to, his standing. His universally admired wife Jean died in January 2000 at the age of 101.

15

The Sum of the Man

THE PRIOR PAGES LAY DOWN THE ESSENTIALS OF MACARTHUR'S LIFE as fairly as possible, neither underplaying the flaws nor overlooking the achievements. But extracting from this story some transferable insights is a daunting task. One of the fascinating findings by biographer D. Clayton James was that interviews with 180 associates produced a cacophony of opinions on MacArthur, but general unanimity on three points. The very first of these was that he was the most complicated person they had ever met. This probably explains why the second point of agreement was that that the public image and the "real MacArthur" were different. Finally, there emerged a corollary that the favorability of the judgment correlated directly with the length of the contact.[1]

Like Franklin Roosevelt, Douglas MacArthur possessed the talents that would have made him one of the supreme actors of his age. He always conducted himself, as Eisenhower discovered, as though he stood before an invisible audience. His chameleon-like "role playing" skills enabled him to guise himself and his message in the manner exactly calibrated to sway his audience, whatever its numbers. It is likely that the only individuals with an exact grasp of his real nature were his parents, particularly his mother, and his second wife Jean. Since these individuals did not share with anyone else their knowledge, the best a biographer can do is to admit defeat on delineating "the real MacArthur."

If MacArthur's true core remains beyond our knowledge, then perforce we must resort to systematically examining what we can discern. Starting with his basic traits, his stellar intellect ranks first. It served as a formidable tool for analyzing any issue or problem before him. When given free rein his mind could identify and assess a challenge from the most mundane detail upwards without losing sight of the total picture. His intellectual makeup incorporated a panoramic curiosity that never left him and propelled him into study of fields far from soldiering—with the admittedly important exceptions of art and literature. This depth of knowledge served him very well as he confronted increasingly complex nonmilitary tasks. His intellect played a huge role in inflating his self-confidence, an indispensable requirement for successfully handling huge challenges. His well-stocked mind supported considerable oral skills, though his public utterances now sound banal and carry a heavy Victorian residue. For most if not all of his life, he believed he was the most competent human being on the planet and there was no job he could not do better than the incumbent, most particularly including the presidency.

His scintillating intellect, however, also generated some nontrivial problems. Professionally, one of the lessons of MacArthur's life for a senior leader is that sheer brilliance is not enough if divorced from mastery of all professional fundamentals. MacArthur never attended a service school that looked beyond battalion or regimental duties. He was, as we might say today, home schooled having done independent reading in the higher arts of war. This left him with a tremendous deficit in one absolutely critical area: logistics. The first clue of this was when, as chief of staff of the Rainbow Division, he set up a staff that omitted any officer with primary responsibility for supply (G–4 in military argot). It is instructive that logistics proved to be the irredeemable error in his strategic direction in the first Philippine campaign—an error his critics properly highlighted but MacArthur, given his outsized ego, could not acknowledge. MacArthur's lack of candor in admitting how defeat in the Philippines spurred him to subsequent masterful management of his scarce logistical support produced a fundamental misjudgment about his greatest achievements as a high commander: whatever stature he is due as a strategist or tactician—and judgments may still differ on this—he earns a salute as one of the stellar masters of logistics in military history.

The second exceptional innate trait was a tremendous constitution. Perhaps ironically, the one thing in life he lacked that he most lamented was first-class athletic ability. Yet he was endowed with a remarkable set of genes that preserved his mental and physical youthfulness far beyond those of virtually any of his peers at the center stage of history. He nurtured this gift by eating and drinking in moderation and maintaining a regular pattern of sleep. What is striking, however, is how elementary was the other key ingredient to his vitality: he converted his office into his workout room by the expedient of pacing as he thought or conversed with visitors. On average, he paced four to six miles per day. He even used the aisle of his command plane for pacing, his pilot once jesting that on flights to Korea MacArthur walked the whole distance. It was the combination of his intellect and his youthfulness that convinced men like Marshall and Eisenhower that he must be recalled to duty for service in World War II.

⊹⇒══⇐⊹

Next we come to a set of fundamental precepts. His parents instilled the first of these: America's future rested in the Far East, not Europe. How Arthur MacArthur, a mid-westerner stationed in the dusty, isolated outposts of the west developed an obsession with the Far East remains an unsolved mystery. But he inculcated this into Douglas, who reached the two greatest peaks of his career during service in the Far East. Since virtually all of his contemporaries in service and his American political superiors were Eurocentric, MacArthur possessed throughout his career a fundamentally contrarian stance toward the country's strategic priorities. Setting aside MacArthur's personality, there is a great deal to be said for having such a contrarian viewpoint to test and temper conventional wisdom in a large institution.

By twenty-first century standards, MacArthur's stance on racial relations might appear constrained. By the standards of his time, however, his views were radically advanced. He basically believed that there was no inherent intellectual or moral defect in nonwhites that would preclude them from achieving equality. In a moving speech in 1930 in Manila he urged the importance of toleration and balance in racial relations. He conspicuously treated Filipino, Japanese, and Korean leaders as his intellectual and moral equals. Moreover, both in the Philippines and in Japan, he not only viewed issues through the eyes of the local people, he could act as their vigorous advocate with U.S. officials. In the Philippines, his identification with the local elites was so complete that he was prepared to use the lives of U.S soldiers to see that the "right" kind of Filipino won. One of the ironies of MacArthur's life is that he was reviled by his political enemies as a hopeless reactionary. They entirely missed the fact that MacArthur's demand that the United States give primacy to the Far East was profoundly subversive to the entire contemporary consensus built upon European and white supremacy.

With the innate sensibilities of a late Victorian, MacArthur stood as an imperfect dissident to the total war philosophy that gained steady hold as the twentieth century unfolded. He refused to imperil Filipino civilians by ruthlessly stripping them of vital foodstuffs to sustain a siege of Bataan. He refrained from humiliation of Japan's representatives at the September 1945 surrender ceremony. Perhaps the most conspicuous episodes revealing MacArthur's attitudes about war involved air power. While he became an ardent disciple of tactical air power, he rejected unrestrained use of aerial firepower, and he particularly abhorred the bombing of cities. He declared Manila an "open city" to spare it the horrors of bombing by the Japanese in December 1941. Then in 1945, as his soldiers faced the daunting task of rooting out Japanese defenders in Manila, he rejected any use of airpower. While there were several reasons why army air force officers contrived to keep the B–29 force in the Pacific out of the control of either Nimitz or MacArthur, at least one reason was their appreciation that MacArthur would never have authorized the incendiary bombing attack on Japanese cities initiated in March 1945. Again in Korea, MacArthur initially rejected air force schemes of city smashing.

But MacArthur compromised his restraints on warfare at several critical moments. In June 1945, he was prepared to contemplate the use of poison gas against stubborn Japanese defenders holding out during battles in the homeland. His participation in the judicial murders of Generals Yamashita and Homma represents further egregious violations of his beliefs. Finally, the catastrophe of Chinese entry prompted him to authorize schemes he had previously rejected for the massive use of aerial firepower against Korean cities.

+≈≈≈+

The foremost misjudgment of MacArthur by his admirers is to extol him as an innovator. The two conspicuous episodes in which MacArthur can rightly be hailed as a radical force for change were his role in transforming army education, and the famous peace provision in the Japanese constitution. His reforms as West Point superintendent and of the army school system as chief of staff were visionary and based on such goals as increasing the breadth of knowledge taught to students, cross-fertilizing army educational institutions with their civilian counterparts, instilling independence of professional thought while reconnecting cadets and soldiers to the civilian society they guarded. He championed them against conventional views and at a cost—his abruptly curtailed tour as superintendent of the military academy.

Although he insisted publicly that the idea originated with Japanese leaders, the fact is that MacArthur authored the stunning provision in the Japanese constitution that rejected war. It remains to this day a singular unfulfilled ideal. Even in Japan, the debate continues over whether the provision actually ruled out the use of force even in self-defense.

But these two episodes are vastly overshadowed by a much more profound and striking pattern in MacArthur's conduct as a military commander and in supreme administrative posts. That pattern is adaptability. At the great crisis of his career in World War I, with his future on the line at the Cote de Chatillon, he adopted a battle plan proposed by one of his subordinates and made it his own. He borrowed from Leonard Wood his scheme for developing defenses for the Philippines. During World War II, he gained mastery of air and amphibious warfare from key subordinates who acted as his tutors, George Kenny and Daniel Barbey. He very belatedly adopted the "bypass" strategy after William F. Halsey, Jr. showed the way. The crown jewel of his campaigns, Hollandia, originated with subordinates, not MacArthur. The excellent policy blueprint he followed for the occupation of Japan was drafted in Washington. What is intriguing and attractive about this trait is that more often than not individuals with vast intellectual gifts deploy them to denigrate the ideas of others rather than dispassionately evaluate them. Moreover, it takes supreme self-confidence and a generous spirit to embrace freely the ideas of others, particularly at a moment of crisis.

Another principle of MacArthur's leadership often cited, but requiring qualification is boldness. That MacArthur exhibited boldness in the latter half of his campaign in New Guinea, at Leyte, and particularly at Inchon is not debatable. Of the Americans who achieved senior leadership positions during his career, only Patton, Halsey, and Nimitz would have done Hollandia and Leyte. No one else would have done Inchon (though a number of leaders would have done a shallower "end run" with nearly the same strategic results, but probably with higher casualties). The campaigns in Kuwait in 1991 and the race to Baghdad in 2003 exemplified the spirit of MacArthur's daring.

As a high commander, however, MacArthur did not exhibit true boldness until after about eighteen months of painfully obtained experience in the Philippines and Papua. The Papua campaign, in fact, marked the lowest point of his generalship and provides a textbook of errors. MacArthur did not display boldness until his forces gained operational maturity and when his codebreakers handed him a picture of enemy dispositions and allowed him to eavesdrop on enemy headquarters. His boldness careened into recklessness in the post-Inchon campaign. Ridgway and the Marine commanders demonstrated that Chinese intervention did not automatically mean that a halt of the UN drive would inevitably result in a serious reverse and withdrawal below the 38th Parallel.

The secrets to MacArthur's ability not just to lead, but to dominate a huge organization such as his Southwest Pacific command and later as SCAP, leave a mixed legacy. MacArthur himself repeatedly extolled loyalty as the first quality he sought in a subordinate. Beginning in 1941 and continuing for the next decade to his firing in Korea, MacArthur surrounded himself with staff officers whose only universally shared trait was loyalty. What MacArthur achieved by placing his foremost emphasis on loyalty was the ability to dominate his bureaucracy by assuring that everything funneled upwards to a handful of men with absolute personal devotion to him and a zealous desire to implement his vision. The price of this benefit, however, was a very serious constriction of information and opinion.

As a motivator within his command, MacArthur's favorite tool was to create rivalries among subordinates and then to play one off against the other. The most conspicuous examples of this are his use of Krueger and Eichelberger and later, in Japan, Whitney verses the rest of the SCAP staff. Contrary to stereotypes about military leaders, MacArthur was very sparing with direct verbal lashings of his subordinates, though he certainly could administer them f required. On the contrary, MacArthur firmly grasped the powerful effect of praise and even flattery as a motivator.

The use of style and symbolism constituted another leadership tool that MacArthur wielded to imprint his personal stamp on a huge bureaucracy. Starting at Vera Cruz and then flowering in World War I, MacArthur used his personal attire to transmit a message of the supreme aristocratic warrior. His visceral rejection of starched creases, bright buttons, and parade ground drill signaled open-mindedness and daring. The uniforms of the army down to the present follow the precedent of MacArthur, not Pershing and Patton. His instincts eventually led him to the insight that in dress, often less is more. He was a certifiable dandy in his nonduty dress prior to World War II and he had an unseemly appetite for every manner of award and decoration all his life. But he recognized during World War II that his hat, sunglasses, a pipe, and a simple open-neck khaki shirt without decorations beyond the minimalist rank insignia could carry more power than the gaudiest uniform.

Perhaps his most powerful uses of style and symbolism appeared in Japan. At the Japanese surrender ceremony, MacArthur brilliantly mixed markers of power and dominance, the democratic participation of all ranks, the understated but unmistakable statement of the presence of emaciated Japanese captives, and then the spare but powerful prose evoking high ideals while totally rejecting humiliation of his enemies. Following this was the partly calculated and partly serendipitous picture with the emperor. Yet another example was the fact that MacArthur drove unescorted twice per day back and forth to his office in Tokyo. In a nation with a recent extensive history of political assassination, this action conveyed his trust in the Japanese people.

Part of MacArthur's role-playing talents appeared in his radically varied direct modes of leadership. In World War I, his extraordinarily personalized frontline leadership won him the accolade of the D'Artagnan of the American Expeditionary Forces. In World War II, he initially abandoned that style in the first year of the war, which opened the way for the calumny "Dugout Doug." As Australian historian Gavin Long noted, "it is part of the business of the good general to make sure that the opportunity to perpetrate such libels does not occur to anyone." MacArthur failed in his critical duty to make sure that there could be no basis for such a charge. Then beginning in early 1944, MacArthur reverted to repeated examples of appearing literally in the front lines, to a degree no other American theater commander could match. But in Japan, he struck the pose of the remote, unapproachable Shogun—and left the glad handing to Hirohito. Except for the 1941–42 year of disasters, in each case he selected the direct mode best designed to imprint his leadership, an example of why one-style theories of leadership fail.[2]

Besides the lessons tucked within MacArthur's own story, his life contains a voluminous treatise on civil-military relations in general, and specifically on how not to deal with an extraordinarily talented but headstrong subordinate. There is nothing inherently sinister about the fact that MacArthur clashed with his civilian superiors over various issues. Simply arguing a point of view is not insubordination, and it would be a tremendous mistake to create a culture in which officers in the armed forces were castigated for forcefully presenting their advice. But MacArthur's challenge to Truman over Korea was not just a candid exchange of private views; MacArthur was properly relieved because he was so manifestly *and* publicly out of step with national policy.

MacArthur's conduct in Korea represented the culmination of a very long process, not an odd aberration. The major shift in MacArthur's willingness to abide by the directives of his military and civilian superiors emerged in the late 1930s. In the first months of World War II, President Roosevelt, Secretary of War Stimson, and Chief of Staff Marshall abided outrageous communications from MacArthur, particularly his paranoid ranting about the navy and fundamental disagreements with national strategy. Only Stimson recognized and acted directly to enforce subordination and thus channel MacArthur's behavior within acceptable bounds. The failure of American senior leadership in World War II to constrain MacArthur leaves its obvious lesson.

Another major milestone came when MacArthur exhibited the effrontery to refuse President Truman's twice-repeated "request" to return to the United States so that he could be accorded the thanks and acclamation accorded other American commanders. Truman failed to enforce his will and thus made MacArthur hold him in contempt. Thereafter, while the Truman administration provided expert guidance overall for the occupation, the Eurocentric outlook of most American leaders gave MacArthur a latitude of discretion he was quick to exploit. A very dangerous situation arose, as MacArthur lacked either a "friend in court" in Washington, or contact with Truman to build understanding. The lesson here is that Truman should have taken steps to secure a much more personal relationship with the man discharging such hugely important responsibilities. To his great credit, Truman belatedly took two steps to rectify this situation. First, after the Korean War erupted, he sent Maj. Gen. Edwin Lowe to Tokyo to open a personal liaison. Had Truman done this, say, two years earlier, it is possible that the confrontation of 1951 could have been avoided. Second, in August 1950, Truman for the first time forced MacArthur to retract publicly his declaration about American policy toward Nationalist China. This action, however, like Stimson's in 1942, while overdue, lost its effect from its belatedness and stark singularity.

⊹⊱══⊰⊹

In view of MacArthur's lack of subordination to civilian authority and his supersized ego, entrusting him with a major command during any subsequent historical period would have been folly. But absent the distorting effects of his own self-interest, MacArthur's keen analytical skills warrant respect and created a record that shows he could be both insightful and confound stereotypical expectations about his thinking. After all, he dissented from nearly all his Western military contemporaries in predicting the survival of the Soviet

Union under German attack in 1941, and in 1951 he would dispute conventional wisdom that Mao was simply the obedient servant of Stalin.

If we venture some informed speculations about MacArthur's assessments of contemporary events, he would demand that we start with the most fundamental national policy issue of his lifetime. Few could now dispute his claim that he and his father were visionaries vindicated by history. In terms of economics and demographics, the brightest future horizons for America beckon in Asia, not Europe. He would be publicly magnanimous to Europeans, with flowery rhetoric about a shared heritage, but privately he would sternly counsel that Europe should play no major role in shaping or guiding American national policy. He would have a still lower opinion of the utility of the United Nations except in such secondary and tertiary roles that overlapped with and reinforced American interests. His attitude would be implacable after what he viewed as the shocking failure of the UN to respond appropriately to a direct attack by China in 1950.

With characteristic immodesty, he not only would take the fair measure of the credit he is due for the emergence of a peaceful and democratic Japanese economic powerhouse, but he would treat attempts to point out that Washington supplied the basic plan as a sort of lèse-majesté. One of the least predictable aspects of his views would revolve around the "peace article" in the Japanese constitution. During his lifetime, he went from an extremely pure idealism that the article meant exactly no armed forces, not even in self-defense, to toleration of some rearmament first to secure an end of the occupation, and then to protect Japan when American troops were sent to Korea. His subsequent views likely would have cycled through several different seasons. He would not have found amiss the modest size of Japan's armed forces during the Cold War and at its end might have talked of how perhaps it was time for the Japanese to reexamine a reversion to a pure interpretation of Article Nine.

With a flourish, he would pronounce that that the running crisis over North Korea's nuclear ambitions and ballistic missile programs, destabilizing the whole region and raising the prospect of sales to terrorists, proves that he, not Truman, correctly weighed what was at stake in 1951. Accepting stalemate rather than victory in Korea only postponed to a later generation a far graver menace than the danger posed to the American homeland by the 1950 invasion. But he would not have urged priority for military action against North Korea at this time, absent some direct act of war. His analysis likely would have stressed that first emphasis should be placed on other, even more ominous, threats to the continued rise of the rest of Asia, particularly China, Japan, and India.

One key part of MacArthur's legacy induced from him an extended silence. That subject was the Philippines. Once MacArthur left the Philippines for Japan in 1945, he severed a family and intense personal linkage of decades' duration. He returned only twice, once for the independence ceremonies in 1946, and then on a nostalgic mission in 1961. He seldom referred publicly to the Philippines again. In this he behaved like a great actor who, once he reaches the premier venues, never again speaks of apprenticeship days in less august theaters.

MacArthur's views on events outside Japan, the Korean Peninsula and the Philippines would likely have been both complex and volatile. His counsel to President Kennedy in 1961 to emphasize domestic matters over events in Southeast Asia strongly implies that he would have advised also against sending Marines to Beirut in 1983, and soldiers or airmen to Somalia, Rwanda, Bosnia, Kosovo, or Darfur. An interesting issue for MacArthur would have been the nation's switch to an all-volunteer military force. His record suggests that he would have pronounced it acceptable for peacetime, but not for wartime. His reasoning on this context would have stressed not just or even mainly the need to muster overwhelming force to ensure victory, but the importance he placed in his reform of army education of maintaining a close relationship between the professional army and the civilian society it served. That relationship was much better served by conscription than by an all-enlistee force—of course, this is the council of "do as I say, not as I do."

He would have been a zealous advocate of advanced technology and quick to chide leaders who failed to use it. But he would also have stressed that changes in technology did not alter the fundamental principles of war. He would have been equally dismissive of Robert S. McNamara and Donald Rumsfeld.

Extracting MacArthur's views on the Middle East and the War on Terror from the complex matrix of his career and beliefs is a challenge. In his late life, he held the classic American "Jacksonian" view that war should be avoided unless vital stakes were at issue, but if it was worth waging war, then there was no acceptable policy short of applying overwhelming force in pursuit of long-term decisive goals. Prior to 1990, MacArthur would have opposed the introduction of American armed forces into any region he regarded as peripheral to American interests, which would have included the Middle East. But MacArthur would have seen a parallel between Korea in 1950 and Saddam Hussein's invasion of Kuwait in 1990. While he would have pointed out the danger of permitting the precedent of naked aggression to stand in the post–Cold War era, he would have attached considerably more emphasis to the strategic importance of oil to the economic advancement of Asia. MacArthur would have been outraged over any proposal that the war should end only with the liberation of Kuwait and not the removal of Saddam Hussein. He would have warned that the most telling analogy to Korea was that letting Saddam survive only guaranteed a greater problem in the future.

The direct attack on the United States on September 11, 2001, coupled with the ongoing threat to oil supplies vital to the economic health of Asia would have certainly found MacArthur advocating action. He would have pronounced it intolerable to permit the Taliban regime in Afghanistan to harbor Al Qaeda and supported the military effort to destroy the Taliban. But MacArthur would have asked, "Why stop at Afghanistan?" He would have pressed for measures against Iraq, Syria, and Iran as part of a comprehensive strategy. This in turn would probably have found his voice raised in favor of a much greater military mobilization than any political leader was likely to contemplate. While he would have admired the boldness and the technological dazzle of the drive to Baghdad in 2003, he would have been critical of the sparseness of American troops—though not for the reasons some might think. In victory he would urge a quiet magnanimous stance of American leaders toward the Iraqis—though had he been in command, he would not have been bashful about claiming more than his full share of credit.

Once the Taliban's power in Afghanistan was broken and Saddam Hussein was toppled, his views would have confounded the expectations of most Americans, historians not exempted, who would assume his advocacy of some American-run interregnum akin to the occupation of Japan. On the contrary, MacArthur's real and often reiterated opinion was that that all occupations end as dark pages in the history of the occupier and the occupied. He would have urged an immediate transition in a period measured in months, not years, to Afghan and Iraqi civil governments. All American combat forces would be withdrawn, apart from a modest and low-profile American mission the training and support role. But this overall design for Iraq would incorporate one major exception: the American army that removed Saddam would be regrouped immediately to the border of Syria for an immediate showdown with Damascus. MacArthur would have hoped that the threat of military action, following upon the spectacle of the collapse of Saddam's regime, would have provided the catalyst for regime change in both Syria and Iran without further military measures, but he would have been prepared to carry the war onward if these two regimes remained defiant. His most fundamental disagreements with the U.S. strategy after 2001 would not be as to the success of the tasks undertaken, but the failure to undertake still larger tasks.

The Australian commander Thomas Blamey tossed off a brilliantly succinct evaluation of MacArthur: "the best and the worst things you hear about him are both true."[3] It follows that MacArthur's legacy is destined to remain in eternal dispute, for it is too complex to admit of an unqualified answer. His great traits and achievements were real. So were his great flaws and failures. Most of the credit and onus for this rests with MacArthur, but his civilian and military superiors bear substantial responsibility for not managing MacArthur, so the balance sheet on his performance is far more heavily positive. His three great career summits leave a far richer casebook on leadership than any other American figure of the twentieth century, save for Franklin Roosevelt. The debate will roll on about MacArthur's virtues or lack thereof, but the question of whether he will continue to fascinate for generations is settled.

Notes

Chapter One

1. Clark Lee and Richard Henschel, *Douglas MacArthur* (New York: Henry Holt and Company, 1952), 9.
2. D. Clayton James, *The Years of MacArthur, vol., 1880–1941* (Boston: Houghton Mifflin Company, 1970) 7–66, 94 [hereafter James, vol. 1].
3. Ibid., 58–61, 67–84. The grip of FDR's mother is well known. For details about the strong grasp of Adlai Stevenson's mother see Porter McKeever, *Adlai Stevenson: His Life and Legacy* (New York: William Morrow and Company, Inc., 1989) 24–8, 30–2, 41.
4. Douglas MacArthur, *Reminiscences* (New York: McGraw-Hill Book Company, 1964) 19 [hereafter MacArthur, *Reminiscences*]; James, vol. 1, 30–43.
5. MacArthur, *Reminiscences,* 30–32; James, vol. 1, 85–109.
6. James, vol. 1, 110–115, 130–31.
7. Ibid., 115–127.
8. Edward M. Coffman, *The Regulars: The American Army, 1898–1941* (Cambridge: The Belknap Press of Harvard University, 2004) 193 [hereafter Coffman, *The Regulars*]; James, vol. 1, 130–5.
9. Timothy K. Nenninger, "American Military Effectiveness in the First World War," Allan R. Millett and Williamson Murray, eds., *American Military Effectiveness. Volume I: The First World War* (Boston: Unwin Hyman, 1988) 137–43; James, vol. 1, 148–50. For a usefully succinct compendium of facts about the AEF, see John F. Votaw, *Battle Orders No. 6: The American Expeditionary Forces in World War I* (Oxford: Osprey Publishing, 2005).
10. James, vol. 1, 155–9; Borch, Frederic L., III and William R. Westlake, *The Silver Star: A History of America's Third Highest Award for Combat Valor* (Tempe, AZ: Borch and Westlake Publishing, 2001) 1–3, 7–8, 10, 67, 240. I am indebted to John Lundstrom for illuminating the issues relating to the Silver Star Medal.
11. James, vol. 1, 158–9; MacArthur, *Reminiscences,* 55–56.
12. James, vol. 1, 165.
13. James, vol. 1, 156, 168–72, 239.
14. MacArthur, *Reminiscences,* 58; James, vol. 1, 174–81.
15. James, vol. 1, 183–95.
16. James, vol. 1, 198–201.

17. James, vol. 1, 201–10.
18. James, vol. 1, 211–12, 221–22; Alan Axelrod, *Patton* (New York: Palgrave Mcmillan, 2006) 55.
19. James, vol. 1, 214–217, 223.
20. James, vol. 1, 218–222, 224.
21. James, vol. 1, 224–37, 239–41.
22. James, vol. 1, 238.
23. James, vol. 1, 254–55.
24. James, vol. 1, 256; MacArthur, *Reminiscences,* 72.
25. Coffman, *The Regulars,* 226–27; James, vol. 1, 259–63.
26. James, vol. 1, 263–94.
27. Geoffrey Perret, *Old Soldiers Never Die* (New York: Random House, 1996) 124–27 [hereafter Perret, *Old Soldiers Never Die*]; James, vol. 1, 295–97, 320.
28. James, vol. 1, 300, 302–03.
29. James, vol. 1, 305–11.
30. James, vol. 1, 319–24; Perret, *Old Soldiers Never Die,* 168–69.
31. James, vol. 1, 325–31.

Chapter Two

1. D. Clayton James, *The Years of MacArthur, vol. 1, 1880–1941* (Boston: Houghton Mifflin Company, 1970) 340–45 [hereafter James, vol. 1].
2. *Ibid.,* 351–52, 354–55, 359–61 (including "Trained officers constitute the most vitally essential element " quote). I am indebted to Edward Drea for pointing out MacArthur's hugely important role in officer education.
3. James, vol. 1, 366–68.
4. James, vol. 1, 370–71.
5. Timothy K. Nenninger, "Organization Milestones in the Development of American Armor, 1920–40," and George F. Hoffman, "Army Doctrine and the Christie Tank: Failing to Exploit the Operational Level of War," in George F. Hoffman and Donn A. Starry, eds., *Camp Colt to Desert Storm: The History of U.S. Armored Forces* (Lexington: University Press of Kentucky, 1999) 43–46, 92–143; Ronald Specter, "The Military Effectiveness of the US Armed Forces, 1919–1939," Allan Millet and Williamson Murray, eds., *Military Effectiveness, Volume II: The Interwar Period* (Boston: Unwin Hyman, 1988) 82–3, 87, 90.
6. James, vol. 1, 376–78.
7. James. vol. 1, 352–53.
8. Stephen Ambrose, *Eisenhower: Soldier, General of the Army, President Elect, 1890–1952* (New York: Simon and Schuster, 1983), 92–93 [hereafter Ambrose, *Eisenhower*].
9. Carlo D'Este, *Eisenhower, A Soldier's Life* (New York: Henry Holt and Company, 2002), 226–28 [hereafter D'Este, *Eisenhower*].
10. Ambrose, *Eisenhower,* 93–95.
11. James, vol. I, 382–84.
12. James vol. 1, 384–7, 407.
13. James, vol. 1, 388–9.
14. James, vol. 1, 392–3.
15. James, vol. 1, 396–7.
16. James, vol. 1, 398–9.
17. James, vol. 1, 400–2; Paul Dickson and Thomas B. Allen, *The Bonus Army: An American Epic* (New York: Walker & Company, 2004) 179–80; Geoffrey Perret, *Old Soldiers Never Die* (New York: Random House, 1996) 159–60 {hereafter Perret, *Old Soldiers Never Die*]; D'Este, *Eisenhower,* 221–3. These sources conflict on whether MacArthur received Hoover's first order, but it seems clear that at a minimum, MacArthur knew or clearly sensed Hoover's intentions and violated them.

18. James, vol. 1, 408–11.
19. Rexford G. Tugwell, *The Democratic Roosevelt: A Biography of Franklin D. Roosevelt* (Garden City: Doubleday and Company, 1957) 348–51.
20. James, vol. 1, 416–23 (including the "a pleasant man" and "whatever the difference" quotes); Geoffrey Perret, *Old Soldiers Never Die* (New York: Random House, 1996), 164–5 [hereafter Perret, *Old Soldiers Never Die*].
21. MacArthur, *Reminiscences,* 101.
22. James, vol. 1, 431–35.
23. Michael Schaller, *Douglas MacArthur: The Far Eastern General* (New York Oxford University Press, 1989) 13–14, 18–20; Perret, *Old Soldiers Never Die* 147–9, 167–70.
24. James, vol. 1, 440–44.
25. James, vol. 1, 445–46.
26. James, vol. 1, 449–53.
27. Forrest C. Pogue, *George C. Marshall: Education of a General, 1880–1938* (New York, Viking Press 1963) 264–66.

Chapter Three

1. Louis Morton, *The United States Army in World War II, The Fall of the Philippines* (Washington D.C.: Office of the Chief of Military History, 1953), 4–5 [hereafter Morton, *The Fall of the Philippines*].
2. D. Clayton James, *The Years of MacArthur, vol. 1, 1880–1941* (Boston: Houghton Mifflin Company, 1970), 470–1; Morton, *The Fall of the Philippines*, 4.
3. James, vol. 1, 470–6; Ricardo Trota Jose, *The Philippine Army 1935–1942* (Manila: Ateneo do Manila University Press, 1992), 216 [hereafter Jose, *The Philippine Army*]
4. Richard B. Meixsel, "Manuel L. Quezon, Douglas MacArthur, and the Significance of the Military Mission to the Philippine Commonwealth," *Pacific Historical Review*, vol. 70, No. 2, 255–292. Meixsel's article builds upon other work and, with due allowances for the incomplete record, makes a strong case that Quezon and MacArthur shared a hidden agenda in creating the Philippine armed forces and the role of the military adviser. For the standard view, see James, vol. 1, 480–81, 493–94.
5. James, vol. 1, 484; Richard Meixsel, "A Uniform Story," *The Journal of Military History* 69 (July 2005), 791–800. Meixsel's excellent piece explains how the mythology of the purported "Field Marshal" uniform arose and spread. Both MacArthur's predecessor and successor as chief of staff also indulged in creating distinctive uniform items, as did another beneficiary of the special authority, General Pershing.
6. Morton, *The Fall of the Philippines,* 9–11; James, vol. 1, 485, 503–4.
7. Jose, *The Philippine Army,* 217–19; Morton, *The Fall of the Philippines,* 6, 10.
8. Jose, *The Philippine Army,* 218; Stephen Ambrose, *Eisenhower: Soldier, General of the Army, President Elect, 1890–1952* (New York: Simon and Schuster, 1983), 105 [hereafter Ambrose, *Eisenhower*]; James, vol. 1, 503, 514, 524, 527–29, 533–35, 543–45, 581, 608–9.
9. James, vol. 1, 531–34.
10. James, vol. 1, 535–39.
11. James, vol. 1, 494–5, 512–3, 555–6.
12. James, vol. 1, 571.
13. Ambrose, *Eisenhower,* 109–11; James, vol. 1, 504.
14. James, vol. 1, 561.
15. James, vol. 1, 565–69 (including "oasis of wit" quote).
16. James vol. 1, 521–26.
17. H. P. Willmott, *Empires in Balance* (Annapolis: Naval Institute Press, 1982) 124; James, vol. 1, 550–1.
18. William C. Bartsch, *December 8, 1941: MacArthur's Pearl Harbor* (College Station: Texas A&M University, 2003) Appendix C [hereafter Bartsch, *December 8, 1941*]; Morton, *The*

Fall of the Philippines, 42; James, vol. 1, 611–12. It was probably the 41st Infantry Division that just missed being sent to the Philippines and captivity. It was one of the first two divisions to join MacArthur in Australia. Exact aircraft strength in the Philippines in December 1941 remains disputed. I follow Bartsch's figures for B–17s and P–40Es.

19. Henry L. Stimson and McGeorge Bundy, *On Active Service in Peace and War* (New York: Harper & Brothers, 1948), 193.
20. James, vol. 1, 527–29, 614–15.
21. Willmott, *Empires in Balance,* 126; James, vol. 1, 546.
22. James, vol. 1, 597–600.
23. "Philippine Department, Plan Orange, 1940 Revision," Record Group 15, Box 49, Folder 4, MacArthur Memorial Archive; Morton, *The Fall of the Philippines,* 26–27; James, vol. 1, 600–601.
24. Morton, *The Fall of the Philippines,* 28–30.
25. Richard B. Meixsel, "Major General George Grunert, WPO–3, and the Philippine Army, 1940–41," *Journal of Military History* (April 1995), 303–24.
26. Morton, *The Fall of the Philippines,* 64–75; James, vol. 1, 595–96, 603–4, 607.
27. Austin Hoyt, Public Broadcasting System, *The American Experience: MacArthur* (Boston: WBGH Educational Foundation, 1999).

Chapter Four

1. Louis Morton, *The United States Army in World War II, The Fall of the Philippines* (Washington D.C.: Office of the Chief of Military History, 1953), 90 [hereafter Morton, *The Fall of the Philippines*]; D. Clayton James, *The Years of MacArthur, vol. 2, 1941–1945* (Boston: Houghton Mifflin Company, 1975), 2, 7–15 [hereafter James, vol. 2]. U.S. casualties ran on the order of 87 killed and 148 wounded and thus born no comparison to the over 2,400 deaths at Pearl Harbor.
2. William C. Bartsch, *December 8, 1941: MacArthur's Pearl Harbor* (College Station: Texas A&M University, 2003) [hereafter Bartsch, *December 8, 1941*] is by far the best study of these events. I respectfully differ with Bartsch on the prospective effect of MacArthur's B–17s had they survived the attack. As to MacArthur's belief that only carrier fighters could provide escorts over central Luzon, see Letter, MacArthur to Marshall, 1 December 1941, Box 2, Folder 1, RG 2, MacArthur Memorial Archive [hereafter MMA].
3. Morton, *The Fall of the Philippines,* 89; H. P. Willmott, *Empires in Balance* (Annapolis: Naval Institute Press, 1982) 186 [hereafter Willmott, *Empires in Balance*].
4. Morton, *The Fall of the Philippines,* 21–30, 47, 49.
5. Morton, *The Fall of the Philippines,* 125–26.
6. James, vol. 2, pp. 16–22.
7. James, vol. 2, 23–26, 831; D. Clayton James, Oral History Collection, Col. Joseph L. Chabot, Cox 1, RG 49, MMA.
8. Willmott, *Empires in Balance,* 208–10.
9. James vol. 2, 28–37.
10. Morton, *The Fall of the Philippines,* 265–346; James, vol. 2, pp. 46–49, 55–60.
11. Willmott, *Empires in Balance,* 369, 383–84.
12. James, vol. 2, 71–76.
13. Louis Morton, *U.S. Army in World War II, The Pacific War, Strategy and Command: The First Two Years* (Washington: Office of the Chief of Military History, 1962) 158–64 [hereafter Morton, *Strategy and Command: The First Two Years*]; President Franklin D. Roosevelt, Proclamation, December 28, 1941, Box 2, Folder 1, RG 2, MMA.
14. Stephen Ambrose, *Eisenhower: Soldier, General of the Army, President Elect, 1890–1952* (New York: Simon and Schuster, 1983), 133–34 [hereafter Ambrose, *Eisenhower*]; Diary of Henry R. Stimson, February 2, 1942, Yale University Library.

15. Morton, *Strategy and Command: The First Two Years,* 190–91; James vol. 2, 91–97.
16. James, vol. 2, pp. 98–100.
17. James, vol. 2, 100–6; 141–43.
18. James, vol. 2, 101–9.
19. Willmott, *Empires In Balance,* 395.
20. Willmott, *Empires in Balance,* 233–34; Morton, *The Fall of the Philippines,* 57.
21. James vol. 2, 89–90.
22. Carol Petillo, *Douglas MacArthur: The Philippine Years* (Bloomington: Indiana University Press, 1981), 204–11, 230; Geoffrey Perret, *Old Soldiers Never Die* (New York: Random House, 1996), 271–73. The officers involved besides MacArthur and the sums received were Sutherland ($75,000) Richard J. Marshall ($45,000) and Sidney I. Huff ($20,000). Petillo made this shocking discovery; Perret provides what can be said in defense of MacArthur. It is perhaps also arguable that Roosevelt and Stimson viewed the sum as a sort of quiet retirement bonus, but I believe by the date they approved the payment they had ample reason to believe MacArthur would not go quietly away.

Chapter Five

1. D. Clayton James, *The Years of MacArthur, vol. 2, 1941–1945* (Boston: Houghton Mifflin Company, 1975), 129–32 [hereafter James, vol. 2].
2. Clark Lee and Richard Henschell, *Douglas MacArthur* (New York: Henry Holt and Company, 1952) 160. James, vol. 2, 136.
3. James, vol. 2, 133–40.
4. Barrett Tillman and Henry Sakaida, "Silver Star Airplane Ride," *Naval History,* April 2001, 25; Borch, Frederic L., III and William R. Westlake, *The Silver Star: A History of America's Third Highest Award for Combat Valor* (Tempe, AZ: Borch and Westlake Publishing, 2001), 1–3, 7–8, 10, 67, 240. A number of reputable historians have accepted accounts provided by a few aging survivors alleging Johnson's plane was attacked. Every reputable aviation historian I know who really understands and actually has examined the records finds this grossly implausible. The recollections at best probably represent the sort of intermingling of multiple unrelated events typical of distant memory.
5. Louis Morton, *U.S. Army in World War II, The Pacific War, Strategy and Command: The First Two Years* (Washington: Office of the Chief of Military History, 1962) 240–56 [hereafter Morton, *Strategy and Command: The First Two Years*]; James, vol. 2, 116–23.
6. Samuel Milner, *U.S. Army in World War II, The War in the Pacific: Victory in Papua* (Washington: Officer of the Chief of Military History, 1957), 21–23 [hereafter Milner, *Victory in Papua*]; James, vol. 2, 86–87.
7. Edward J. Drea, *MacArthur's Ultra: Codebreaking and the War Against Japan, 1942–45* (Lawrence: University Press of Kansas, 1992), 20–26, 62 [hereafter Drea, *MacArthur's Ultra*]. This is an indispensable source in understanding MacArthur's campaigns in World War II.
8. Morton, *The Fall of the Philippines,* 405–67, 471–97, 520–84.
9. John Lundstrom, *Black Shoe Carrier Admiral* (Annapolis: Naval Institute Press, 2006), 154–217.
10. Richard B. Frank, *Guadalcanal* (New York: Random House, 1990), 32–35 [hereafter Frank, *Guadalcanal*].
11. Frank, *Guadalcanal,* 33–34.
12. W. David Lewis, *Eddie Rickenbacker: An American Hero of the Twentieth Century* (Baltimore: The Johns Hopkins University Press, 2005), 414–15, 443–44.
13. Frank, *Guadalcanal,* 21–25, 43–44, 598–99.
14. SWPA MIS Daily Intelligence Summaries, July to October 1942, Folders 1–3, Box 26, RG 3, MacArthur Memorial Archive; Milner, *Victory in Papua,* 56–91; Drea, *MacArthur's*

    Ultra, 40–42; David Horner, *Blamey: The Commander-in-Chief* (Sydney: Allen & Unwin, 1998), 320 [hereafter Horner, *Blamey*].

15. Horner, *Blamey,* 320–38; Dudley McCarthy, *Australia in the War of 1939–1945, Series One, Army, Vol. V, Southwest Pacific Area, First Year: Kokoda to Wau* (Canberra: Australian War Memorial, 1959), 108–11.

16. Milner, *Victory in Papua,* 204; James, vol. 2, 265; Horner, *Blamey,* 339–84.

17. Milner, *Victory In Papua,* 205–364.

18. Perret, *Old Soldiers Never Die,* 325; Milner, *Victory in Papua,* 369–72; James, vol. 2, 267–71; Frank, *Guadalcanal,* 613.

Chapter Six

1. William Manchester, *American Caesar, Douglas MacArthur 1880–1964* (Boston: Atlantic, Little and Company, 1978) 279.

2. Robert W. Coakley and Richard M. Leighton, *The U.S. Army in World War II, The War Department, Global Logistics and Strategy 1943–45* (Washington D.C. Center of Military History, 1986), 494–99 [hereafter Coakley and Leighton, *Global Logistics and Strategy 1943–45*].

3. Col. John Lada, Editor in Chief, *Medical Department, Department of the Army, Medical Statistics for World War II* (Washington, D.C.: U.S. Government Printing Office, 1975), 27, 71 [hereafter Lada, *Medical Statistics for World War II*]. In rates per thousand men per year, disease admissions in MacArthur's command averaged 807 from 1942 to 1945. For the European theater it was 464; the continental United States, 598; and Pacific Ocean Area, 523. The Middle East and Africa was the worst, at 917. The annualized disease death rate was 1.035 in the Southwest Pacific, compared to .551 in Europe.

4. Mary Ellen Condon-Rall and Albert E. Cowdrey, *The United States Army in World War II, The Medical Department: Medical Service in the War Against Japan* (Washington, D.C.: Center of Military History, United States Army, 1998), 253–54, 256–58 [hereafter Condon-Rall and Cowdrey, *Medical Service in the War Against Japan*].

5. D. Clayton James, *The Years of MacArthur, vol. 2, 1941–1945* (Boston: Houghton Mifflin Company, 1975), 354–56 [hereafter James, vol. 2].

6. Condon-Rall and Cowdrey, *Medical Service in the War Against Japan,* 264.

7. Geoffrey Perret, *There's a War to Be Won* (New York: Random House, 1991), 447–455; Robert R. Palmer, Bell I. Wiley, and William R. Keast, *The United States Army in World War II, The Procurement and Training of Ground Combat Troops* (Washington, D.C.: Office of the Chief of Military History, 1948), 489–93; Shelby L. Stanton, *Order of Battle: U.S. Army, World War II* (Novato, CA: Presidio, 1985).

8. David Horner, "The ANZAC Contribution," *The Pacific War Companion: From Pearl Harbor to Hiroshima* (Oxford: Osprey Publishing, 2005), 143–57.

9. Samuel Eliot Morison, *History of United States Naval Operations in World War II, vol. VIII, New Guinea and the Marianas, March 1944 to August 1944* (Boston: Little, Brown, and Company, 1964), 47–48.

10. Steve Birdsall, *The Flying Buccaneers: The Illustrated Story of Kenny's Fifth Air Force* (Garden City: Doubleday & Company, Inc., 1977) 184. The Far East Air Forces was in operation provisionally from June 15, 1944.

11. Kenn C. Rust, *The Fifth Air Force Story in World War II* (Temple City, CA: Historical Aviation Album Publication, 1973), 6; Kenn C. Rust and Dana Bell, *The Thirteenth Air Force Story in World War II* (Temple City (CA): Historical Aviation Album Publication, 1981) 4. The 22nd Bomb Group initially flew B–26 medium bombers before converting to B–24 heavy bombers.

12. Coakley and Leighton, *Global Logistics and Strategy, 1940–43,* 496–503; James, vol. 2, p. 174.

13. James, vol. 2, 469–70.

14. D. Clayton James, *The Years of MacArthur, vol. 3, Triumph & Disaster 1945–1964* (Boston: Houghton Mifflin Company, 1985) 657.
15. Forrest C. Pogue, *George C. Marshall: Organizer of Victory 1943–45* (New York: The Viking Press, 1973) 168, n626 (quote from Marshall); Samuel Eliot Morison, *History of United States Naval Operations in World War II, vol. VI, Breaking the Bismarcks Barrier* (Boston: Little, Brown, and Company, 1964), 32; Gerald E. Wheeler, *Kinkaid of the Seventh Fleet: A Biography of Admiral Thomas C. Kinkaid* (Washington: Naval Historical Center, 1995), 343–49 [hereafter Wheeler, *Kinkaid*]; Paolo E. Coletta, "Daniel E. Barbey: Amphibious Warfare Expert," William Leary, ed., *We Shall Return! MacArthur's Commanders and the Defeat of Japan 1942–45* (Lexington: University of Kentucky, 1988) 208–243 [hereafter Leary, *We Shall Return!*]; Thomas Buell, *Master of Sea Power: A Biography of Fleet Admiral Ernest J. King* (Boston: Little, Brown and Company, 1980), 197, 219, 320. Kinkaid was the losing commander at the Battle of the Santa Cruz Islands in October 1942. Halsey believed Kinkaid displayed faulty leadership in the Naval Battle of Guadalcanal in November 1942 and effectively relieved him. Kinkaid's availability, more than talent, got him subsequent jobs first in the Aleutians and then with MacArthur. He failed to take adequate measures to meet the Japanese at Leyte Gulf, negligently exposed an escort carrier group, and then grossly failed the survivors. It was subordinates, not Kinkaid, who arranged the belated rescue which cost many lives.
16. Herman C. Wolk, "George C. Kenney, MacArthur's Premier Airman," Leary, *We Shall Return!*, 88–117; Donald Goldstein, "Ennis C. Whitehead, Aerial Tactician," Leary, *We Shall Return!*, 178–207; James, vol. 2, 197–201; Geoffrey Perret, *Old Soldiers Never Die* (New York: Random House, 1996), 302–4 [hereafter Perret, *Old Soldiers Never Die*].
17. Horner, *Blamey,* 296, 305 (the quote from Curtin), 526 (the quote from Rankin); David Horner, "Blamey and MacArthur, The Problems of Coalition Warfare," Leary, *We Shall Return!*, 23–59; James vol. 2, 265–66. For an example of the type of scorn heaped upon Blamey (and MacArthur) in more recent histories, see Jack Galloway, *The Odd Couple: Blamey and MacArthur At War* (Queensland: University of Queensland Press, 2000).
18. Perret, *Old Soldiers Never Die,* 335–37, William M. Leary, "Walter Krueger, MacArthur's Fighting General," Leary, *We Shall Return!*, 60–87.
19. Jay Luvaas and John F. Shortal, "Robert L. Eichelberger, MacArthur's Fireman," Leary, *We Shall Return!*, 155–77.
20. Mark A. Stoler, *Allies and Adversaries: The Joint Chiefs of Staff, The Grand Alliance, and U.S. Strategy in World War II* (Chappell Hill: University of North Carolina Press, 2000), 84–102.

Chapter Seven

1. Louis Morton, *U.S. Army in World War II, The Pacific War, Strategy and Command: The First Two Years* (Washington: Office of the Chief of Military History, 1962), 364–411 [hereafter Morton, *Strategy and Command: The First Two Years*]; Edward J. Drea, *MacArthur's Ultra: Codebreaking and the War Against Japan, 1942–45* (Lawrence: University Press of Kansas, 1992), 63, 67–72 [hereafter Drea, *MacArthur's Ultra*].
2. William F. Halsey and Joseph Bryan III, *Admiral Halsey's Story* (New York: Whittlesey House, McGraw-Hill, 1947) 154–55.
3. John Miller, Jr., *The United States Army in World War II, The War in the Pacific, Cartwheel: The Reduction of Rabaul* (Washington: Officer of the Chief of Military History, 1959), 15, 26, 45–47 [hereafter Miller, *Cartwheel: The Reduction of Rabaul*].
4. Ibid., 67–188; Samuel Eliot Morison, *History of United States Naval Operations in World War II, vol. VI, Breaking the Bismarcks Barrier* (Boston: Little, Brown & Company, 1964), 138–224 [hereafter Morison, *Breaking the Bismarcks Barrier*].
5. Morison, *Breaking the Bismarcks Barrier,* 225–27.
6. Morison, *Breaking the Bismarck Barrier,* 225–39; Miller, *Cartwheel: The Reduction of Rabaul,* 172–84.

7. Miller, *Cartwheel: The Reduction of Rabaul*, 189–96; David Horner, *Blamey: The Commander-in-Chief* (Sydney: Allen & Unwin, 1998), 408 [hereafter Horner, *Blamey*]; Drea, *MacArthur's Ultra*, 79–84.

8. Miller, *Cartwheel: The Reduction of Rabaul*, 198–99; Drea, *MacArthur's Ultra*, 84–85.

9. Morison, *Breaking the Bismarcks Barrier*, 259–60; Miller, *Cartwheel: The Reduction of Rabaul*, 200.

10. David Dexter, *Australia in the War of 1939–1945, Series One, Army*, vol. VI, *The New Guinea Offensives* (Canberra: Australian War Memorial, 1961), 328–29, 332, 365 [hereafter Dexter, *The New Guinea Offensives*]; Morison, *Breaking the Bismarcks Barrier*, 262, 265–66.

11. Dexter, *The New Guinea Offensives*, 338–40; Miller, *Cartwheel: The Reduction of Rabaul*, 207–11.

12. Dexter, *The New Guinea Offensives*, 339.

13. John R. Galvin, *Air Assault: The Development of Airmobile Warfare* (New York: Hawthorne Books, Inc., 1969), 109–18.

14. Dexter, *The New Guinea Offensives*, 351–57.

15. Ibid., 363–65, 370–71, 377, 385–86, 386–89.

16. Ibid., 391–92; Drea, *MacArthur's Ultra*, 85.

17. Miller, *Cartwheel: The Reduction of Rabaul*, 212–16; Drea, *MacArthur's Ultra*, 86–87.

18. Miller, *Cartwheel: The Reduction of Rabaul*, 217–21.

19. Morison, *Breaking the Bismarcks Barrier*, 279–349, 392–409; Miller, *Cartwheel: The Reduction of Rabaul*, 222–71, 351–78.

20. Morison, *Breaking the Bismarcks Barrier*, 389–91; Miller, *Cartwheel: The Reduction of Rabaul*, 272–305; Drea, *MacArthur's Ultra*, 91–92.

Chapter Eight

1. Edward J. Drea, *MacArthur's Ultra: Codebreaking and the War Against Japan, 1942–45* (Lawrence: University Press of Kansas, 1992), 62, 92–93 [hereafter Drea, *MacArthur's Ultra*].

2. D. Clayton James, *The Years of MacArthur, vol. 2, 1941–1945* (Boston: Houghton Mifflin Company, 1975), 443–45 (including "lousy" quote) [hereafter James, vol. 2]; Drea, *MacArthur's Ultra*, 96–98.

3. Roger Olaf Egeberg, M.D., *The General: MacArthur and the Man He Called "Doc"* (New York: Hippocrene Books, 1983), 28–33, 154–57.

4. John Miller, Jr., *The United States Army in World War II, The War in the Pacific, Cartwheel: The Reduction of Rabaul* (Washington: Officer of the Chief of Military History, 1959), 316–50 [hereafter Miller, *Cartwheel: The Reduction of Rabaul*]; Drea, *MacArthur's Ultra*, 98–104.

5. Drea, *MacArthur's Ultra*, 104–06; Robert Ross Smith, *The United States Army in World War II, The War in the Pacific, The Approach to the Philippines* (Washington, D.C.: Office of the Chief of Military History, 1953), 9–12 [hereafter Smith, *The Approach to the Philippines*].

6. Smith, *The Approach to the Philippines*, 29–32.

7. Drea, *MacArthur's Ultra*, 106.

8. Smith, *The Approach to the Philippines*, 208–212; James, vol. 2, 455.

9. Drea, *MacArthur's Ultra*, 135–37.

10. Smith, *The Approach to the Philippines*, 212–279; Drea *MacArthur's Ultra*, 133–34.

11. James vol. 2, 458–61; Drea, *MacArthur's Ultra*, 135–37; Smith, *The Approach to the Philippines*, 280–396. I am indebted to Edward Drea for sharing a copy of his forthcoming article, "Biak: A Tale of Two Commanders," which reveals the actual evolution of Japanese defense plans on Biak.

12. James, vol. 2, 461–63; Drea, *MacArthur's Ultra*, 139–41.

13. Drea, *MacArthur's Ultra*, 134, 141–42; James, vol. 2, 463–64; Smith, *The Approach to the Philippines*, 397–424.
14. Drea, *MacArthur's Ultra*, 142–43; James, vol. 2, 464–65; Smith, *The Approach to the Philippines*, 425–49.
15. James, vol. 2, 464; Drea, *MacArthur's Ultra*, 143; Edward J. Drea, *In Service of the Emperor: Essays on the Imperial Japanese Army* (Lincoln: University of Nebraska Press, 1998) 91–109.
16. Drea, *MacArthur's Ultra*, 147–51; Smith, *The Approach to the Philippines*, 103–205.
17. James, vol. 2, 408.
18. James, vol. 2, 403–40; Geoffrey Perret, *Old Soldiers Never Die* (New York: Random House, 1996), 383–89.

Chapter Nine

1. Samuel Eliot Morison, *History of United States Naval Operations in World War II, vol. XII, Leyte: June 1944–January 1945* (Boston: Little Brown and Company, 1963), 9–10 [hereafter Morison, *Leyte*].
2. Grace Pearson. Hayes, *The History of the Joint Chiefs of Staff in World War II: The War Against Japan*, (Annapolis: Naval Institute Press, 1982) 543–68, 603–24 [hereafter Hayes, *History of the Joint Chiefs of Staff*] ; M. Hamlin Cannon, *The United States Army in World War II, The War in the Pacific, Leyte: The Return to the Philippines*, Washington, D.C.: Office of the Chief of Military History, 1954), 1–9 [hereafter Cannon, *Leyte*]; Edward J. Drea, *MacArthur's Ultra: Codebreaking and the War Against Japan, 1942–45* (Lawrence: University Press of Kansas, 1992), 153 [hereafter Drea, *MacArthur's Ultra*]; Morison, *Leyte*, 19–25.
3. Morison, *Leyte*, 65–73.
4. Drea, *MacArthur's Ultra*, 152–59
5. Cannon, *Leyte*, 60–84; D. Clayton James, *The Years of MacArthur, vol. 2, 1941–1945* (Boston: Houghton Mifflin Company, 1975), 552–58 [hereafter James, vol. 2].
6. Cannon, *Leyte*, 35–36, 45–53, 85–102, 185–88, 306–8.
7. Drea, *MacArthur's Ultra*, 163–69, 178; Morison, *Leyte*, 159–338.
8. Morison, *Leyte*, 339–360.
9. Drea, *MacArthur's Ultra*, 168–73.
10. James, vol. 2, 585–56.
11. Cannon, *Leyte*, 367–70; Drea, *MacArthur's Ultra*, 178.
12. Hayes, *History of the Joint Chiefs of Staff*, 620–624; Robert Ross Smith, *The United States Army in World War II, The War in the Pacific, Triumph in the Philippines* (Washington, D.C.: Office of the Chief of Military History, 1978 reprint), 43–53 [hereafter Smith, *Triumph in the Philippines*].
13. Drea, *MacArthur's Ultra*, 186–87.
14. Smith, *Triumph in the Philippines*, 22–25; Gerald E. Wheeler, *Kinkaid of the Seventh Fleet: A Biography of Admiral Thomas C. Kinkaid* (Washington: Naval Historical Center, 1995), 409–13.
15. James, vol. 2, 589–91.
16. Drea, *MacArthur's Ultra*, 189–91; Smith, *Triumph in the Philippines*, 73–84.
17. Drea, *MacArthur's Ultra*, 192–96; Smith, *Triumph in the Philippines*, 85–87, 139–43; James, vol. 2, 623–31.
18. Drea, *MacArthur's Ultra*, 193–95; Smith, *Triumph in the Philippines*, 217, 222–24; Roger Olaf Egeberg, M.D., *The General: MacArthur and the Man He Called "Doc"* (New York: Hippocrene Books, 1983), 115–16, 122–23, 135–36; James, vol. 2, 639–40; Douglas MacArthur, *Reminiscences* (New York: McGraw-Hill Book Company, 1964), 247–48.
19. Smith, *Triumph in the Philippines*, 237–307; Richard Cannaughton, John Pimlott, Duncan Anderson, *The Battle for Manila* (Novato, CA: Presidio, 1995), 172–76, 195–96.

20. Carol Petillo, *Douglas MacArthur: The Philippine Years* (Bloomington: Indiana University Press, 1981), 227–30; James, vol. 2, 691–700.
21. James, vol. 2, 670–81; Smith, *Triumph in the Philippines,* 167–210.
22. Smith, *Triumph in the Philippines,* 335–50; Drea, *MacArthur's Ultra,* 199.

Chapter Ten

1. Robert Ross Smith, *The United States Army in World War II, The War in the Pacific, Triumph in the Philippines* (Washington, D.C.: Office of the Chief of Military History, 1978 reprint), 449–579 [hereafter Smith, *Triumph in the Philippines*]Smith, *Triumph in the Philippines,* 449–579; D. Clayton James, *The Years of MacArthur, vol. 2, 1941–1945* (Boston: Houghton Mifflin Company, 1975), 686–88 [hereafter James, vol. 2].
2. James, vol. 2, 737–38. Geoffrey Perret argues that President Roosevelt made a pledge to liberate all of the Philippines in December 1941, but his language was ambiguous as to whether he promised to liberate them before the end of the war. *Old Soldiers Never Die* (New York: Random House, 1996), 463.
3. James, vol. 2, 642–43, 697, 738–39.
4. Smith, *Triumph in the Philippines,* 583–648; Samuel Eliot Morison, *History of United States Naval Operations in World War II, vol. XIII, Liberation of the Philippines* (Boston: Little Brown and Company, 1965) 213–51; Edward J. Drea, *MacArthur's Ultra: Codebreaking and the War Against Japan, 1942–45* (Lawrence: University Press of Kansas, 1992), 200–01 [hereafter Drea, *MacArthur's Ultra*]; James, vol. 2, 740.
5. Smith, *Triumph in the Philippines,* 651–58; James, vol. 2, 690.
6. James, vol. 2, 702–05; David Horner, *Blamey: The Commander-in-Chief* (Sydney: Allen & Unwin, 1998), 510–29 [hereafter Horner, *Blamey*].
7. James, vol. 2, 713–15 (including "my purpose in projecting this campaign" quote), 751–57; Horner, *Blamey,* 529–42.
8. James, vol. 2, 710–17; Horner, *Blamey,* 517–18.
9. Richard B. Frank, *Downfall: The End of the Imperial Japanese Empire* (New York, Random House, 1999) 33–34 [hereafter Frank, *Downfall*]; James, vol. 2, 763–67.
10. Frank, *Downfall,* 34–37.
11. Sixth Army Field Order No. 74, July 28, 1945, Center for Military History, Washington, D.C.
12. Frank, *Downfall,* 117–18, 140–41.
13. Ibid., 81–86.
14. "Magic" Far East Summary, April 1 to August 15, 1945, Entry 9001, RG 457, NARA; Joint Intelligence Committee, Japanese Reaction to an Assault on the Sendai Plain, J.I.C. 218/10, August 10, 1945 (final revision August 20, 1945). Geographic File 1942–45, CCS 381 Honshu (7–19–44) Section 4, Record Group 218, National Archives and Records Administration, Washington, D.C. [hereafter NARA].
15. "Magic" Far East Summaries, July 19, 1945, August 9, 1945.
16. SRMD–008, p. 266, July 16, 1945, p. 297, August 13, 1945, RG 457, NARA.
17. United States Strategic Bombing Survey, Report No. 62, Military Analysis Division, *Japanese Air Power* (Washington, D.C.: U.S. Government, 1946), pp. 24–25, 70. For a discussion of the various numbers offered concerning Japanese air strength in the homeland see Frank, *Downfall,* 182–83 and notes.
18. General Headquarters, United States Army Forces Pacific, Military Intelligence Section, General Staff, "Amendment No. 1 to G–2 Estimate of the Enemy Situation with Respect to Kyushu," July 29, 1945, p. 1, Gen. John J. Tolson Papers, United States Army Military History Institute, Carlisle, Pennsylvania (A copy is also in Record Group 4, Box 22, MacArthur Memorial Archive).
19. Frank, *Downfall,* 273–77.
20. Ibid., 322–24, 357–60.

21. James, vol. 2, 763–67.
22. James, vol. 2, 728–30.
23. James, vol. 2, 776–85; Frank, *Downfall*, 296–99, 308–12, 315–22, 326–30.
24. James, vol. 2, 790.
25. James, vol. 2, 786–92.
26. Typical is the claim by one biographer that MacArthur's casualties from Buna onwards were fewer than those in the Battle of Bulge alone. William Manchester, *American Caesar: Douglas MacArthur, 1880–1964* (New York: Dell Books, 1978), 4.
27. *The History of the Medical Department of the United States Navy in World War II: The Statistics of Disease and Injury,* NAVmed P–1318, Vol. 3, United States Navy, Government Printing Office, 1950, 171–74 [hereafter *The Statistics of Disease and Injury*]. On page 84, this same document gives slightly lower totals of 54,863 casualties and 29,263 deaths. The difference seems to be omission in the latter of some Pacific-area losses not specifically linked to one of the battles or campaigns.
28. Richard B. Frank, "Pacific Battle Casualties and the MacArthur Myth," *Armchair General Magazine,* June/July 2006, 93. For the record, losses among army and Marine Corps personnel in the operations in the Solomon and Bismarck Islands post-Guadalcanal under MacArthur totaled 11,891 including 3,355 deaths.
29. Ibid.
30. Ibid., 94.
31. Statistical and Accounting Branch, Office of the Adjutant General, *Army Battle Casualties and Nonbattle Deaths in World War II, Final Report, 7 December 1946,* 92–93 [hereafter *Battle Casualties and Nonbattle Deaths in World War II*].
32. *The Statistics of Disease and Injury,* 84.
33. U.S. Army losses during the Papua Campaign were 343 battle deaths among a total of 947 casualties. Of these numbers, ground forces sustained 239 battle deaths and 817 casualties. Air units lost 104 dead among 130 total battle casualties. Australian losses during this campaign totaled 5,698 casualties, among them 2,165 dead and missing. Samuel Milner, *U.S. Army in World War II, The War in the Pacific: Victory in Papua* (Washington: Officer of the Chief of Military History, 1957), 370. Thus, the total for the Kokoda-Buna-Gona campaign was 6,645 casualties and 2,508 dead. Army casualties on Guadalcanal totaled 1,434, including 712 deaths. Of the casualties, there were 150 deaths among 166 casualties in air units. *Army Battle Casualties and Nonbattle Deaths in World War II,* 94. Marine Corps casualties on Guadalcanal totaled 3,868, including 988 deaths. *The Statistics of Disease and Injury,* 171. This would give total casualties in non-naval combat at Guadalcanal as 5,292, with exactly 1,700 deaths. (My research showed that ground losses among army and Marine Corps personnel came to 1,769. Frank, *Guadalcanal,* 614). The Papua campaign therefore resulted in about 1,353 more casualties and at least 808 more deaths than parallel losses on Guadalcanal. Other sources reflect somewhat different numbers for Australian losses on Papua and Marine Corps losses on Guadalcanal, but the basic point that there were substantially more casualties, and particularly deaths, in Papua holds.
34. John Dower, *War Without Mercy: Race and Power in the Pacific War* (New York: Pantheon, 1986), 297.

Chapter Eleven

1. While there is a vast library of publications on the occupation, I found D. Clayton James, *The Years of MacArthur, vol. 3, Triumph & Disaster 1945–1964* (Boston: Houghton Mifflin Company, 1985) [hereafter James, vol. 3]; Eiji Takemae, *Inside GHQ: The Allied Occupation of Japan and Its Legacy* (New York: Continuum, 2002) [hereafter Takemae, *Inside GHQ, Inside GHQ*]; and John W. Dower, *Embracing Defeat: Japan in the Wake of World War II* (New York: W.W. Norton & Company, 1999) [hereafter Dower, *Embracing Defeat*] the most comprehensive and soundest in overall judgment. For the rug story see James, vol. 3, 59–60.

2. Geoffrey Perret, *Old Soldiers Never Die* (New York: Random House, 1996), 488 (with the "interesting tidbits" quote) [hereafter Perret, *Old Soldiers Never Die*]; James, vol. 3, 61–62.

3. James, vol. 3, 36, 43–44, 50–55, 60–67; Takemae, *Inside GHQ,* 65–67, 96–99, 174–75.

4. Takemae, *Inside GHQ,* 76–79, 105, 405–09 (including "the general's most noble" quote); James, vol. 3, 153–56 (including the "Give me bread" quote); Richard B. Frank, *Downfall: The End of the Imperial Japanese Empire* (New York, Random House, 1999) 350–52 [hereafter Frank, *Downfall*].

5. Takemae, *Inside GHQ,* 192, 425; James, vol. 3, 47, 276–79.

6. Robert P. Newman, *Truman and the Hiroshima Cult,* (East Lansing: Michigan State University Press, 1995), 134–39; Takemae, *Inside GHQ,* 243–54; James, vol. 3, 93–105. The Soviets could only chose their war criminal defendants from approximately 500,000 Japanese soldiers and the only senior officers were from the Manchuria based Kwantung Army. This makes their record of war crimes trials extraordinary, quite apart from the ratio of executions to trials.

7. Takemae, *Inside GHQ,* 222, 256–60 (including quotes from January 25, 1946 message); James, vol. 3, 105.

8. SRH–090, 16–19, Record Group 457, National Archives and Records Administration; Edward J. Drea, *MacArthur's Ultra: Codebreaking and the War Against Japan, 1942–45* (Lawrence: University Press of Kansas, 1992), 225. Due to the extreme secrecy surrounding ULTRA, linking retention of the emperor to the Imperial Navy message confirming his role in the surrender must remain a speculation as Drea notes. But at the September 1945 meeting with Hirohito, MacArthur's comments can be read as demonstrating his confidence about the real role the emperor played in the surrender. It is easy to believe that confidence stemmed form the ULTRA intercept.

9. James, vol. 3, 77–78, 87–91.

10. Takemae, *Inside GHQ,* 110–13; Dower, *Embracing Defeat,* 51–58.

11. James, vol. 3, 11–15; Takemae, *Inside GHQ,* 104–5.

12. James, vol. 3, 17–21; Takemae, *Inside GHQ,* 61–64.

13. Takemae, *Inside GHQ,* 73; James, vol. 3, 275.

14. Dower, *Embracing Defeat,* 292–97; James, vol. 3, 320–23; Takemae, *Inside GHQ,* 235–36. The emperor's interpreter wrote down a record after the meeting that is presumably the most reliable account. It contains no passage that sounds like the emperor took responsibility for the war. Dower makes the fair point that the photograph also conveyed the message that MacArthur would work with the emperor.

15. James, vol. 3, 114–16; Takemae, *Inside GHQ,* 236–40.

16. James, vol. 3, 117.

17. James, vol. 3, 119–39; Takemae, *Inside GHQ,* 270–92. An extremely clever SCAP lawyer and "flaming New Dealer," Charles Kades, prepared an opinion that MacArthur had the authority to intervene to change the Japanese constitution. But Takemae is correct that MacArthur had orders to the contrary. Even if he thought he had authority, in such circumstances he should have asked Washington first.

18. James, vol. 3, 143–46.

Chapter Twelve

1. Eiji Takemae, *Inside GHQ: The Allied Occupation of Japan and Its Legacy* (New York: Continuum, 2002), 307–8 [hereafter Takemae, *Inside GHQ*].

2. D. Clayton James, *The Years of MacArthur, vol. 3, Triumph & Disaster 1945–1964* (Boston: Houghton Mifflin Company, 1985) 183–91 [hereafter James, vol. 3]; Takemae, *Inside GHQ,* 339–46.

3. James, vol. 3, 174–183;

4. Takemae, *Inside GHQ,* 334–39; James, vol. 3, 165–74.

5. Takemae, *Inside GHQ* 348–71; James, vol. 3, 295–300.

6. James, vol.3, 193–217.
7. James, vol. 3, 221–29.
8. James, vol. 3, 232–35.
9. Takemae, *Inside GHQ,* 457, 473
10. James, vol. 3, 229–31, 233, 238–40, 458–59; Takemae, *Inside GHQ,* 469.
11. James, vol. 3, 330–32; Takemae, *Inside GHQ,* 469 (including ""impact on the Japanese during the occupation" quote), 485. James provides these figures: 1950, 184 million; 1951, 592 million, 1952 824 million, 1953 806 million.
12. James, vol. 3, 477–78
13. Takemae, *Inside GHQ,* 483.
14. Takemae, *Inside GHQ* 468–76; John W. Dower, *Embracing Defeat: Japan in the Wake of World War II* (New York: W.W. Norton & Company, 1999), 547–48 [hereafter Dower, *Embracing Defeat*].
15. Takemae, *Inside GHQ,* 487–90.
16. Takemae, *Inside GHQ,* 116.
17. Takemae, *Inside GHQ,* 426–35; Dower, *Embracing Defeat,* 559–60.
18. James, vol. 3, 287–95.
19. Takemae, *Inside GHQ,* 235; James, vol. 3, 323–25.
20. Michael Schaller, *Douglas MacArthur: The Far Eastern General* (Oxford University Press, 1989).

Chapter Thirteen

1. For general background on the Korea War, including the key period between August 1945 and June 1950, sources consulted included William W. Stueck, *The Korean War: An International History* (Princeton: Princeton University Press, 1997); Chen Jian, *China's Road to the Korean War: The Making of the Sino-American Confrontation* (New York: Columbia University Press, 1994) [hereafter Chen, *China's Road to the Korean War*]; and Alan R. Millett, *The War for Korea, 1945–50, A House Burning* (Lawrence: University Press of Kansas, 2005) [hereafter Millett, *The War for Korea*]. For the period of the war itself, in addition to the sources cited, I am deeply indebted to Dr. Allan Millet who generously provided a copy of his draft manuscript chapter on period from the liberation of Seoul to the Chinese intervention from the second volume of his series on the war [hereafter Millet manuscript) other material, particularly Office of the Secretary of Defense, "Analysis of MacArthur Issues, 1951," Marshall, Secretary of Defense Collection, Marshall Papers, Box 195, Folder A/22, George C. Marshall Library, Lexington, VA [hereafter "Analysis of MacArthur Issues"].
2. D. Clayton James, *The Years of MacArthur, vol. 3, Triumph & Disaster 1945–1964* (Boston: Houghton Mifflin Company, 1985), 399–403, 412 [hereafter James, vol. 3].
3. James, vol. 3, 411–12, 414–18; Chen, *China's Road to the Korean War,* Chapters 1 to 4; Edward Drea, "Military Intelligence and MacArthur," in William M. Leary, *MacArthur and the American Century: A Reader* (Lincoln: University of Nebraska Press, 2001), 198–99 [hereafter Drea, "Military Intelligence and MacArthur"].
4. James, vol. 3, 420–21, 425, 431.
5. James, vol. 3, 425–33. See also James W. Schnable, *U.S. Army in the Korean War: Policy and Decision, The First Year* (Office of the Chief of Military History, 1972).
6. James, vol. 3, 436–38.
7. For the desperate struggle in the summer of 1950 prior to Inchon, see Roy E. Appleman, *South to the Naktong, North to the Yalu* (Washington D.C.: Office of the Chief of Military History, 1966). Also very informative is the Millet manuscript.
8. James, vol. 3, 450–464.
9. James, vol. 3, 433–482 (with both "We drew up a list" and "5000 to 1 gamble" quotes). James at his best. Clay Blair, *The Forgotten War: America in Korea, 1950–53* (New York: Times Books, 1987), 223–37, has a discussion of the alternatives to Inchon.

10. Millet manuscript; James, vol. 3, 483–517 (including "We want you to feel unhampered' quote). The popular versions containing the gross distortions of events in at Wake Island were Merle Miller's *Plain Speaking* (a 1973 best seller), Samuel Gallu's play *Give'em Hell Harry!* (1975) and the ABC television "historical drama" titled "Collision Course: Truman vs. MacArthur" (1976).

Chapter Fourteen

1. Chen Jian, *China's Road to the Korean War: The Making of the Sino-American Confrontation* (New York: Columbia University Press, 1994), ix to xii, 175–77 [hereafter Chen, *China's Road to the Korean War*].
2. Edward Drea, 'Military Intelligence and MacArthur,' in William M. Leary, *MacArthur and the American Century: A Reader* (Lincoln: University of Nebraska Press, 2001), 199–201 [hereafter Drea, 'Military Intelligence and MacArthur']; Chen, *China's Road to the Korean War*, 111–13, 288n.
3. D. Clayton James, *The Years of MacArthur, vol. 3, Triumph & Disaster 1945–1964* (Boston: Houghton Mifflin Company, 1985), 536–38 [hereafter James, vol. 3]: "Analysis of MacArthur Issues." The following pages also profit from William W. Stueck, *The Korean War: An International History* (Princeton: Princeton University Press, 1997); Roy E. Appleman, *South to the Naktong, North to the Yalu* (Washington D.C.: Office of the Chief of Military History, 1966); and James W. Schnable, *U.S. Army in the Korean War: Policy and Decision, The First Year* (Office of the Chief of Military History, 1972).
4. James, vol. 3, 538–40, 546.
5. James, vol. 3, 542–50.
6. For Ridgway's extremely interesting messages, see 'Eyes Only,' Ridgway to Collins (no date but apparently about 26 December 1950); Letters (two) Ridgway to MacArthur, 6 January 1951; Letter MacArthur to Ridgway, 7 January 1951. Also of interest is a Ridgway message to General Doyle Hickey, 18 January 1951 expressing his concern about the prospect of the Soviets employing atomic bombs against any evacuation from Pusan. Papers of Maj. Gen. Courtney Whitney, Record Group 16, Box 5, Folder 17 'Personal for Ridgway,' MacArthur Memorial Archive. I am indebted to James Zobel for bringing these to may attention.
7. James, vol. 3, 571–7.
8. James, vol. 3, 602, 604 (including 'there is no substitute' quote); Perret, *Old Soldiers Never Die,* 564–7.
9. In his fascinating memoir, George M. Elsey describes how he helped 'leak' the transcript of the Wake Island Conference which the *New York Times* published with the intention of showing MacArthur's erroneous predictions about Chinese intervention and how soon the war would end. While demonstrating MacArthur's shared responsibility for these misjudgments is fair, using these minutes to try to place primary responsibility on MacArthur is not. *An Unplanned Life* (Columbia: University of Missouri Press, 2005), 198–208.
10. James, vol. 3, 603–4, 608.

Chapter 15

1. James, vol. 3, 366.
2. Gavin Long, *MacArthur as Military Commander* (Princeton: D. Van Nostrand Company, Inc. 1969), 82.
3. As quoted in David Horner, *Blamey: The Commander-in-Chief* (Sydney: Allen & Unwin, 1998), 570. Horner makes the observation that exactly the same thing could have been said about Blamey!

Index